Barbara E Evans

SURVIVAL ON THE FAST TRACK

Also by Barbara E. Kovach:

The Flexible Organization: Effectiveness and Organizational Change
Organizational Sync: Making Your Job Work for You
The Experience of Adolescence: Development in Context
Power and Love: How to Work for Success and Still Care for Others
Outsiders on the Inside: Women in Organizations
Sex Roles and Personal Awareness

SURVIVAL ON THE FAST TRACK

Barbara E. Kovach

DODD, MEAD & COMPANY   New York

1 2 3 4 5 6 7 8 9 10

Library of Congress Cataloging-in-Publication Data

Kovach, Barbara E.
  Survival on the fast track.

  Bibliography: p.
  Includes index.
  1. Leadership.   2. Executive ability.   3. Job stress.
4. Organizational behavior.   I. Title.
HD57.7.K69 1987   658.4'092   87-19940
ISBN 0-396-09027-3

Contents

Preface

This book has been written almost of its own accord. I did not plan to write a book on fast-trackers. I did plan, at some time, to write a book on leadership. In fact, I was drafting a book on leadership when I had a telephone call from a corporate colleague about one of that institution's bright, young managers. "Why," my colleague wondered, "was this young manager arousing animosity among his seniors in the company? What did he need to know in order to keep himself out of further trouble?"

I knew the manager in question as well as the organization, but I did not give this conversation much thought at the time. A few days later, however, I met on other matters with Dan Fishman, a professor in our graduate school of psychology, and mentioned the comments made about the young manager. In succeeding weeks, we talked about this manager and generalized his difficulties into a framework that fit well with our knowledge of what was happening to other bright, young corporate stars. It came slowly to us, it seems now, that this was most likely representative of a "fast-tracker phenomenon."

At one point a month later, I sat down and wrote up the basic steps that had emerged in my conversations with Dan. On his urging, I sent it out for review—not only for publication but to other friends and colleagues in the professional and corporate worlds. The article (which this paper became shortly) struck a nerve. Colleagues in five major companies called about the article, saying, more or less, "I know people like that!" Lynne Lumsden, Publisher of Dodd, Mead, called and said, "I want the book."

There was no book. What I knew about fast-trackers had been written in the twenty pages of the article. Little else was known on fast-trackers. There was not any particular literature to review. In the consulting work that my husband and I have done over several years with more than three hundred General Motors managers at component operations, there were a number of fast-trackers but not enough to establish patterns for a group as a whole. It was a month or so later that it struck me that one way to find out if there were a book in the fast-tracker phenomenon was to follow up on the spontaneous comments of my corporate friends and to talk with the people they had thought about on reading the initial paper. I called them up and asked them if they would be willing to nominate individuals—and they agreed.

There was still no book. I had no notion of what I would find in talking to these individuals. I went with some skepticism to the first interview session that was described to those interviewed as a study on exceptional managers. I went with less skepticism to the next and the next. And by the time I had completed the first five interviews I was fully caught up in what this group of people, collectively, was telling me—about themselves, their work, and their organizations. What was most astonishing was the degree to which in different companies, different functions, different settings, these exceptional managers of different ages and backgrounds were echoing each other. The patterns that became apparent early were reinforced by the remainder of the interviews. They were shaped and changed in the succeeding sessions but the clarity with which similarities emerged was tremendously exciting. Yes, there was a book in this material—a significant book—that talked not only about individuals, about families and organizations, but about the prospects for corporate survival.

My excitement continued as I processed the information and wrote the preliminary manuscript. As I look back now, I remember the sense of discovery that led to these pages. The strengths in this book are the result of the strengths of the individuals whose stories are in these pages. The weaknesses arise from the fact that the writing may not fully communicate the astonishing clarity with which their lives illuminate our own work and our understanding of living and working well. It is now many weeks—and many, many revisions—later and I hope that the sense of discovery and excitement is still evident in the book and is clearly communicated to the reader.

There are many who have been significant in establishing the fact that material for a book did indeed exist. Foremost among these are my corporate colleagues who were willing to nominate individuals for the sample and then pursued their choices—eliciting the commitment of those identified as fast-trackers in this book. Without their efforts and support this material would never have been gathered. Much appreciation is, therefore, due to Joanne Start, Director of Personnel at General Motors; Warrington Parker, Director of Executive Development at Rockwell International; Jim Rose, Vice-President of Human Resources for Orthopharmaceuticals, a division of Johnson and Johnson; Douglas Quinn, a Division Manager at AT&T; and Jack Gorman, a District Manager at IBM. The book began with the initial responsiveness and interest of these five people.

In shaping the final product, there are many others who have been essential to the process. At the heart of what I know and do lies the wise advice of my husband, Randy, my partner in all of our consulting ventures. A recent comment of his shifted the focus of one part of the book and added immeasurably to the final product. My older daughter, Deborah, never one to withhold criticism, recently sent one whole version of two chapters into the wastebasket so that much better versions could emerge. The careful reading of the book by my husband's parents, Dona and Lou Kovach, took this manuscript another step along the way. However, throughout the rewriting process, the most constant assistance has come from Sharon Greenfield, a graduate student in psychology, who has read and reread the manuscript many times and *never* finds it satisfactory—thus provoking another session with the computer and a new and cleaner version. Without Sharon's efforts, this book would not have emerged from its infancy.

Then, in writing the book, I have become even more aware of how no one manages to achieve anything significant totally alone. I am aware of the debt I owe to the people I work with on a daily basis who do their job so well that I have the freedom to be preoccupied with other matters—and who, in a way, have provided the support for me to accomplish this work. In particular, I think of my Associate Dean Gabby Hartmann and my administrative assistant, Carolyn Broadbelt, both of whom are superb administrators and colleagues. My appreciation extends as well to the Assistant Deans John Rutan and Ed Regan and our Business Administrator, Al Gynn.

In another context, I have a new appreciation for those I used to live with on a daily basis: my parents, my sister, and my brother. As I talked with the fast-trackers about their lives and families, I have seen more clearly how my parents contributed to my own career path. People of strong opinions and somewhat eccentric viewpoints, they did much in my early years to shape the course I now take. They continue to express their opinions in their own individualistic manner today. My mother read an early manuscript and wouldn't speak to me for several weeks—not an uncommon event—but I learned that some sections of the book required significant changes. My sister too read part of the book and said she would read further when it was "fixed." I think it is "fixed" now, and not only my family but many others will enjoy and profit from the stories of those on the fast track to the top.

Finally, I must thank Lynne Lumsden again and her new partner Jon Harden—now steering their own publishing firm from the top—and the conscientious work of Barbara Beckman, the primary editor of this book.

It is my hope that the book itself does justice to the outstanding contributions of the many individuals who have brought this work into being.

Barbara Kovach
New Brunswick, New Jersey
January, 1987

Introduction

*Leadership in corporations today demands broadly
able, flexible, agile individuals. Protecting
executives from unfavorable or incompatible work
environments prevents them from learning to adjust
and work around problems.*
ALLAN COX
THE COX REPORT ON THE
AMERICAN CORPORATION

*. . . the essence of leadership is choice, a singularly
individualistic act in which a person assumes
responsibility for a commitment to direct an
organization along a particular path.*
ABRAHAM ZALEZNIK
"MANAGEMENT OF
DISAPPOINTMENT"

In big corporations, junior stars receive one set of messages and senior statesmen receive another. The result of these contradictory signals is that we are programming the brightest and best among our young junior managers for derailment.[1] We put them on the fast track and promise them the moon. If, however, at the midpoint of their flight through space, they do not jettison the baggage that brought them to this point, they will plummet back to earth . . . limping along with the rest of their corporate peers through the remainder of their careers.

In fact, corporations require that managers on the fast track go through a metamorphosis in mid-career that transforms them from independent actors on the front lines to team builders in the background, at the same time as they move inward from the outer edges to the center of the organization. Mid-career is the time of transition and the time in which managers are most alone. Surviving the transition depends on individual strengths, for there is little group support. It is individually that young stars face the process of transformation and determine whether or not they will

---

The Key Questions about the Fast-Trackers

1. How and why do some people survive on the fast track to the top in major corporations?
2. What do the stories of their lives mean for other people—on other tracks or in other places?
3. Are there guidelines in the stories of the fast-trackers that are applicable to the development of leadership in general?
4. Do the lives of the fast-trackers give any indication about the future of American corporations? of America itself?

---

bring together the paradoxes of leadership and survive on the fast track to the top.

Perhaps this is not as strange as it may seem. Jack Welch, President of General Electric Corporation, reminds us that at the heart of all organizational change is the individual:

> . . . consider that organizations are really nothing more than collections of people, and it's at that level—at the level of the individual—that you really deal with the issue (of change) most effectively. People decide. People act. People respond to change.[2]

If we accept that the individual's strength and flexibility are at the basis of an organization's capacity to change—to adapt and survive—then perhaps it is less paradoxical than we might first think that our senior statesmen have arrived at the top only after trials that test their individual adaptability, resilience, and ability to face contradictions. The difficult transition of mid-career requires, in fact, that junior stars shed many of the behavior patterns that brought them to this point and take on new ones appropriate to senior statesmen close to the core of the organization. Mid-career is the time of Executive Transition, which may, indeed, be an appropriate rite of passage for those who are going to assume the seats of power in major organizations. Making sense of the apparent contradictions of this career phase may be an appropriate measure of the necessary strength of our future leaders.

DEFINING AND REDEFINING INTENTIONS

This book was undertaken in order to answer questions about the nature of the career track and the individuals who survive the intensity of a high-speed journey to the top of our corporations. Seeking answers to these questions, five high-level individuals in major corporations nominated peers and superiors perceived within the company to be racing up the fast track to the top. Each of these fast-trackers was interviewed about family, educational, and work history in sessions of approximately three hours. Their answers provide the data for this book.

As the interviews progressed, it became clear that these individuals not only spoke for themselves and their career paths but also gave clues to the future of American corporations. These fast-trackers are part of the "ascendancy group" in our biggest corporations. They are among those who will form tomorrow's leadership. As they told their own stories, they provided guidelines for others to follow in the workplace, but they also said something important about the future prospects of American organizations.

Their message was reassuring. In a time of economic instability and societal transition, it is comforting to know that those who might guide our corporations in the future, demonstrate integrity and compassion in the present. We are at a time of shaping new directions. The policies and procedures that worked yesterday are a dismal failure today. The patterns of behavior that put us on top of the world in the years from 1945 to 1980 have not insured continued success. Those who will shape our future directions may be the men and women in this sample. In knowing more about them, we learn more about ourselves and our own future.

It is apparent to many who read this manuscript that these fast-trackers represent a special group. They have each chosen to make a personal, life-time journey within big American corporations, and they each made this choice relatively early in adult life. Their choices were appropriate for their talents, and their priorities matched the opportunities that existed in big corporations at the time at which their careers began. Other individuals have assessed their priorities *and* matching opportunities in the larger world and have chosen to make their personal journeys in other spheres both in and out of the work world. Many of these are also on a fast track to the top in their own areas of expertise. The same task faces those who are now entering or reentering the work world—to assess their own talents, interests, and priorities *and* match these talents and priorities with opportunities in the current world. The opportunities and choices of these newcomers to organizations will not, cannot, be the same as those of the fast-trackers in the book: not only does each individual differ, but organizations—and organizational opportunities—have changed dramatically in the last few years. The fast-trackers' life histories illustrate only one result of the process of matching individual strengths and organizational needs. Moreover, their message is strong and clear enough to transcend the particular setting in which it was shaped.

This message is applicable to everybody, of every age, in every occupation. The way in which the fast-trackers speak about themselves, their families, and their work outlines with bold strokes many of the behavior patterns happening around us every day. Further, the way in which they speak of their work, their unanimity or near-unanimity on certain issues, and the commonalities in background, suggest certain hypotheses about the development of leadership. In a time in which the demand for leadership has become imperative, we must pay attention to any new guidelines on the development of leadership. We may test these guidelines in our own lives, explore them in larger scope, but the directions that they offer are vital to our future welfare.

For it is not only in big corporations that we need leadership but in every walk of life. Unless many more of us emerge as leaders, the United States will not survive this time of economic instability and transformation as a significant force in the world. Unless many more of us are willing to take up the responsibilities of leadership, the story of America as a world leader will be told in the history books and not in current affairs. The fast-trackers have a message for anyone who might move toward the path of leadership in any sector—willing to live their life in bold strokes—and assuming the responsibilities and enjoying the satisfaction of a personally chosen career on the fast track.

This book began, as noted above, with a reasonably modest intention: to determine how and why some bright and talented people survive along the fast track and others do not, and to uncover some of the paradoxes that they meet along the way. As it became clear that these individuals represented the leadership of tomorrow, a second intention was added to the first: to assess the commonalities in their behavior as leadership characteristics and behaviors. Finally, a third intention emerged: to view the leadership behavior of the fast-trackers within the context of the future of American corporations and hence of America itself. Thus, this book not only examines individual histories but also draws out from these histories the lessons that are here for individuals both personally and collectively. From the stories in this book, we may learn not only about ourselves, our families, and our careers, but also about the future of American leadership as a whole.

All of the initial and emergent intentions eventually became woven together as part of the same fabric. The first part of the book introduces the fast-trackers and their message in the context of *leadership*—described as a combination of substance and style. The second part discusses their career histories with an emphasis on the similarities between the junior and senior phases in contrast to the difficult years of mid-career, and sets this in the context of the interplay of substance and style. The third part explores the early and current families of the fast-trackers with an emphasis on style, concluding with an overview of significant factors in leadership development. The fourth and last section spells out the specific attitudes and behaviors common to all the fast-trackers that form the *essentials of leadership*. Following their path, we might all learn to resolve contradictory messages, find the common thread in paradox, prepare ourselves for success along our chosen track, and so increase the odds that American organizations and America itself might survive and prosper in this time of transition.

PART I

The Fast-Trackers and Their Message

The Substance and Style of Leadership

> *Managing complex diversity and interdependence in an effective and responsible way requires, first, sufficient power to make up for the power gap inherent in leadership jobs and then, second, the willingness to use that power to manage all the interdependencies in as responsible a way as possible. The power one needs comes, of necessity, in many forms. It has multiple bases, including ones associated with information or knowledge, good working relationships, personal skills, intelligent agendas for action, resource networks, and good track records.*
>
> JOHN KOTTER
> *POWER AND INFLUENCE*

The Essentials of Leadership
LEADERSHIP

SUBSTANCE	STYLE
1. Knowledge	1. Communication
2. Understanding	2. Commitment
3. Awareness	3. Confidence
4. Knowing oneself	4. Being oneself

The values, beliefs, and judgments of these fast-trackers affect thousands of people each day in five major corporations. In the immediate future, it is likely that at least two of these fast-trackers may sit at the very top of two of these large corporations. In the more distant future, several others may be in that position in all five of the organizations. What they think matters—for individuals and for organizations as a whole. What they do today is what is often termed "leadership."

Leadership has multiple meanings, but simply put, leadership is going in advance of others, showing the way, choosing new directions, and bringing something new into being. In working with hundreds of managers over the last few years, it has been useful to talk about two components of leadership: substance and style.[1] Substance is the knowledge that we bring to our work: the accumulation of people- and task-related understanding that is the foundation of any consistently successful effort. Style is the way in which we communicate that knowledge to others, elicit commitment and motivation, and guide people toward the accomplishment of common goals. Substance is the *what*, and style is the *how*. Substance is the foundation of success, the basis for establishing appropriate priorities and fine-tuning judgments; style is the way in which we communicate our knowledge, priorities, and judgments to others.

When there is much substance, but style is not strongly developed, we have people with talent and knowledge who are minimizing their range of influence by limiting their communication. When an individual's style is strongly developed and there is little substance, we have the "operators" of the world who are selling little of genuine value to others. When there are high levels of substance, and style is well developed, we have leaders who are influencing people to move in directions chosen on the basis of knowledge and shaped by the values, beliefs, and judgments of these leaders and their followers.

It is important, then, that we understand both the substance and style of those who affect the outcome of matters that concern all of us. We tend to understand substance better than style. We have been to school and know what constitutes essential, functional knowledge. As adults, we have been workers and/or parents and understand what constitutes on-the-job training. As individuals in families and organizations, we have acquired some degree of awareness of self and others and recognize the process of learning about human behavior. It is harder to identify and understand style, that intangible "something" referred to as charisma, as "getting one's point across," as "being heard." Style is more variable than substance and is an outward manifestation of a unique personality. Style may be flamboyant or reserved, warm or cool, energetic or calm. However style is demonstrated, it is unique to each individual.

All of the fast-trackers demonstrate high levels of substance and strongly developed styles. They know their business and they communicate well with others. They know themselves and they are not afraid—for the most part—to be who they are in their dealings with the world. It is the combination of these two essentials of leadership, substance and style, that has put them on the fast track to success. It is the continuous development of both substance and style that may allow most of them to continue learning, to continue growing, and to survive the intensity of their journey along the fast track. It is the life-long willingness to learn and relearn that may allow them to resolve the paradoxes of the journey along the fast track, emerging as leaders today and tomorrow.

We begin in this section with three chapters that introduce the fast-trackers and their organizations, spell out their message, and describe the basic categories of style exemplified by the fast-trackers. Then, in Part II, the interplay of substance and style are viewed in the fast-trackers' progress along their career paths. In Part III, style again takes center stage as a focus for the examination of their personal and family lives, and finally in Part IV, both substance and style are the foundation for enumerating the essentials of leadership.

CHAPTER 1

The Corporate Fast-Trackers

The Setting and the Characters

> *The leader uses his imagination for strokes of genius
> geared to the present; the imitator perverts his
> imagination by trying to find the right action for
> conditions long consigned to the dustbin of history.*
> HENRY M. BOETTINGER
> "IS MANAGEMENT REALLY AN
> ART?"

The business of America is business. Those perceived as stars in the business world live out the dreams of many Americans and stand as examples for many of their fellow citizens. Yet there are many myths and stereotypes about these people that all of us are often inclined to believe. We think that those who succeed in business are particularly interested in power, in the accumulation of dollars, and the pursuit of self-interest. If these myths were to be true it would bode ill for America as a whole. If, on the other hand, we showed them to be definitively untrue, the picture for America would be much brighter. For it is the stars of the business world, those whose hearts and hands shape corporate America, who illustrate what our future might be, both in terms of the national economy, *and* as exemplars of American values and beliefs.

Moreover, if our concerns lie with the future as much as the present, it is those corporate stars who have been picked out as future leaders of America who must concern us. These are the men and women who form the ascendancy group and will take over the leadership in American corporations over the next three, ten, and twenty years. These are the people who will have a large hand in determining the fate of our economic

—————————⋯◁∞▷⋯—————————

The Corporations and the Fast-Trackers

THE CORPORATIONS

American Telephone and Telegraph
(AT&T)

General Motors Corporation
(GM)

International Business Machines
(IBM)

Johnson and Johnson
(J&J)

Rockwell International

THE FAST-TRACKERS

	Rich
	Andrew
Senior Statesmen:	Hal
	Tom
	Jon
	Art
	Larry
Those in Mid-Career:	Hank
	Jerry
	Ken
	Don
	Christine
	Brian
	Sandra
Junior Stars:	Alec
	Pete
	Sam

—————————⋯◁∞▷⋯—————————

well-being; they will stand, for decades, as examples of what Americans believe is worthwhile. While we are surviving the present, it is the future that worries us, and glimpses into that future may be provided by studying those who will participate in creating the economic and social stance of America in the years just ahead.

As a consequence of these concerns, I undertook a study of a small sample of fast-trackers in our major organizations. These fast-trackers were those perceived as moving ahead of their age group on a fast track to the top. These are the people who might, within the next twenty years, be sitting in the highest seats of corporate power. The sample included seventeen people in five of the biggest corporations of the world. I talked with them in manufacturing plants in the Midwest, in corporate offices of the high-rent district of Manhattan, in the corporate centers of the larger Detroit and New York metropolitan areas, and in an executive helicopter over the city of Pittsburgh.

The fast-trackers worked, at one time or another, in the east, west, north and south; currently they have offices in California, New York, New Jersey, and throughout the Midwest. They range widely in age and in position on the corporate ladder. They all work, however, in major companies that are undergoing processes of transformation in response to new economic conditions of the last five to ten years. The context in which they work—the commonalities across companies—sets the stage for the stories of the fast-trackers.*

THE FAST-TRACKERS' ORGANIZATIONS

Turbulence, the threat posed by new competition, instability . . . transformation. American organizations and the American economy have been characterized in a variety of ways, but traditional ways of doing business have been shattered by the economic upheavals of the late 1970s and 1980s. Employees at all levels of corporations are now seeking new directions, creating new procedures, and seeking to find a profitable path through an unpredictable and unanticipated economic landscape.

From 1945 to around 1980, corporations and "successful" corporate behavior were semi-predictable. Corporations were hierarchical and became increasingly encumbered through these years with layers of management. The way through these layers was up the corporate ladder. There *was* a ladder. It was assumed that the most talented—or sometimes the most wily or shrewd—were the ones who were able to climb from one rung to the next. The fact that many did not rise very far on that ladder was attributed to lack of talent or lack of motivation or lack of any other number of valuable characteristics. The fact that some did not rise on that ladder was rarely, if ever, attributed to lack of opportunity. This was the world in

*See Appendix A for a brief description of each fast-tracker.

which the fast-trackers in this study first came into their own as junior stars and the world in which some of them (the eldest) rose to senior statesmen.

This does not, however, represent the world in which the fast-trackers live now nor the world which young men and women, aspiring to career success, are now entering. The corporation is still hierarchical, but, in many, the layers of management have disappeared as the hierarchies have flattened and the top of the corporation now lies closer to the ground. Most leaders in major corporations today know—and knowing is sometimes different from doing—that their corporations will only survive through full involvement of their people, through teamwork and participation. Without drawing every ounce of commitment and creativity from the people in their employ, our giant organizations will falter and eventually succumb to the competitive pressures from newer businesses in our own country and abroad.

In this context, it is no longer so clear that there is a ladder to the top. Layoffs, hiring and promotion freezes, and down-sizing represent the current state of affairs in most major corporations as they reshape themselves to meet the challenges of an unanticipated future. Lack of opportunity, circumstances beyond one's control, and the unexpected, are now clearly important factors in individual career paths. It is not so clear that talent and motivation are the primary characteristics that guide careers. On every hand, highly paid executives, with every reason to believe that they held lifetime jobs, have been abruptly sent out into the world in order to lighten company costs and increase chances that the company can maintain a shaky foothold on profitability.

The companies in which the fast-trackers work are some of the biggest in America and all are reeling from the economic challenges of this age. Brief descriptions of each of the companies are given below:

General Motors, the largest corporation in the world, is currently posting quarterly losses, has announced that eleven plants will close by the end of the decade, and is communicating a new ethic and a new imperative to its people. Challenged first by the Japanese in the late 1970s, GM, along with the entire automotive industry, is relearning how to design, make and sell cars—and experiencing the difficulties of moving into new fields with troublesome acquisitions.

American Telephone and Telegraph, now (according to some) the fourth largest corporation, is moving through a chaotic transformation as it copes with the competitive environment created by divestiture and government deregulation. Employees as well as the general public may wonder along with customers what business AT&T is really in. It is clear from the newspapers, however, that one of its businesses is down-sizing and restructuring the company for a new and unexpected future.

IBM has recently been in the news as analysts have examined what is wrong with "Big Blue," an unassailable leader in the technological field since the 1930s. Now beset by new competition on all sides, IBM too is posting diminishing returns—although still one of the most profitable businesses in America—and reexamining past choices. Its reputation as one of America's best-managed companies may, in the ensuing events, be put up for recall.

Johnson & Johnson, another model of excellent management, received kudos for its smooth handling of the Tylenol crisis. Yet, as pressures from both the government and private sector to reduce health care expenditures have increased and as the patents on products expire and generic drugs compete successfully with mainstays that have provided a base income over the last several years, Johnson & Johnson has found itself facing the pressures of new competition, a rapidly changing market, and a turbulent economy.

Finally, Rockwell International, which has recently soared to number 30 on the charts of the Fortune 500, has acknowledged the same needs for transformation as the four companies above and is setting a new course in order to meet new and tougher competition.

In all of these companies, changing circumstances are calling for new individual and corporate directions, reevaluation of past priorities, and new and innovative leadership. There are no guarantees that the track followed by the men and women in this sample—nor the one that they expect to take—will be as clearly outlined in the next decades as it has been in the past. Certainly, there are sufficient challenges and responsibilities within each of these companies to test the mettle of any who thrive on difficulties and seek out opportunities for growth and innovation. Yet the nature of these challenges and responsibilities has changed and the predictability with which they could be outlined just a few years ago has also diminished.

At the same time as the shape of corporate ladders is dimming and prospects for climbing them receding, another matching phenomenon has transpired. A new cultural orientation has developed among young (and not-so-young) people. Since the early- to mid-1970s, those entering organizations are not at all certain that they are interested in climbing any ladder. Raised in the anti-establishment 1960s and the personalized orientation of the 1970s, young employees in corporations are more interested in their personal satisfaction—as well as their economic well-being—than they are in "corporate success." The new set of values has led to a greater emphasis on enjoying work at any level and on doing one's own thing in the work world, than on speeding up a track to the top. This is the world in which the youngest fast-trackers came of age, and the world in which all the fast-trackers now live and work.

What does this mean for the fast-trackers? It means that they must, if they are to continue to succeed, show maximum adaptability in shifting gears, in rethinking their priorities, and taking a sense of the new imperatives. They must, in fact, reevaluate the meaning of success, for their future is less certain than it might have been just a few years ago. Their careers, as well as those on slower or different tracks, are subject to pressures outside their control. Their individual efforts are only one factor in determining the outcome of their course.

INTRODUCING THE FAST-TRACKERS

The individuals who form the basis for this book each work for one of the five companies listed above. Seven come from one of the companies, four from another, and two each from the remaining three. The fast-trackers range widely in age and are found from the ranks of middle management up through inner executive circles. All of them are perceived by others in their companies, however, as moving faster than their peers on a course that may take them to the top. The fast-trackers, here and throughout the book, are referred to by age-graded categories as juniors or junior stars, those in the middle or mid-level managers, and seniors or senior statesmen.

The junior stars include three men and one woman between the ages of 30 and 34, all with middle-management positions. Those at the point of mid-career transition include seven men and one woman from 36 to 43 who are at the senior steps of middle management or the junior steps of the senior ranks. Finally, the senior statesmen are represented by five men between the ages of 46 and 52 who are near the top of the corporate ladder, presidents and vice-presidents of subsidiary corporations or of the corporation itself.

The names under which the fast-trackers appear in this book, along with brief histories, appear below under each age classification. (Fuller descriptions appear in Appendix A and the reader may want to turn to these from time to time for reference; Appendix B describes the interview setting and approach to interpreting the interview material; Appendix C gives a sample of the questionnaire used as a guide during the interviews.)

(a) The senior statesmen

————••⌖∞⌖••————

The Senior Statesmen

Pseudonym	Age in 1986	Title
Rich	52	Divisional President
Andrew	51	Group Vice-President
Hal	48	Senior Vice-President
Tom	48	Divisional Vice-President
Jon	46	Vice-Chairman

————••⌖∞⌖••————

Rich and Tom are both at or near the top of their division of their companies; Andrew, Hal, and Jon work in the corporate center. All have worked for the same company through their entire career. All are married, Hal and Tom for the second time, and all have children and/or stepchildren. The fast-trackers themselves come from familes of various sizes, but all are either first- or second-born in their own families. Among the senior statesmen there are two first sons, one first-born twin, one only child, and one second son. The parents (and in one case grandparents) of these men include a highly educated professional, a business manager, two small business owners, and a blue-collar worker.

(b) Those in the middle

————••⌖∞⌖••————

The Mid-Career Managers

Pseudonym	Age in 1986	Title
Art	43	Divisional General Manager
Larry	41	Divisional President

Hank	39	Divisional Vice-President
Jerry	39	Divisional Manager
Ken	38	Divisional Director
Don	38	Divisional Manager
Christine	37	Divisional Manager
Brian	36	District Manager

———————◦∞◦———————

Art, Larry, and Hank are either at or near the top of their division and are considered part of the senior management team. Ken is one step down, with Jerry, Don, Christine and Brian one step further down from him— each within the upper ranks of middle management. Half of these fast-trackers began their careers in a company other than the one in which they are now working, whereas the other half remained with the company they entered at the beginning of their careers. All are married, Art and Don for the second time. Exactly half of this group of eight have children and/or stepchildren and half do not. Among these fast-trackers themselves, in relation to their early families, there are two first children (eldest boys), and six second children. Among the parents of this group, there is one professional, one business manager, a farmer, a small business manager, three blue-collar workers, and a single mother on welfare.

(c) The junior stars

———————◦∞◦———————

	The Junior Stars	
Pseudonym	**Age in 1986**	**Title**
Sandra	34	District Manager
Alec	33	Division Director
Pete	31	District Manager
Sam	30	District Manager

———————◦∞◦———————

Alec is at the top rung and Sandra, Pete, and Sam are at the lower rung of the middle-management hierarchy. Alec and Sam have both worked for three companies. Sandra and Pete are making their careers now in the same company they entered initially. All are married, Sandra for the second time, and all have children and/or stepchildren. Sandra and Sam are first children, Alec and Pete are second children. The parents' occupations include one professional, one business manager, one white-collar worker, and one small business owner.

The titles given above are not always those that the fast-trackers use in their particular organizations. Instead, their titles have been translated into one particular rank order—from president through vice-president, director, division and district manager—in order to indicate their status relative to each other. However, even this translation of their titles lacks accuracy, because the weight of their responsibilities depends upon the size of their corporations and the positioning of their division within the corporation. Nonetheless, these titles do roughly align the fast-trackers on the same hierarchy.

From a quick review of the fast-trackers' histories, it is clear that the younger fast-trackers have changed companies more often than the older ones have, which is in part a response to the recent changes in corporations and the narrowing of opportunities. The older fast-trackers entered a relatively stable organizational world. The younger ones entered a world that was already feeling the first tremors of change. The dramatic changes in organizations of the last several years, in fact, make it even less likely that people of talent may follow directly in the paths laid out by these fast-trackers. The fast-trackers have succeeded because their not inconsiderable talents and abilities were matched by opportunities to use those talents in big corporations. The setting in which they work has been a key component in their success and that setting has and is changing. What then may we learn from the fast-trackers?

SIGNIFICANCE OF THE FAST-TRACKERS' EXPERIENCES

The changes in both organizations and in cultural values that have occurred in the last few years make it unlikely that in the future young men and women might duplicate the career tracks of the men and women in this book—and, perhaps more importantly, that they would want to do this. These changes also mean that in companies that are meeting the challenges of a turbulent economy, the ladder climbed by the fast-trackers may not even be visible; and if visible, it might shift or disintegrate at any given time.

What, then, does it matter what the men and women in this book have done if they do not provide a blueprint for talented and motivated young men and women to follow? It *matters*. It matters because *who* these people are, as people, has led them to find *one* road to success. They demonstrate many of the characteristics that can be applied, in a general way, to other settings, other fields, other disciplines. They have found success along one particular road. It is a road that may not exist for others and it is a road that, if available, may still not be chosen by others. Yet, in the behavior of these fast-trackers, individually and as a group, there is a clear message about living life well. Although there certainly are other ways to live life well, the fast-trackers clearly illustrate one way in which to live at the top of one's capacity: drawing a full measure of satisfaction from work and family. All people, in any field, who seek to live fully and use all their capacities, will identify at some point with the fast-trackers, and in so doing learn more about themselves, their career path, and their organizations.

In addition, corporate business is still in some sense the hallmark of America and the source of much American power in the world at large. What these men and women do in the heart of corporate America will stand as an example to many others who are yet to come and who will, in time, look back on our collective history and judge the value of those who went before. Those who are concerned about the future of this country can ill afford to ignore the message of those who may, within the relatively near future, stand at the helm of our biggest corporations.

CHAPTER 2

The Message from the Fast Track

The Real Meaning of Success

Leadership is the assumption of responsibility for the
pursuit of excellence in group life.
PHILIP SELZNICK
CHRONICLE OF HIGHER
EDUCATION

The fast-trackers collectively convey an impression of health and vitality. In contrast to many popular conceptions about those who succeed in business, they also clearly enunciate many "home truths" about their lives that reside in a basic American value system. Their lives, they say, are guided by ethics related to hard work, integrity, and compassion. For the most part, their work histories bear this out, showing that, indeed, it is not the shrewd and the cynical with their eye on the dollar but the honest and hard-working who have risen to the top of American organizations in the 1980s.

These corporate stars demonstrate the substance and style of leadership. They are able, they know what they are doing, they do their homework—often into the small hours of the night. They also have style and their styles vary widely from each other reflecting individual personalities. Yet even the fast-trackers, on reading this first chapter, wonder if they are really *that* good and if some shrewd cynicism and pursuit of the dollar does not enter into their calculations. Indeed, it is most likely that they *do* serve their own personal interests in their work, but the telling fact is that in doing so, they also serve their organizations. Human beings are

15

————•◦◦◦◦•——

The Message of the Fast-Trackers

1. Time and energy can be stretched if managed wisely.
2. Self-responsibility is central to success.
3. Well-developed interests outside of work enhance career activities.
4. Achieving important goals requires long hours of work.
5. Work is a primary source of satisfaction.
6. Families are primary sources of learning.
7. Success occurs only because people help each other.
8. Honesty about personal strengths and weaknesses is essential.
9. Personal success is making the world a better place to live in.
10. Informal career training begins in childhood.
11. Problems are really opportunities.

————•◦◦◦◦•——

neither all one way or all another: a mix of motivations lies behind most actions. On balance, however, all of the fast-trackers agree with the major points listed below. Although they are aware that they sometimes falter in their course, and are sometimes moved by personal interests instead of more altruistic ones, by and large they are working to make a contribution to the whole. The message that they illustrate individually and collectively is reassuring. What this says about the future leadership of this country and its organizations may be taken as giving some measure of comfort in an uncertain age.

There are eleven characteristics of these fast-trackers that appear in all of their stories of their family and work lives. These characteristics, it could be argued, are at the heart of their success, and are applicable as well to those who are successful in other settings at other times. These characteristics reflect their orientation toward time, toward responsibility, toward people, and toward ethical concerns. Each of the eleven is described below with excerpts from the stories of individual fast-trackers.

1. High level of energy and efficient management of time.   All of these people have managed to fit so much into each day that the immediate inference is that their energy levels are superhumanly high. On closer analysis, however, it is not the level of energy but more particularly the *management* of that energy which is unusual. They put their energy where it counts and do not waste time on unproductive matters.

This is most clear as they talk about their early lives. From adolescence on, often even earlier, they have been unusually busy. They did not sit in front of the television, or whatever the counterpart was before the television era, but were actively engaged in school, in part-time jobs, in sports, and in other extracurricular activities on a continual basis. Several early examples illustrate this.

Sam and Pete, both of the youngest group, demonstrate two patterns that are representative of the early lives of these fast-trackers as a whole: the fast-trackers were either highly involved in school experiences and worked as well, or put highest priority on working and were still involved in some school activities. In other words, almost all of the fast-trackers invested time and energy in both school and work; for some school absorbed most of their time, for others it was part-time work experiences that came first.

Sam went to a high school miles from his home so that daily, both going and coming, he walked a mile, took two city buses, and then the school bus. In school he was in dramatic plays, part of the cheerleading squad, and an Honors student. When he got home he raked leaves or shoveled snow and then delivered papers. Twice a week he had professional tennis training; he was then, and still is, close to professional in his tennis skills. Pete, on the other hand, was less involved in school activities but equally busy with work. Part of a large family, Pete worked every day in his father's business from the age of 10 and took a second job in a fast-food restaurant at the age of 16. He says he only played football—and not other sports—because he was expected to work.

In the middle group, those now around 40, the same two patterns are evident. Some of the individuals were highly involved in school activities and also worked part-time, others were more heavily involved in working but did participate secondarily in school acitvities. Brian, Ken, Christine, Jerry, and Hank, for example, did *everything* there was to do in high school and also worked part-time. Larry was involved in a similar amount of activity but with a different focus: He joined his four brothers and his father working on the family farm on a daily basis and was excused to play only one sport a year.

Those now in their forties and early fifties also talk enthusiastically about their high school years and their involvement in continual activity: Jon, Hal, Tom, and Andrew reminisce about school activities from participation in drama and music activities to the more traditional involvement in sports (Jon was, at one time, a professional baseball player); faced with different opportunities Rich held a job after school every day, gaining significant daily experience in learning to work with people.

The level of activity in the early years is matched by that in their current life. Larry and Pete both said that they now spend almost all their time at work or with their families—and it is no different than the way that they grew up. Pete described one of his typical days from a recent week. He went to work at 5:30 A.M. and was on the move until 4:30 P.M., at which time he jogged three miles and worked out. Then he went home and took his wife to dinner, returning to load his minivan with the bicycles of his two little girls and to take them to a distant park, where their friends would not see their stumbling beginnings in learning to ride their bicycles. Home by 8:30, he put the girls to bed, showered, and was back at work by 9:30 P.M. until close to midnight.

Such a life clearly requires physical health, but not necessarily superb physical health. These fast-trackers have the usual ailments of their particular age group and at least one was thought to have a rather severe life-long physical restriction. More importantly, however, these fast-trackers spend their time and energy on high-priority projects. The result is that to others they appear to be almost superhuman. Larry describes this process: "I learned long ago from my father not to waste my time on unproductive things. Lots of people do this. They spend time on things they can't control, can't fix. I don't."

2. Sense of responsibility. All of these individuals accepted responsibility for themselves and their own welfare prior to, or occasionally during, adolescence, and felt accountable for their actions. They sensed that whatever they were to make of their lives was up to them. This is clearly reflected in their early financial affairs. Many of them had full responsibility for earning any money they needed (beyond room and board) by the time they were 10, 12, or 14. This continued into their college years. Almost without exception, all of the fast-trackers paid their own way through college even when their parents were financially able to do so. In addition, many contributed their time and energy to helping their families survive crises and difficulties.

For example, both Pete and Sam paid all their own expenses from the time they started working just prior to adolescence. Hank, president of his student body class, worked in his parents' home business, and took care of his older sister's "tribe of children" (only a little younger than he), all at the same time. Hal worked with his father around the house on a regular basis, and is puzzled by the fact that his older brother never agreed to help out. He finds it ordinary or usual, as well, that he chose to go to the local state college (rather than a more prestigious one) because he could pay for it himself rather than rely on his father.

Many of these individuals were offered the choice to take care of themselves or to be taken care of by their parents, and chose the former. Others did not have the same choice; the options available were more highly charged and problematic. Andrew chose to pitch in to help his mother and grandparents; thus, although he was involved in almost every high school activity, he worked every night on the switchboard of a local business, and did his shift taking care of an ailing grandfather. He could have chosen not to be an active and contributing member of his family—a choice made by a few of the older brothers and sisters of this group—but found the alternative to not helping grimmer than might have been the case in more affluent families. Arthur also had a choice: he could stay on welfare, as his mother and sister did, or he could work. He chose to work and took on two jobs in order to provide for his family. He is the only one he knows from his childhood, he says, who is no longer standing in the welfare lines. "Everybody else I grew up with is still there."

> Larry took it as a matter of course that he would help on his father's farm although his older brother opted out as soon as he could and joined a motorcycle gang and got involved with drugs. Larry, on the other hand, worked every day of his childhood and adolescence. He remembers lying under the tomato truck in the nearby city at 5:30 A.M., waiting for the market to open so he could sell his vegetables and get home in time for school, and laughing at the classic painting of the farmer and his wife staring calmly ahead as if this characterized the life of a farm family.

So along with the management of their time and energy, these people all took on responsibilities early and contributed not only to their own but to their family's well-being.

3. Diversity of interests.   Each of these individuals has a variety of well-developed interests, many of which are not directly related to their work activities; instead of a simple single-mindedness in their approach to life, there is a complex diversity. In their early school years they took part in dramatic and musical productions, played almost all sports regardless of their level of skill (two were professional or nearly so in sports, others just went along for the fun of it and were admittedly not very good), rode horses, raised animals, or were involved in small, sometimes self-started businesses.

> These interests have, for many, continued into their adult lives. Until recently, Sam continued to play tennis many hours a week, coaching every weekend. Pete and Arthur run regularly (Arthur is preparing for his first marathon) and Christine spends winter weekends and vacations on skis with her husband. Ken is part of a family business raising and training horses for show, Hal has rehabilitated old trailer parks throughout the west, and Tom is two years away from having the *very best* garden in his state.
>
> The involvements of these fast-trackers outside of work are as often the focus of their enthusiasm and excitement as is work itself. Jon's austere face lights up when he talks about his last fifteen years of rebuilding houses, collecting folk art, and acquiring a superb collection of Oriental carpets. Initially, pressed by monetary necessity in his first move from the Midwest

to the East, he and his wife moved into an old, rambling house on the seacoast that lacked heat or plumbing. Once renovated, they sold this house and bought a semi-converted barn left unfinished by an impoverished architect. Jon and his wife completed the remodeling of this building, and later sold it, buying another 200-year-old farm house that they turned into their present home. In regard to houses, Jon says clearly, "If you have a *vision* . . ."

The visions of the fast-trackers range across a complexity of different interests, only some of which are directly related to work.

4. Willingness to work hard and long hours.   In whatever areas these fast-trackers have time invested, from childhood through the present, they are willing to put in long hours and to pursue their dreams to the end. They know, as Larry was cited as saying above, that if the dream is nonproductive they will pull out and turn their energy elsewhere. But if there is a chance of making a dream a reality, they will give everything they have to bring it into being.

In a recent article, a Nobel Prize winner in economics clearly states that doing well at anything takes time—generally at least 10 years of long and continuous effort.[1] This length of time is required for excellence in any discipline. Creativity and innovation may then build upon this level of expertise, and they may not. It is clear that in the world of business, as in a variety of other interests, the fast-trackers have devoted the requisite time. Starting in childhood, they have spent most of every day learning how to make things work, for themselves and for others.

5. Joy in work.   The fast-trackers love their work. They like the *process* of doing what they do and are pleased by but not caught up in the results that they achieve. Time after time they spontaneously and exuberantly describe their joy in work.

Alec most clearly describes the feelings voiced by many fast-trackers: "I work hard because I'm having fun. I won't work for a living. I don't know what I'd do if at some point it becomes just work." This feeling is voiced in other words by Larry, Christine, and Hal. Hank states, "You can't suceed if you're not having fun." Andrew describes his own sense of excitement: "I love it when a plan comes down." Tom and Pete say they love their work, and add that they love their respective companies.

The excitement of the *process* of working is described by Andrew in recalling an early job assignment. His facility was given the charge to develop a new product and a time limit of six months. Another facility was given the same charge; the choice of product would occur at the end of the time limit. Andrew clearly recalls the sense of excitement that energized him and his people as they put everything they had into the creation of something new. "There was," he says, "a real sense of unity—we were in this thing together." His team met the time limit and developed what he still views as the "best" product. However, it was not chosen by corporate headquarters ("Their loss," he smiles gleefully, "to the tune of several millon dollars"). Yet, this was a *good* time, and he gives the impression that in the remainder of his career he has sought to generate that same kind of excitement and commitment again and again. The fact that the product was buried does not interfere with his delight in the process.

Clearly, there are strong emotional rewards for these people in doing what they do. Rich says of his work on two occasions: "It was an emotional experience—very powerful." It is not the dollar value on their work that excites them (Tom had trouble describing the actual material benefits, he couldn't remember the numbers) but the process of making things work and, for some of them, creating a way of being that did not exist before.

6. Importance of family connections.   In talking about their early lives, the overwhelming importance of family members in the thoughts and feelings of these fast-trackers is clearly spelled out. More than any other mentors, sponsors, or helpers along the way, the early family is credited with shaping their orientations and influencing their career decisions.

For both men and women the fathers are important figures and often serve as models of how to make things work. Larry and his brothers all worked long hours on the farm, and Larry spoke often of his father's ability to manage—to take a small opportunity and turn it into a big one. Pete too worked in his father's business (a second job for the father in addition to working on the railroad). Pete's father told his boys that the business was for them, to teach them their responsibilities as men. This meant that they were to do the best possible job, work long hours, and keep the customer happy. For Pete, his father's model is the one he still follows in guiding his own management style.

Other fast-trackers who did not work directly with their fathers still mention them frequently and attribute many of their own characteristics to their father's advice or example. Christine talks about her caring, empathetic, father. Hal's father told him he could do anything he wanted to do as long as he relied on himself and didn't depend on others. For Hal, his father was an example too of a creative mind and a person willing to change and explore new ideas. Brian, specifically, states an often-repeated theme when he says: "Dad always said 'When you leave the world try to leave it better than you found it.' He did what he thought was right." The fast-trackers as a whole accept an obligation to make this world a better place to live.

Mothers are often seen as supportive and supplying the "brains of the bunch." They are perceived as having held high expectations for their children and believing that the children could meet these expectations. Pete's mother taught all her children to be open and to be frank about who they were and what they felt. She emphasized the importance of integrity and said her children were never to take advantage of anybody else—nor allow themselves to be taken advantage of by others. Pete says, in general, "Our parents thought we were pretty good."

Sometimes, the fast-trackers draw their models and find support from others than their parents. Although Sam thanks his parents for the "tone" of his life because they expected their children to be honest, moral, and true to themselves, it was his uncle that he wanted to emulate: "My uncle saw me as a precocious kid and always took time for me. I wanted to be like him." Alec wanted to do as well as his "perfect" older sister, and Larry, among others, credits his wife with his success: "She says I only succeeded in college my second time around because of her, and I think she's right."

7. Interdependence with others.   The fast-trackers had help not only from their families but from their school, work, and community associates. The fast-trackers did not make it to the top by themselves. An absolutely key factor in their success is that they were helped—and often helped in invisible ways that were almost so unnoticeable as to be overlooked. Hank states a common point of view: "I'm amazed at those who think they get ahead by *themselves*. People get ahead because of what other people do."

Fast-trackers receive help in their adult lives in much the same way they received it in their childhoods. The patterns of helping and being helped are established early, and seem not to vary much as the individuals grow older.

> When Brian was in sixth grade he was an "odd-ball, skinny red-haired kid," who was singled out for attention by a teacher and given leadership responsibilities. This teacher, Brian says, sort of took him under her wing. Now in his thirties, he still regards himself as a maverick, and has been singled out for his new job and transported half-way across the country by a vice-president who sees that he has unusual talent. Brian says, "I've always been lucky. It's like I have a fairy godmother or something."
>
> Hank was in second grade when he got into trouble partly for his own actions and partly because he was not part of the "in" group of his small town. His teachers gave him a very hard time and his mother wondered if he would survive second grade. Hank, however, had made friends with the son of an "in" family and the members of that family reached out to help him, teaching and advising him, and cautioning his teachers to go easy on him. In his adult life, as a junior vice-president, he was again an outsider, partly because he was younger than his peers and was consequently isolated in his company (see Chapter 7). Individuals higher up in the corporation, and

professional friends outside the corporation, quietly gave him advice and told him to sit tight. He did, and his more recent rise up the vice-presidential hierarchy was the result. In both his early and his current life, Hank has received help from others on the sidelines who have recognized and accepted his talents. The help was not direct, however, but just as important as if it had been more obvious to others.

Rich has been "adopted" by whole crews of people since he was a teenager and maybe before. All of the men that worked with his father took him on as one of their own. ("I was sort of adopted by all the crews on the railroad; I had a lot of help but not a lot of funds.") His fraternity brothers in college must have felt the same way, for they saw him through a rough first year and taught him how to study. Now in his role as president of a major division of his company, his people are again rallying round and participating in their success and his. Rich's approach to people allows and encourages this style of group helping.

All of the fast-trackers admit to considerable help from others somewhere. Ken remembers a basketball coach who set him on the right path in high school. "He was an absolutely remarkable man who had given his life to helping kids turn their heads around." Sam draws lessons from the people he met in the sports world; one woman in particular, who ran a sports club, knew how to get the most out of employees and customers and believed the customer was most important. Lessons and help come from unlikely places sometimes. Alec remembers a boss who did all the wrong things but "he's the one I'd like to work for." Tom is more specific when he says he learned from this "absolutely archaic man who had an unfailing sense about people even though he needed guides to get to the men's room." Part of being helped along the way is recognizing the odd places in which one might find that help.

Arthur, one of two fast-trackers without a father in residence while growing up, is the most emphatic about help he received from college instructors. He traces most of his coming of age back to a teacher at a community college who, he says, "challenged my basic values and led me to think about God and love and major concepts. I am a very emotional person and this unnerved me and forced me to think about things. His teaching had a long-term impact." Arthur credits his work success to his own ability to think things through, and remembers this instructor as a catalyst in beginning this process.

It is important to recognize that these men and women are not just helped by but help others. To receive the kind of help that is absolutely critical for success follows upon helping others oneself. Hal, as several of the others, views this mutual interaction in terms of establishing partnerships: "I select my boss and he selects me. We work out a partnership together, helping each other. I've had a lot of good examples."

The result of this investment in and reliance on interaction with others shows up in the strong feelings these fast-trackers have about their people. Most of them care enormously about the people with whom they work. Rich said, "This is what motivates me: my feelings about these people." Tom says even more simply, "This is my family."

8. Honesty about themselves and others.   Strikingly, these fast-trackers do not dress up bad situations, nor do they show undue modesty about their own accomplishments. They know what they have done well and what they have done badly and they are comfortable in admitting both. Their clarity about themselves is matched by a clarity about others and their organizations. In this way they appear to be well-grounded in the reality of their work lives; this perception of reality is the foundation for their decision-making about their own careers. In recalling past decisions or forecasting their career futures they are very clear about their strengths and the political and organizational world in which they live.

> Alec's description of his relatively short but rapid climb up the corporate ladder is one example of this clarity. Starting as an assistant to a manager in his first company, he quickly moved through the ranks to become a product manager of one of this company's secondary products ("a weak sister"), then product manager of the company's major product. In this role he encountered more supervision and more executive demands than in his previous assignments. He had originally come to the attention of the top executives as manager of the "weak sister" of the line where, with plenty of autonomy and room to experiment, he had dramatically increased sales. In his new job, however, as manager of the main product line, he found he had less freedom and there was more concern that any experimentation might in some way damage the firm's primary money maker.
>
> He learned from these experiences that he wanted to work in an area in which he had autonomy and freedom to experiment. He was able to define his own talents as best used when working on something "new" (or rapidly changing) as opposed to established ventures. And, from his mentors, he had learned it was okay to be different—if one were outstanding. And Alec planned on being outstanding.
>
> Consequently, when he was approached by another company (Company X) with a job managing an established product (electronic widgets) for a greatly increased salary, he said, "No. I prefer to manage new products." Company X responded that there was no such job in the company, and Alec went back to work. Two days later , a representative of Company X called and offered Alec an even greater salary for a new job they had just created as Manager of Widgets and New Products. Alec again said, "No," and went on to explain, "in that job I would be spending 95 percent of my time on widgets and 5 percent on new products and I am not interested." Two days later, Company X was again on the line, this time with an outrageous salary

offer for a Manager of New Products. Alec said, "Yes," changed companies, and developed a concept for a revolutionary new product now coming on the market.

With this behind him, he was called by Company Y and asked to manage their established line of electronic superwidgets. Again, Alec said no, and after three separate calls, Company Y had created a job that included a strong component of new product management, and again Alec changed companies. In this, his current position, he is again working with new products and also changing the way existing ones are managed. As he points out, if this process does not repeat itself, and work becomes routine, he will leave and start his own smaller company, beginning something new again. Part of Alec's success is that he knows what he does well and he is not persuaded to do anything else, and he has developed contingency plans down the road to continue doing what he does well.

In a different sort of way, Jon is equally clear about his career path, but part of the clarity is provided by his wife's commentary and reluctance to buy into the corporate belief that up is always better than staying where you are. In his first major move, Jon's wife hung up the telephone when he called her and refused to move with him. Jon went anyway—his wife had a profitable business venture and no children at the time—and they commuted between states for eleven years. Now, with another offer pending, one small child and another on the way, Jon has yielded to his wife's judgment and has turned down an important and prestigious post in another country. He laughs as he remembers, "Margaret said that if they have to come to America to find good men then it is not the place she wants to raise her children. And that's the end of it." It is in Jon's recounting of Margaret's viewpoint that one glimpses the clarity he brings to his own career, the importance of his own and his family's priorities, and an unwillingness to be moved from this track by lucrative offers that do not fit their needs and talents.

Rich is a third example of the clarity all these fast-trackers show about their career course. Perceived as the most likely successor to the current Chief Executive Officer of the corporation, he smiles and says, "not likely." He is pleased that others view him in this light but aware that the political realities of his world make this a most unlikely possibility. He is relieved by this rather than saddened. He too, much like Alec, performs at his highest levels when he is running an experiment and not guiding the mainstream activities of the company.

The clarity about themselves fits with other characteristics of these fast-trackers. They do not do nonproductive things. They do not waste time. Being honest about what they do well and doing it means that their energy is well-focused and expended in areas which have the greatest impact. They lose little time in pretense but make their time count for themselves, for their families, and for their organizations.

9. Strong ethical concerns. Most of these fast-trackers spontaneously voice concerns about values and ethics. It is important to them that they are doing what they believe is right, rather than those things which bring in the most dollars. "Integrity," "being who you are," and "honesty" were values that they learned in the family home.

> Tom's statement about his father as *the* ethical man is typical. Tom now says, "I can lie, but I can't lie and be comfortable because of him." This is borne out by Tom's own career; one of his first victories at work came when his boss, who had not yet accepted him, moved into his corner and said, "Finally, I have found an honest man."
>
> Rich is viewed not only as a caring man but one who has a strong core of integrity. He relates two incidents in his early life that reflect the origins of his own sense of ethics. In his early childhood he once stole a comic book and was taken back to the store by his mother not only to return the book but to work in the store sweeping floors until he had earned the price of this book. Later, as a teenager in a summer job in a manufacturing plant, all the people with whom he worked threw a party for him at the end of summer and brought him many gifts. "I was astonished," he said, "to find that all of the gifts were things they had taken from the company that they thought would help me in school. They felt that this was all right and that the company owed them." He refused the gifts but thanked them and has worked since to create quite a different attitude in his people—to give them ownership in the work of the company, and not in its materials and products. He believes that if they feel that it is *their* company they will not take from it but rather give more to it in terms of their time, energy, and commitment. Experience has proved him right.
>
> Alec has worked for three companies: his first was *very* ethical, he's less sure about the second, and he has been testing the waters in his current company (a very recent occurrence was reassuring when a profitable product was withheld from the public until more-than-sufficient evidence demonstrated that safety was ensured). He says, "An ethical question would be a sufficient reason for finding a new job."

All of the fast-trackers want to make a difference in the world, want to make a contribution, want to leave the world better than they found it. This set of beliefs includes an often unspoken set of assumptions that this can only happen when one supports basic human values that support the health and well-being of all involved, and not one at the expense of another.

10. Early exposure to a business environment. Since childhood the fast-trackers have been building their expertise in business. Given a different setting, they might have directed their talents in other directions. For most of them, however, early exposure to the business world formed an appropriate context for their own activities and they channeled their energies in ways that led to business success. Again, if it takes ten years to acquire expertise, the clock started running for these people at six, ten, and 14—not later. They have been building their careers for a long time although they may not have consciously accepted this until their mid-twenties.

> Four of the fast-trackers were involved in the businesses run by one or both of their parents: Tom's parents had a laundry and Tom learned *that* business, though he more often worked for one of his father's associates than his father himself; Hank's parents ran a telephone service and the front room of the house was always more business- than family-oriented; Larry learned from working on his father's farm; and Pete grew up working next to his father in the business that the father said was "to turn his boys into men."
>
> Others of the fast-trackers, such as Alec and Ken, were exposed to the business world through their fathers' work as managers and presidents of manufacturing operations. Two learned from their grandparents: Christine from her grandmother and Andrew from his grandfather. Still others, such as Sam, learned by listening to their parents' friends and talking with other family members.
>
> Each of the fast-trackers then incorporated their learning into their own lives by going to work early and taking responsibility for their own financial welfare. Many of them had at least two jobs from early in adolescence so that they could pay for their own expenses. All of them worked in the summers and most put themselves through college. Yet for most of them, this training was informal. Alec was the only one involved in Junior Achievement, dedicated to preparing young people for business, and the only one to experience the more formal training provided in this setting.

Only one woman among these fast-trackers recalls a family pattern that might have set her on a different course—the rest of them do not talk of parents reading poetry, writing books, or doing scientific experiments. It seems likely that the activities of the immediate family and the interests of the parents shape the direction in which people choose to use their energy later—and form the training ground that is a springboard for later success.

11. Viewing problems as opportunities. The fast-trackers have met with considerable success in their careers, but each one has also encountered and overcome difficulties. It is striking that in telling their stories, however, the difficulties are not described as defeats, but as incidents that eventually promoted further growth and learning. The most severe difficulties surfaced during mid-career and for some, derailment loomed as a real possibility. Skillful negotiating of this time of crisis, however, led to new and bigger opportunities in the succeeding years.

It would almost seem as if a clock is ticking that cannot be hurried along by outstanding achievements so that those who progress most rapidly in the early years must slow down at mid-career, at least for a time, and allow their years to catch up with their achievements. Among the senior members of this sample, all individuals were able to let this happen, and the time of sidelining, of potential derailment was passed through and followed by a time of increased opportunity.

> At mid-career, Tom was frustrated and dissatisfied because he felt sidelined, but this time of waiting gave him an opportunity to learn more about another side of the business. Larry felt angry and almost left the company at about the same time in his career, but a new job opened up in a different area and he learned more about the business in a short period of time than in any such comparable period before. Hank too learned to wait (see Chapter 9). The lessons learned by these fast-trackers were probably similar to those learned by all who survive the crises of mid-career and successfully traverse the Executive Transition. They learned to run slowly as well as fast and that versatility may well take them to the top of the line.

In summary, the fast-trackers demonstrate many characteristics of fully functioning human beings and have learned to make the most of their own and their peoples' potential. They do so by managing their time and energy, assuming responsibility for themselves, developing a variety of interests, working hard and enjoying their work tremendously, valuing their families and recognizing their interdependence with others, being honest and maintaining a high standard of values, and by utilizing their early training to forge ahead—turning difficulties into new pathways to success. This does not mean that they are always successful . . . and indeed, as will be noted later, several have come close to falling off the track at one time or other, and others may yet face this same experience. Yet these characteristics have, to date, brought them to their current status, a status evaluated as successful by those with whom they work.

CHAPTER 3

Diversity on the Fast Track

Varieties of Style

*Differences in leadership style seem to revolve
around differences in basic orientations to ideas,
things, and people.*
ABRAHAM ZALEZNIK
"MANAGEMENT OF
DISAPPOINTMENT"

*An effective leader must be the master of two ends of
the spectrum: ideas at the highest level of
abstraction and actions at the most mundane level of
detail.*
THOMAS PETERS AND ROBERT
WATERMAN
IN SEARCH OF EXCELLENCE

Although in basic characteristics and values the fast-trackers have much in common, in manner and expression they are very different from each other. Different degrees of calmness or activity, outward warmth or inward thoughtfulness characterize each of these fast-trackers. Jon is cool, contained, possibly stern; Ken is warm, effusive, impulsive. Rich is steady, consistent, and caring. Hal is quick to show interest in others and to get excited about ideas. Christine is calm, attentive, and thoughtful. Pete talks non-stop and sits still only momentarily. Clearly, however, the differences in personal manner and outward expression are the vehicles for expressing the common characteristics of confidence, ability to communicate, and commitment that are characteristic of the style of the entire fast-track group. Differences in manner and expression are an overlay on the basic similarities among the fast-trackers.

Varieties of Style

	CREATORS	CONTRIBUTORS
COOPERATORS	Doing things differently in partnership with others	Making things better for the entire team
COMPETITORS	Doing things differently and winning	Making things better and being first

Although there are basic commonalities in style, there is also great diversity; each fast-tracker has developed a personal style that is unique. Still, two sets of differences *can* be identified. These differences reflected some basic distinctions among the group. The differences became apparent in noting the frequency with which some fast-trackers used words like "vision" and "change," while another group more often talked about "making something better," "solving a problem," and "meeting a challenge." The first group used the terms "creating" and "building" as they described their career paths. The second group more often used the terms "contributing" and "making it work."

The difference in language suggested that the fast-trackers positioned themselves differently along a dimension that ranged from "doing things differently" to "doing things better." Some individuals were distinctly at one end or the other but some were close to the middle zone in which doing things differently and doing things better had a more equivalent place in their priorities. All the fast trackers, however, could be classified on one side or other of the middle point. Those more interested in doing things differently were called *creators*; those more interested in making things better were called *contributors*.

The differences in language were indicative of differences in style. Those characterized as creators, by and large (but not in every instance), talked more and longer than those characterized as contributors. The creators also told more stories and more often strayed from the point at hand; they spent more time talking about people and less about specific tasks. Noting these differences, it became clear that style is not just a pattern of interaction but also reflects an underlying orientation toward self and others. The sober accountant concerned about numbers and quantitative measures is unlikely to be a garrulous, hail-fellow-well-met type. The outgoing salesman who spends time polishing his persuasive skills is unlikely to be the non-talker in any given group. People's values, attitudes, and beliefs affect and influence their interpersonal style. Style is a reflection of one's orientation to the world.

One other set of differences in style became apparent in the interview sessions, again noticeable in the choice of language that each fast-tracker used. This set of differences suggested another dimension characterizing the fast-trackers, one that cut across the groups defined as creators or contributors. Some fast-trackers more frequently mentioned their delight in competition, whereas others never mentioned it at all. Some fast-trackers talked of their joy in sharing power with all their people, whereas others mentioned this only briefly. This second dimension, then, extended from those who emphasized cooperation and partnership at one end to those who emphasized competition and individual achievement at the other. Again, the fast-trackers ranged across the entire spectrum, with some at the ends and some closer to the middle. It was possible, however, on the basis of the relative frequency of the terms used, to categorize each of the fast-trackers as competitive or cooperative in style and orientation. These categories cut across the ranks of both creators and contributors.

The fast-trackers were not asked directly about any of these differences. However, the number of spontaneous references to creation and contribution, competition and cooperation were used as indicators of the importance of these orientations in their thinking. Among the fast-trackers as a whole these terms—or their synonyms—were used with great frequency. Then, for each individual telling his or her own story, the number of references to each concept reflected the category most consistent with his or her viewpoint. On this basis, two groups of fast-trackers were delineated—those tending toward the creator end of the continuum and those closer to the contributor pole. Then, each fast-tracker was also categorized as either cooperative or competitive, resulting in four subsets among the fast-trackers as a whole.

In thus categorizing the fast-trackers, it is noticeable that the emphasis on competition is stronger among the junior members and less strong among the senior ones. The emphasis on non-competitive or cooperative activities may be something that comes to these corporate stars more readily with the passage of years. This may reflect a common process of development in organizational growth and maturity.

The distinction between the creators and contributors, however, is more likely to be one that is maintained throughout adulthood. Other writers have reported on similar distinctions such as that between artists and scientists: the artists work intuitively, guided by an inner sense of rhythm, and create a whole out of existing parts; the scientists work rationally, guided by the demands of the task, and step by step arrive at a new synthesis of existing parts.[1] Our creators are the corporate artists creating new structures, cultures, and ways of managing; whereas the contributors are the corporate scientists building a better mousetrap with the knowledge now at hand. Creators do things differently, and contributors make things more effective. Yet within each group, some are more competitive than others.

Eight of the fast-trackers were categorized as creators and nine as contributors. Some in each group were categorized as more competitive than cooperative. The following groups resulted from this breakdown:

------------◆------------

Styles of the Fast-Trackers

Cooperative Creators: Rich, Hal, Tom, Ken, Don
Competitive Creators: Art, Larry, Alec
Cooperative Contributors: Andrew, Jon, Hank, Jerry, Christine, Brian
Competitive Contributors: Sandra, Pete, Sam

------------◆------------

Part of the success of the fast-trackers is due to the fact that they know who they are, they know what they do well and what they do less well. They spend their time doing what they do well—in and out of organizations. The creators find themselves in jobs where they are charged with doing things differently, the contributors in jobs where they are asked to do things better. They manage their time and energy well and they work in jobs that are well matched to their abilities. In terms of self-understanding as well as management development, the four categories that emerged from this sample are useful to a group far beyond this sample. The statements of the fast-trackers clarify each of the four subsets, defining four different orientations reflected in their personal styles.

COOPERATIVE CREATORS

The creators are identifiable by their references to "vision," "change," "experimentation," and their frequent comments about having fun. They are working more often in accord with an inner sense of timing. In their job changes, they move on, not when the company calls but when they are bored, lacking challenge, or have completed their personal agenda. They are motivated by what they believe can be. None of them describes taking a pattern that already works and making it better. Each describes the implementation of a new pattern.

The cooperative creators are identifiable by their references to partnership, working through and with people, taking care of others, making it happen for everybody in the company. The most salient distinction between these fast-trackers and their more competitive peers is their emphasis on the word *partnership*.

Hal represents the more senior members with this orientation when he describes how he is going to change his corporation. Like the other creators, it becomes clear that he did not become this way on the job but rather has a history of doing things differently that reaches back into his childhood. It seems that his personality (along with that of the other fast-trackers) matched the needs of a specific company in developing innovative approaches to particular and yet far-reaching tasks.

Hal describes his job as follows: "My job is to be the architect for change in this company in a well-ordered, consistent way . . . We have unbelievable potential if we can just learn how to manage it." He follows this with a description of his own orientation: "I am an 'incurable optimist.' I always seem to have ideas on how to do things differently, and I did these things." In speaking of his work and his organization he uses the word *vision*: "We had a vision to put together a new financial organization. We spent seven days a week at work or on airplanes and we achieved our goal." And he says spontaneously about each point of his career: "it was an exciting time," and over and over again, "it was fun." (None of these men, by the way, sees fun as associated with leisure or frivolity. Their "fun" is dead serious and describes the satisfaction they find in doing what they believe must be done, in having a vision and turning it into a reality.)

Throughout Hal's story he emphasizes the importance of people and partnership in creating change and turning a vision into reality. At one point he says clearly, "I believe in working with and for people." And as he talks about his current job he says first, "I always had a *vision* of what this company could be and the vision is now shared," and, later, "I'm doing what I've always wanted to do. I believe in continually creating change in your life."[2]

Ken is a younger representative of the cooperative creator orientation who has a long history of creating new ways of doing things. Doing things differently got him in trouble in his early school years but began to pay off in graduate school, where he created his own program using new technology and thus set a pattern for others. He then created his own small business and spent 18 hours a day "bouncing from item to item to item," a condition he sees as a prerequisite for personal satisfaction. In a later corporate job, he trained new recruits and, in the process, isolated what he sees as the most important quality needed to succeed in business, the "ability to take relatively disconnected events and weave them together into a larger whole and create a common understanding." Of his current task, he says, "I want to change the perspective and culture of this organization." His dream someday is to take another business that is totally ineffective and turn it around.[3]

COMPETITIVE CREATORS

The competitive creators were distinguished from their more cooperative peers only by the fact that, at some time during the interview, they said clearly either "I want to win," or "I hate to lose," or spontaneously described themselves as competitive. Their emphasis on the "I" was at least as strong as their emphasis on the "we" of partnership. Each of these individuals, however, also affirmed his or her belief in working with and through people. It is notable that the competitive group as a whole (including both creators and contributors) includes all of the junior people, a mere quarter of the middle group and none of the senior members of the sample. This suggests rather strongly that the emphasis on competition may be a result of youth and may not necessarily represent a distinct orientation.

The two representatives of this group at middle levels, Art and Larry, are at the very top of this group in age, experience, and status. Both of these men, while demonstrating a competitive streak, also emphasize the importance of creation and building new patterns, and both are in charge of innovative divisions within their companies. Art's description of his experience is similar to that of other creators—but he emphasizes his desire to win.

Like other creators, Art does things because they feel right. Early in his career, he was on the engineering side of the business and transferred to marketing as fast as he could. Of this decision, he says, "I'm not an engineer. I despise the mentality of engineering. Engineers do it because it makes sense, not because it feels right." In contrast to his perceptions of engineers, Art believes his talent lies with people: "I am masterful at making people feel important." Describing his career path since that time, Art says that early on, "We worked to build a new sales program." And of more recent years, he states: "I am always creating something from nothing. My boss and I created this thing, this company."

He is ambivalent about the prospect of further steps up the ladder that loom in the immediate future. He says, practically in the same breath and with great emphasis at first, "*I only know how to win*," and then follows this with, "I think being number two is more comfortable than number one," and "I'm not sure I want to move up and have to do all the right things— maybe I don't want to."[4]

The one representative of this orientation at the junior level is Alec, only 33, who has a job title comparable to those of the men closer to 40 than 30. He too is junior for his status, and faces, most likely, a developmental transition in the near future. His job, with its emphasis on new products and new ways of managing, is one that is clearly designed to match his innovative approach. In addition, he said, "I like to compete." Both innovation and competition are driving forces in Alec's life at the moment.

COOPERATIVE CONTRIBUTORS

The emphasis in this group is not on building or changing things but on making them work, making them effective. The fast-trackers with this orientation often refer to themselves as "contributors," people who are making the system work better. When asked why they made career choices, unlike the creators they do not respond in terms of visions and challenges, but say simply, "because it was there." The focus of the career path is guided more by the perceived needs of tasks than by an inner rhythm or personal dream. During the course of the interview, they never sponta- neously refer to the creation of a new pattern but document instead the increased effectiveness of the ventures that they have managed.

The cooperative contributors are distinguished from their more com- petitive peers by the fact that they emphasize the people aspects of their jobs. They use the word partnership less than the creators, but they state in other words that their work is with people. In much of what they say, however, there is a greater task-orientation than in the words of the creators: they are not building something new, they are doing the task—whatever the task may be—very well.

The two most senior representatives of this group, Andrew and Jon, are comparable to Rich and Hal in status and in years. The differences between the two sets of men (Andrew and Jon vs. Rich and Hal) are, thus, not reflective of differences in age or status. According to the perceptions of those who work for them, their career possibilities are very much the same. Of the four, three have been mentioned for the top slot in their corporate hierarchy. Consequently, it seems likely that differences between them reflect differences in well-developed and mature personality *orienta-*

tion.[5] The orientations have been developed over time and have found a good fit in terms of company needs. Style, in this sense, is the outward expression of orientation.

There is, however a clear difference in the functions that these creators and contributors fulfill near the top of their megacorporations. Whereas Rich and Hal are charged with innovating within their setting, Andrew and Jon are within the mainstream of corporate management and are expected to increase the effectiveness of the total organization. They are not expected, not in their own words nor in those of others, to innovate. Instead they do well, perhaps better than anybody who has gone before them, the major work of the organization.

> Andrew, in describing his career track, highlights two experiences that he found especially positive: the first was when an entire facility drew together to accomplish a major task and achieved their goal, and the second when he had the opportunity to manage an extremely well-designed and well-run facility where the structure had been put in place by his predecessor. The first instance he described as exciting and stimulating, the second as delightful and pleasant. (Note that the creators want to take something that is ineffective, and dramatically change it by making it effective, whereas the contributors enjoy improving upon the management of a well-run outfit.) Andy sums up his position as, "I always do the next thing to be done," and "I want to be a *positive contributor* rather than top dog."
>
> Andrew works well with people and sees his career moving back and forth between accomplishing new tasks and helping others to accomplish these tasks. Since he was young he has always pitched in to help when necessary and never questioned that he would contribute to the general good.[6]

The individual contributors at middle levels are also similar in status to the creators who are their peers, but like the senior contributors are most concerned with doing well what has to be done. In their descriptions of their career history, they do not clearly outline new projects that they set in motion, but some of the enthusiasm of the mid-level creators is also evident in their stories.

> Both Christine and Brian emphasize the importance of making a contribution. Christine is emphatic (in a calm way) about her role as a cooperative contributor. She says, "I want to contribute to society in a positive and meaningful way; I want to know that I have helped the world to be a better place." Brian wants to have an impact on his company but mostly he wants to carry out the message given him by his father: "When you leave the world, just leave it better than you found it."

COMPETITIVE CONTRIBUTORS

The more competitive of the contributors are those who are the youngest in the entire sample, and who are still in the process of determining their potential path through the organizational ranks. As a group, they are more diverse than the other three groups, and individually may still be developing their own orientations. Yet, in their career histories they do not mention creating or building—rather they talk about doing it well.

Sandra, more than any of the others, describes her career track as following a plan that is under her control and that was created before she entered the career world. Pete, who is more exuberant and runs at a rapid pace, says more than once, "I have a personal drive to succeed," and "I love responsibility, I love to take the heat and come out on top." Sam sums up his position simply, and in this accords with many of the others with a competitive orientation: "I hate to lose."

In summary, the fast-trackers are very different from each other in style (overt expression) and in orientation (underlying approach to the world). The differences among the fast-trackers are apparent in descriptions of their early experience as well as their current lives. The development of their orientation as creators and contributors began early and has continued as they have undertaken tasks in the business world particularly suited to their individual orientation.

The clear distinction between the creators and the contributors is best seen among the senior representatives of this sample: They are very clear about who they are and what they do. The lack of differences in status and age highlights the differences that do exist—the differences in orientation as creators and contributors. The distinction is fuzzier among the younger members of the sample, who nonetheless show definite inclinations toward creator and contributor orientations. Yet the younger people have had less opportunity to test, to refine and hone, their orientations in the world; their orientations are still developing and are not yet fully mature.

The age distinction between cooperators and competitors is suggestive of some differences in expectations at different career stages. All of these individuals are doing well—and, therefore, it is likely that their attitudes and behavior are, at this time, reinforced by others in the organization. In other words, their attitudes and behavior are meeting expectations, suggesting that expectations for attitudes and behavior vary at different stages. It may well be that cooperation is the norm at highest levels of management, defining corporate expectations for senior executives, and a competitive orientation is expected in early career stages and may even be helpful in moving rapidly through junior levels, and the expectations for those in the middle are not as clearly defined. If this is the case, those from 36 to 43 may be proceeding through an Executive Transition in which a competitive orientation fades away and a cooperative orientation takes hold, at least among those who continue to succeed. The competitive orientation, persisting through mid-career and into the senior years may well be the primary reason for mid-career difficulties and a chief cause of derailment of those on the fast track to the top.

The fast track itself may represent a learning experience in which corporate stars move into new galaxies and, having established their place through individual achievement, turn to creating a new pattern or heightening the effectiveness of the old one by working in conjunction, in partnership, and in teams with others. Within the cooperative view of the world, moreover, there is room for, in fact it is essential that there be, both creators and contributors. The contributors are pulled by the direction of the company to solve the next problem and to meet the next challenge. The creators more often create their own problems and their own challenges by seeing clearly what may be . . . and working to bring it into being. Both creators and contributors are therefore essential for our corporations to survive and prosper in an age marked by drastic economic change.

The origins of differences in style will become the focus of Part III of this book. In the next section, we follow the fast-trackers along their career paths, from career entry and then the journey from star to statesman as they move up the corporate ladder.

PART II

Growing Up in Organizations

The Interplay of Substance and Style

*I think I had a flair for [politics] but natural feelings
are never enough. You have got to marry those
natural feelings with really hard work—but the hard
work comes more easily when you are doing things
that you want to do.*
MARGARET THATCHER
NEWARK STAR LEDGER
*The pertinent question is not how to do things right
but how to find the right things to do, and to
concentrate resources and efforts on them.*
PETER DRUCKER
MANAGING FOR RESULTS

The Career Stages: Substance and Style

	CAREER TIMELINE			
				SENIOR
			MIDDLE	
		JUNIOR		
			Executive Transition	
	ENTRY			
AGE:	21–25	25–35	35–45	45 +
P A R A L L E L S T A G I F E E L S	PRE-SCHOOL	CHILDHOOD	ADOLESCENCE	ADULTHOOD
F O C U S	PREPARATION IN SCHOOL INTERPERSONAL SKILLS	INDIVIDUAL ACHIEVEMENT SKILL BUILDING	RELEARNING RELATIONSHIPS REEVALUATING PRIORITIES	CONCEPTUALIZING STRATEGIES ESTABLISHING DIRECTIONS
R E A S O N A S C R E N T	OUTSTANDING PREPARATION OR SKILLS	OUTSTANDING INDIVIDUAL ACHIEVEMENT	LEARNING TEAM BEHAVIOR	EMPOWERING TEAMS AND ORGANIZATIONS
L D R S H P D E V M T	SUBSTANCE OR STYLE	SUBSTANCE	STYLE	INTEGRATE SUBSTANCE + STYLE

The fast-track career path has its own course: it has a beginning, a middle, and an end, with transitions and crises along the way. In many ways the stages of the career may be compared to the early developmental stages of life: just as young people grow up first in families and then the world at large, those entering the career world have the new task of growing up in organizations. Entry onto the career track is much like the pre-school years in life when children first learn to walk and talk as preparation for the rest of their development. The junior level parallels childhood or pre-

——••⟨∞⟩••——

Substance in the Career Stages

SUBSTANCE

. . . .	KNOWLEDGE
. . . .	UNDERSTANDING
. . . .	AWARENESS
. . . .	KNOWING YOURSELF

CAREER STAGES	RELEVANCE OF SUBSTANCE
Entry	"Apparent" substance determines balance of choice or chance
Junior years	Importance of learning about self and organization
Middle years	Reevaluating learning in terms of expanded awareness of self, others and the organization
Senior years	Teaching others about themselves and their organization; foundation for establishing priorities and creating a philosophy

——••⟨∞⟩••——

adolescence with its emphasis on building skills and developing tentative alliances. The difficult mid-career transition finds its counterpart in adolescence, which in the career and in life, is a time of ambivalence and reevaluation. The senior career years then are similar to adulthood, in which individuals use their now-developed skills in a new context—in the best cases for the benefit of others.

Getting on the fast track, proceeding through the junior, mid-career, and senior years are the stages of a journey that is completed by only a few. The trip is arduous and of high intensity and events are written on a larger screen than in many other lives. These are the same stages, however, that with less visibility, describe the lives of many: people, in general, begin a lifework (paid or unpaid) around 21; acquire the skills to pursue this work from 21 to 35; proceed through a time of reevaluation in mid-life from 35 to 45 that often results in life changes (and sometimes, an unwillingness to continue learning and growing); and then arrive at a higher level of skill and understanding after 45 (at least those who continue to be open to new learning do) and turn their attention to improving the world for others.

In the progression of these career stages, *substance* and *style*, the two components of leadership, alternate in emphasis. The accumulation of substance or knowledge is important in the junior career years. A reevaluation of past learning and a modification of style then occurs in the middle career. Finally, both substance and style come together in the senior years as a prerequisite for leadership on a large scale.

The *style* of each of the fast-trackers is highly developed and marked by self-confidence, a flair for communication, and strong commitment to achieving goals. In addition (as described in Chapter 3), each of the fast-trackers developed an orientation (underlying approach) and style (external expression) as a creator or contributor, cooperator or competitor. The origins of style in early family life and the effects of style in the current families of the fast-trackers are the subjects of Part III of this book.

Substance, the other leadership component, is knowledge—knowledge of self, others, and of information in specific fields. People begin to accumulate substance early in life as they are open to and learn from their experience. But the necessary knowledge for specific endeavors is varied, and exposure to new situations or the assumption of new responsibilities requires the learning of new knowledge. The key to substance is, therefore, the *ability to learn*, and the willingness to move through the learning process again and again.

The fast-trackers are all people of substance. They are not, in any sense, lightweights, floating up the corporate hierarchy on the strength of their ability to influence others on matters of which they know little. They know and love what they are doing. They know their businesses, themselves, and their organizations. The fast-trackers do their homework, often into the small hours of the morning. They are, by and large, willing to learn from their experience. They are willing to accept the feedback and the criticism that is so essential to further growth and development.

Accumulating substance takes time in the long term: to know oneself, others, and an organization takes years, years in which the door to new learning is kept open. Accumulating substance also takes time in the short term: time that is often countable in the hours after five that are spent on preparation, on getting ready for what is to come.

It is managers who *know* things that matter, who document what they know, and who offer this knowledge to the group, who have an opportunity to move up the corporate ladder or make a contribution in another setting. It is the managers who know things that matter, who have stood up for what they know, who can be relied upon the next time a serious issue is at stake. However those who *know* are also those who say "I don't know" when such is the case. Only those who truly know something can recognize and own up to the situations in which this is not so. Those with substance say both "I know" and "I don't know." Regular and appropriate use of both these phrases is a sign of influence and power in groups and organizations.

Substance is often confused with *apparent* or *perceived* substance. When selecting people for new jobs, for example, decisions are often based, naturally enough, on the *apparent substance* reflected in the college transcript or the resume. When first-hand knowledge of an applicant is not available, paper credentials stand in for this knowledge. However, as many employers are aware, the substance reflected on paper is not always demonstrated on the job itself. Yet the perception of substance, whether or not this is real or apparent, is an important factor for individuals moving into new jobs or situations.

For the fast-trackers, apparent substance was a critical factor in determining their mode of entry into the work world. A strong college education in a field perceived as relevant was viewed as a measure of substance for the fast-trackers entering the corporate sphere. At time of career entry, the perception of substance affected their lives as much or more than the actual accumulation of knowledge. Yet for a career on the fast track to actually begin, once the doorstep has been crossed, the perception must be backed up by the reality of genuine knowledge.

The variety of ways in which the fast-trackers entered the work world bears a direct relationship to their perceived degree of substance at time of entry. Their movement up the track, however, is determined by their actual substance, based on a willingness to learn—about themselves, about others, and the organization. Successful in accumulating and using knowledge in these junior years, they then approach the door of the Executive Transition, where a new set of rules, guidelines, and associates awaits them. In moving into mid-career, the new expectations often jolt them into reevaluating their knowledge and refining their styles. They succeed in surviving the Executive Transition only by being willing to learn a new set of rules, develop new sets of connections with others, and modify the competitiveness of early style with the team-oriented spirit required for life at the top of the corporation. Those who succeed become the senior statesmen who provide guidance for large numbers of people to accomplish common goals.

This is not easy to do. Young fast-trackers are rewarded for learning new skills quickly, for carrying out individual projects, for moving into the front lines. Faced with the mid-career transition, they are shocked that they must rethink their behaviors, attitudes, and values. As one young fast-tracker said: "You mean I am supposed to give up doing all the things that got me where I am? You're nuts!" Nuts or not, this is exactly the task of mid-career. The learnings in mid-career, if achieved, will prepare the way for the integration of substance and style, the hallmark of leadership at the senior level.

Substance is the foundation of the climb up the corporate ladder. Style is the process, the motion, the way in which the climb is made. Substance is knowledge, and those with substance are comfortable saying "I don't know" and then, if it matters, proceeding to turn not knowing into knowing. Style, on the other hand, is confidence, communication, and commitment, and those with style are comfortable saying "yes" and saying "no," making commitments and withholding them, standing firmly on their consciousness of themselves and their degree of responsiveness to the environment. Substance is the basis for establishing priorities and style is the way in which we communicate our priorities and our intentions to others. Together substance and style equal leadership.

Those with substance and little style hold their knowledge to themselves and wonder why the world is not listening to or profiting from their advice. Their knowledge is not shared. These are represented by the many technocrats of our universe. Those with style and little substance are the "politicos," the "operators," the "hucksters" of this world—selling to others things of which they have little knowledge and in which they have no belief. They operate for their own advantage, for their own profit. Substance without style is a structure built only to house those few who live within; style without substance is hot air selling emptiness—no house at all—to others who are gullible enough to pay for lack of structure, lack of strength.

People with both substance and style help build open structures through which new information flows; and pass along to others the means with which to build their own structures. Substance and style together are the foundation of a life-long learning process, of strength *and* flexibility, of knowledge of self and adaptation to a changing environment, of receptivity and activity. Substance and style equal leadership.

The next chapters trace the fast-trackers' journeys through the career stages from entry through the senior stages, noting the interplay of substance and style in their journey to the top.

CHAPTER 4

Choice and Chance at Career Entry

Perceptions of Substance and Style

> *Success in real life depends on how well a person is able to find and exploit the opportunities that are available to him, and, at the same time, discover and deal with potentially serious problems before they become critical.*
>
> J.S. LIVINGSTON
> "THE MYTH OF THE WELL-
> EDUCATED MANAGER"

Choice is a rather dignified word for the way many fast-trackers fell into what turned out to be productive career paths. Some, indeed, did choose their careers following interview sessions customarily held on college campuses. Most, however, stumbled onto an opportunity and turned it to their advantage, which resulted in the initial positions that began their careers. Finally, a very few had to work at finding an opportunity at all; opportunities did not fall into their laps, but had to be actively created over a period of several months in which job-seeking was made into a career in itself.

Some of the fast-trackers, then, credit their first jobs to choice. More of them describe their initial opportunities as a result of chance or a lucky event. On closer examination, their views of choice and chance are directly related to *perceptions* of their substance and style at the time of career entry. As noted earlier, college degrees, in particular those from schools evaluated by national committees as "very good" or better and with course

Choices and Chances at Career Entry

PERCEPTION OF CHOICE	PERCEPTION OF CHANCE
STRENGTH IN "APPARENT" SUBSTANCE Strong school record or on-the-job training	STRENGTH OF STYLE Initiative and strong interpersonal skills
ASSETS AT ENTRY: SUBSTANCE	ASSETS AT ENTRY: STYLE
EARLY CAREER TASK: INCREASE STYLE + SUBSTANCE	EARLY CAREER TASK: INCREASE SUBSTANCE

matter in subjects directly related to potential careers, are perceived as a measure of substance or knowledge. Such degrees do reflect a measure of substance, but a narrow measure, because they take no account of the self- and people-knowledge integral to a full definition of substance. College degrees also do not indicate an ability to apply this knowledge in a constructive way, which requires a concomitant amount of style. Yet the fast-trackers who had acquired such degrees—or who had extensive on-the-job training—perceived themselves as *choosing* their first jobs. Those who did not have such a degree nor applicable training, relied more heavily on the strength of their style, confidence, communication skills, and commitment, in order to get across the doorstep of the corporate world. These fast-trackers, the majority, perceived themselves as lucky, finding their jobs by *chance*.

INTERPLAY OF CHOICE AND CHANCE

Regardless of the fast-trackers' perceptions, however, some degree of choice and chance played a part in their initial entry onto the fast track. Among those who perceived themselves as having *chosen* their jobs are several who actually selected their organization because of prior connections with that organization: through their own work experience, that of friends, or that of friends of their parents or parents of their friends. In this way, the interpersonal connections that they had developed, resting on their own interpersonal skills, played a role in their job choices. In the eyes of the fast-trackers, these prior connections lie in the realm of *chance*; yet this group focuses on the degree of *choice* in their selection of a first position.

On the other hand, all of the individuals who perceived themselves as finding their jobs by *chance* had also prepared themselves for these opportunities. They had done their homework and studied the companies; in effect, they had accumulated substance, although this might have been less apparent to others. They had experience in other areas of the workplace that they were able to generalize to the settings that they wished to enter. They may not have *seemed* as prepared as some others, to either themselves or to job recruiters, but they had acquired the necessary substance to begin their career on the fast track. Their ability to convince those making hiring decisions of this, however, drew upon strengths in *style*. Although the fast-trackers had, in fact, *chosen* to prepare themselves to take advantage of opportunities in the corporate world, they viewed the fact that they were able to do so as coming their way by *chance*.

These perceptions of substance and style—for example, an over-valuation of substance (actually *apparent* substance) at the expense of style—are common in the workplace and suggest the reason why many suffer career disappointments for reasons that are ill understood. Those on the lower rungs of organizations tend to view substance as meritorious; actual or even *apparent* substance is expected to open up choices on any career track. These same people often regard strength in style with skepticism and a certain lack of understanding. Advances made because of strength in style, when personal attributes and interpersonal skills carry the day, are often viewed as a result of *chance*. However, as those further up the ladder are often aware, leadership requires *both substance and style*. It is the combination of substance and style that increases the chances of success on any career track.

The necessity for balancing substance and style carries yet another message: those who are strong on substance (perceived or otherwise) are in danger of derailment unless they develop the necessary interpersonal skills associated with style by the time of the difficult mid-career transition; likewise, those who are strong on style must be certain of acquiring the essential substance before they too hit the bumps and potholes of mid-career. The journey up the fast track requires strength in both areas, in knowledge and interpersonal skills. Neither substitutes for the other beyond the first few rungs of the corporate ladder. In terms of the common association, then, of substance with choice and style with chance, a career on the fast track is the result of the interplay of both choice and chance.

"PERCEIVED" SUBSTANCE, CHOICES, AND CHANCES

In spite of the need for both substance and style, choice and chance, to be successful on the fast track, all who desire to make this journey must recognize and respond to perceptions of others on these matters, regardless of whether or not they are *mis*perceptions. The ways in which the fast-trackers entered the corporate world were determined as much by others' perceptions of their preparation for this step as by this preparation itself. In fact, their mode of entry was determined to a large extent by perceptions of *apparent* substance drawn from the kind and quality of their college education.

All but one of the fast-trackers entered their career track with a college degree. In earning their degrees, all of them had performed fairly well, graduating with at least a B average, and half of them were on the Dean's list, graduating with honors. However, the subjects in which they majored, whether or not they changed majors, and the apparent quality of the schools from which they graduated all affected the degree of choice or chance with which they perceived their entry onto the fast track.

The fast-trackers, however, had *chosen* their schools and had done so on the basis of priorities that included many factors beyond the quality of education itself. Some schools, usually the "very good" ones, were chosen primarily on educational factors. Other schools were chosen for their proximity to home or work, the financial aid that they offered, or the opportunity to play sports. With the aid of loans and scholarships, and with part-time (and sometimes full-time) work, all of the men and one woman put themselves through school, paying for most of their education. One of the striking characteristics of the fast-trackers is that they assumed financial responsibility for themselves at an early age (and not always because of necessity) and this governed many of their choices in regard to higher education. Their work experience, therefore, affected the choices that they made in terms of college, which, in turn, affected their mode of entry into the corporate world. Both work during college and the nature of the college experience themselves are, therefore, related to choice and chance.

Putting Oneself Through School

The fast-trackers worked enormous numbers of hours while they were in school. When the number of hours a week that they worked is taken into account, it is astonishing that they performed as well as they did. All but one of the fast-trackers worked during the school year at college, and everybody worked during the summers. Three of the fast-trackers were part of a "co-op" college program in which they worked half time and studied half time, graduating in five years. Nine other fast-trackers worked fifteen to forty hours a week during the school year. Pete worked 55 to 70 hours a week. Despite the heavy load that they were carrying, all but one of the fast-trackers graduated within the expected amount of time: normally four years, and five years for those in co-op programs. Pete with his heavy work load graduated in four and one-half years.

As was typical of the fast-trackers' earlier lives, their college existence was extremely busy, and they packed more things into one day than most. Sam, who worked a minimum of 40 hours a week, graduated first in his major with honors. He describes an average school day with the following schedule:

8:00 AM to 12 Noon	Classes
12:30 PM to 4 PM	Taught tennis
4:00 PM to 6:00 PM	Practiced tennis
6:00 PM to 7:00 PM	Dinner
7:00 PM to 12 Midnight	Taught tennis
12 Midnight on . . .	Studied for classes

Their involvement in work and other activities throughout college reflects the orientation of the fast-trackers and, to some extent, their priorities. Most of the fast-trackers would have been accepted at very good schools and were capable of graduating from those schools with honors. However, their own sense of values led them to work their way through college, often spending as much if not more of their time in non-academic pursuits. The fast-trackers were clearly bringing more to the business world than a college education. In going through college and working along the way, they demonstrated the same management of time and energy, the same complexity and diversity that are found in their current lives. This was not, however, always initially clear to the fast-trackers or to recruiters. Turning these experiences into the foundation for a career on the fast track, therefore, was not a foregone conclusion as they sought to enter the business world, and introduced a large element of perceived chance into the career entries of many.

Nature and Quality of Education

It is within the context of their devotion to work and other activities that the college education of the fast-trackers must be understood. In effect, their high levels of activity in a variety of areas, including work, constitutes for most a large part of the *substance* that they brought to the work world. The characteristics developed in their early years—for example, their management of time and energy—saw them through college and are in large part responsible for their survival along the fast track.

Their entry into the work world, however, was perceived by many as related to *chance,* because of the importance of perceptions of "apparent" substance on entry into new situations. Consequently, the way in which they entered the work world is strongly related to college major and, secondarily, to the quality of the school they attended.

College Majors and Career Entry

Majored in Business, Economics, or Engineering

Creators:

Rich	Choice
Larry	Chance
Alec	Choice

Contributors:

Andrew	Choice
Jon	Chance
Hank	Choice
Jerry	Choice
Brian	Chance
Pete	Choice

Majored in Liberal Arts, Other Area, or No Degree

Creators:

Hal	Chance
Tom	Chance
Art	Chance
Ken	Chance
Don	Chance

Contributors:

Christine	Chance
Sandra	Chance
Sam	Chance

The fast-trackers who majored in business-related subjects, other things being equal, more often believed that they had chosen their jobs than those who majored in liberal arts. Both Larry and Brian, who perceived a strong element of chance in their career entry, were the two who had majored belatedly in business but had started in another field. In addition, Jon, Larry, and Sam went to schools that did not rank as highly as those of some of the others. There is clearly a direct one-to-one relationship between major in school, with adjustment for the quality of school, and the perception of choice and chance in entering the work place. It is interesting to note as well, that choice was more often perceived by contributors than creators, again, related to the fact that contributors were more likely to major in business-related subjects.

PATTERNS OF ENTERING THE FAST TRACK

As is evident in the above table, six fast-trackers perceived themselves as choosing their first job. These six were spread across all age groups among the fast-trackers, with four contributors and two creators forming part of this group. Nine fast-trackers perceived themselves as stumbling onto unexpected opportunities. Again, this group ranges across all ages, with six creators and three contributors making up its composition. Finally, two of the fast-trackers worked hard to create opportunities to enter the business world—although they found their jobs by "chance" they *chose* to actively create that opportunity. Both of these are among the youngest in the sample, and both are contributors. The fast-trackers' stories themselves demonstrate the variety of ways in which choices and chances were related in their initial leap onto the fast track.

Choosing A Job

The fast-trackers who perceived themselves as choosing their first career jobs had majored in business, economics, or engineering from the outset of their college careers. Five had attended "very good" schools, and two had been at the top of their class. Pete was the only one of this group to attend an "average" school; however, he had worked full-time for his company during his college career and chose to stay in his job. Andrew, Hank, and Jerry also chose to stay with the companies where they had prior experience. Only Rich and Alec moved into jobs with companies that were new to them.

> Hank—with a good undergraduate and graduate degree and a number of job offers—"chose" to return to the company at which he had worked as a student, despite the fact that their job offer was definitely less attractive than several others. Andrew, too, chose to maintain his prior association with the company for which he had worked part-time, as did at least three others. Still

other fast-trackers opted for companies that they had heard about from friends or, more often, from the parents of friends. Certainly some among this group of fast-trackers were given a "choice" among various options upon leaving school. Yet their past experience, their connections and associations, may have narrowed the field so that, in fact, there were fewer real options and *chance* may have played a larger role than might be suspected.

Stumbling Onto Opportunities

Most fast-trackers perceived themselves as having found their first career jobs by "chance." They had for the most part not majored in business-related subjects, three of them changed their college major at least once, many of them graduated from schools recognized as having "average" standing by company recruiters, and Don went only briefly to college, having to drop out when his father became terminally ill and required continual care. Those among this group who went to "very good" schools did not major in business—in fact, winding up in business at all was not something they would have predicted during college.

> Jon's first career-oriented job occurred because of a chance meeting on the golf course, and the coincidental reading of a job advertisement in the newspaper. Jon had just left the sports world and taken a job with a small company in order to support himself (the sports world in his day, he points out, did not carry the same financial rewards as it does now). He tells the rest of the story this way: "In the fall of that year, I read an ad in the paper which didn't specify the company but looked like an A Company ad . . . I was out on the West Coast working for a small company, and I met a man from A Company playing golf in the evenings. After we'd played a while, he had said, 'If you ever want to go into sales, give me a call.' His name was Alan Jones. So when I saw this ad, I called his home. He wasn't there but I talked to his wife and she said she would talk to him. He called me back—and we began a long hiring process. I was evaluated on a psychological battery of tests, had several interviews, and finally got a job working for this very man."

Many of the fast-trackers made first job decisions for reasons unrelated to specific information on the company itself. Sometimes, certain possibilities were chosen over others because of mistaken information and *mis*-connections with past experience. Larry, for example, went to a job interview with B Company because he thought, at the time, that this company made products that his father had used on the farm. It turned out that this was an entirely different B, which made a quite different line of merchandise, and which bore no relationship to work on the farm. Larry joined the company anyway and has stayed there ever since. Thus, even to those who may have actually had the opportunity to choose, the actual decision may be perceived as more directly related to chance.

Other fast-trackers made spontaneous decisions about the job world based on prior experience and immediate opportunities. Tom, for example, found himself unexpectedly in the business world.

> Tom first went to school planning to be a lawyer, but later majored in English and committed himself to becoming a college professor; in fact, he was nominated for a major national fellowship and traveled to Washington, D.C., for the interview. "But when I got there," he says, "and sat through that interview I got so upset at the arrogance of the people doing the interviewing that I rushed home, walked right over to C Company where somebody-or-other's father worked, and immediately signed up. I started work the next day."

All of these fast-trackers perceived their initial job decisions as largely based on unpredictable factors; in other words, a question of "chance." They each took advantage of, and made the most of, unanticipated opportunities, relying on their self-confidence and their interpersonal skills to carry the day during the decision-making process and once the decision had been made.

Actively Seeking Opportunities

Two of the youngest men in the sample actually perceived the interplay of both choice and chance in their initial career decisions. Their choice was not *which* job to take but to actively seek out job opportunities. Both of these young men, Brian and Sam, graduated from "average" to "good" schools. Sam did not major in business and Brian did so only belatedly. Neither of them had worked in big business prior to or during college. These two young men came into adulthood along with large numbers of others entering the job market during the 1970s, at a time when the economy was showing the first signs of economic downturn. For these young men finding a career job in big business was initially a career in itself. In the stories they tell of their job searches, the interplay of choice and chance is seen most clearly.

Brian and Sam came of age at a time when the job market had tightened up considerably in response to an unprecedented number of job applicants and the early rumblings of economic turbulence. In the stories of Brian and Sam the job search was more difficult and the interplay of choice and chance more evident.

Brian had worked throughout college, often at two jobs, as a ride-operator at one of the Disney facilities and as a furniture salesman. Upon graduation from college, he applied for a number of jobs but was not offered an interview. Eventually, the father of a girl he knew invited him to come in for an interview—at one of the companies that had already turned him down. At the interview he was able to persuade the company, a large retail chain, that his prior part-time experience suited him for their management training program. He was offered the job.

In the first three years, he took on all sorts of departments and sold appliances "no college guy had ever sold before." On a national scale, he came out third in the company. He knew, however, that given the current climate his chances of advancement there were slim, so he began to explore other opportunities. From a list of several companies, he finally zeroed in on one. "It took me eight months to get an interview," he says, "but once I got the interview I got the job." In this company, his record as a top salesman eventually took him out of direct sales and into financial marketing and more recently to his new job as a regional manager.

Sam's story is similar to Brian's. It is also similar to Jon's because both men were leaving a possible sports career and moving into the business world, and yet differs from Jon's because of the different eras in which the two came of age. In Jon's time, sports players were generally not well paid and opportunities outside of sports were numerous. Fifteen years later, Sam faced a different world. His work in sports was already paying extremely well, and opportunities outside of sports were limited. Consequently, Sam gave up more immediate benefits in opting to join the business world, and had a more difficult time doing this at all.

For several months after college, Sam wrestled with whether or not to give up the idea of a career in the sports world. Giving up sports as his career meant giving up a good cash flow, and lots of the comforts of an affluent life style. Sam brags a bit about this: "By the time I was twenty-one, I had bought my own home, was driving a marvelous sports car, and had everything I wanted." He had everything, that is, but a new challenge and good long-term prospects. Consequently, he started looking for another job. There was a hiring freeze on at the company of his choice, but he saw an advertisement for another company's new training program. To apply for the program required previous sales experience or a Masters of Business Administration degree. Technically, Sam had neither. He built upon his own experience, however, and convinced someone that he had the necessary talent. Sam says, "I parlayed my sports experience into marketing experience—convincing the company that my sports experience *was* marketing experience—and finally, after several months, I got an interview." This was just the beginning of a long screening process that, eight months after college graduation, resulted in his first job in the business world. In the training program, he was the only one without an advanced degree. He did not find this intimidating, however, but rather challenging. He says, "Everyone else in this training program had an MBA or a Ph.D. —yet I came out number one. I felt good about that."

Sam's early experience was repeated more than once; he is now in his third company and still on the fast track. At each turn, he was able to persuade the people with decision-making power that his previous experience was a good substitute for the qualifications they thought they were seeking. Brian, on a similar track, did the same. Neither had the specific experience required for the job. Yet, they were able to bring together their past experience in such a way that they convinced decision-makers to make them job offers and to bring them on board. Once inside, both of these men were willing to go all out to achieve their goals and won every award in the company. They are both excited about recent promotions, and look forward to the challenge of continuing steadily on the next lap of the fast track to the top.

THE BALANCE OF SUBSTANCE AND STYLE

For some of the fast-trackers, entrance into the business world was earned because of how others perceived the *substance* that they brought with them from prior experience in college and in business. For many more, entrance into the business world was earned because of characteristics associated with *style* which, in effect, earned them the right to keep on accumulating knowledge or substance. Yet for all the fast-trackers, their leap onto the fast track, as well as the chances of their continued survival on this track, is related to the interaction of substance and style. Substance is knowledge of people and the task. Style is the way that this knowledge is communicated to others. At entry level, other people associate substance with external credentials, generally from colleges; style is more difficult to measure but encompasses the confidence, ability to communicate, and the commitment to accomplishment demonstrated by all the fast-trackers.

The characteristics associated with style are perceived as more nebulous, harder to define, more difficult to write into a job description. Yet, for all the fast-trackers (particularly those who had to actively seek out job opportunites) these characteristics are absolutely essential for success. In fact, the characteristics of style—confidence, communication, and commitment—when in association with substance, give a basis for understanding why the fast-trackers are able to take advantage of opportunities, create opportunities when there appear to be none, and walk through walls that appear impenetrable to others by opening doors where none have been before. Each of these characteristics of style merits further elaboration in terms of the fast-trackers' entry-level experience.

Confidence

All of the fast-trackers are self-confident. For example, Tom said, "I always thought of myself as successful." Brian announced, "I'm good and I'm lucky, which is different than being lucky and lucky," and Sam, along with others, stated, "I rarely lose."

They do admit to being insecure or having little confidence at various junctures of their careers or in their early lives. Both Jon and Rich talk about their early shyness. Yet their insecurities did not keep them from taking the initiative with others, and moving forward to take on new challenges. Art is most emphatic about his insecurities and lack of self-confidence. However, each time he mentions his insecurities, he also recounts significant achievements that followed closely upon the heels of times of doubt. Self-confidence does not preclude a realistic—and sometimes even unrealistic—questioning of one's abilities. Research on leadership has found that the self-confidence carrying great leaders through difficult times is paired with an awareness of vulnerability and the possibilities of failure. Thus, awareness of strength is accompanied by awareness of weakness. All people have areas in which they are more comfortable than others; the trick for the fast-trackers was to put their major efforts into the areas of greatest comfort, and even there, to stretch their limits to the utmost.

The self-assuredness that led Brian and Sam to continue a difficult job search in the initial stages, a sure sign of strong style, is one of the reasons for their success. The confidence that Tom showed (however impulsively) in simply signing up for a job in a company he had not consciously considered is a unique manifestation of the strength found in all of the fast-trackers. As they all say in one way or another, and Alec says specifically, "I just believe that everything turns out OK."

Communication

All of these stories reflect the use of more than adequate interpersonal skills, and the fast-trackers' ability to develop and sustain connections with others. Jon's job emerged from a casual acquaintance with a man on the golf course and an initial telephone conversation with this man's wife. Brian got his first chance because of a prior connection, and through the parent of a friend. Many of these individuals also had personal connections that focused their attention on specific companies, and that helped them get their foot in the door.

Unexpected opportunities often arrived through relationships with others. Having important connections with other people cannot and does not guarantee success in specific endeavors, yet these connections may influence decisions about who gets up to the door and who does not. For Brian and Sam in particular getting an interview was difficult. Once at the door of the company, however, their own skills earned them entry into the business itself.

Commitment

The fast-trackers are, almost above all, committed to the goals that they set for themselves. They persist in working toward the objectives they have chosen. They are willing to double back in their tracks, to take detours, to slow down for a while—but by and large they continue to keep the same objectives in front of them until they have accomplished what they set out to do. This is more evident in the stories of Brian and Sam than in the others when initial job entry is the topic. However, persistence characterizes every one of the lives of the fast-trackers overall.

In short, the fast-trackers' lives illustrate the interplay of both choice and chance, substance and style. They prepare for opportunities although not always in the commonly perceived manner. Then they rely on their interpersonal skills to make the most of opportunities when they arrive. Their sense of control rests in their ability to learn and to be aware of themselves and their environments; they are thus ready to make the most of those events that occur outside of their control.

The fast-trackers did not have more opportunities than other people, but with a combination of substance and style they did create more opportunities. They were not offered written invitations to join the world of big business; they found ways in which to write those invitations for themselves. They were prepared to take advantage of situations about which they had no immediate knowledge. Given a slight possibility, they had the self-confidence, interpersonal skills, and commitment to turn it into a solid reality. All of these are essential characteristics of those on the track to the top.

The fast-trackers' careers thus go far beyond what they might have predicted during high school or college. In fact, what they do now surprises them in many ways, though the foundations were laid early in their personal histories. They credit much to luck, which is simply the arrival of unexpected opportunity—opportunity to use what they already know (substance) and to make use of the interpersonal characteristics (style) that they have already been refining, through a variety of experiences, since early in their childhood.

CHAPTER 5

Being Number One in the Junior Years

The Importance of Substance

> *The common romantic scenario for the creative hero postulates an underdog willing to risk all to achieve his visionary goals, and who finally reaches those goals, after surviving many perils and overcoming many obstacles. We have seen that a more realistic scenario pictures the creative person as a professional gambler who prefers odds that are stacked in his favor, and who secures those odds by acquiring superior knowledge about the domain in which the gamble is taking place.*
>
> HERBERT SIMON
> "WHAT WE KNOW ABOUT THE
> CREATIVE PROCESS"

Fast-trackers enter the work world prepared to do as much as they can as fast as they can. They are open to learning their business and they are open to learning about themselves. They are prepared to accumulate *substance*. This first career stage parallels the lifetime developmental stage of childhood. In childhood, very young people focus on building skills and identifying a tentative "place" in their community of peers in terms of task- and people-oriented skills—even as they learn the customs of the larger society. In the first year of the career, people on the way up the ladder focus on individual achievement and the development of support networks—as they learn the customs of their organization. Both children in elementary school (newcomers to the school society) and junior fast-trackers in

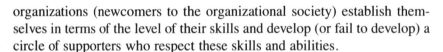

The Junior Years

SIGNIFICANT LEARNINGS

1. SUBSTANCE:
   to learn the technical side of the business
   to learn the informal rules of the organization
   to understand visions and dreams of bosses and co-workers
   to stretch self and thinking in new ways

2. STYLE:
   to believe in own abilities
   to grow in communication skills
   to share visions and dreams of bosses and co-workers
   to believe that the impossible can be achieved

IMPORTANT BEHAVIORS

Utilize talents to the fullest—often becoming #1
Acknowledge and accept company expectations
Become good managers and motivators of people
Develop positive relationships with co-workers
Bring dreams down to earth in creation of new products and processes
Achieve visibility for creating a difference in organization
Accomplish what nobody believed could be done

organizations (newcomers to the organizational society) establish themselves in terms of the level of their skills and develop (or fail to develop) a circle of supporters who respect these skills and abilities.

The tasks then of young managers are to discover and accept the customs of their organizational culture (what is expected and what is not, what is allowed and what is not, both of which vary by organization), learn new skills, identify their skill levels in comparison to others, and develop allies, mentors, and other supporters who are willing to help them along the way. The competitive orientation common among the young fast-trackers in this sample is not inappropriate for this career stage. It is a time of learning and evaluation. Young people in their twenties and early thirties are measuring themselves against standards that have been created by others, flinging themselves against an already-established grid to see at what level and in which function they operate most effectively.

The organization generally aids and abets them in this goal. Promising newcomers to organizations are given challenging jobs, and large doses of constructive criticism, in order that they may learn as rapidly as possible. They are supported and sometimes sponsored by those who appreciate their skills and potential. Those newcomers who are not given difficult jobs, who are sheltered from critical feedback and who neglect to develop support networks, have already determined their course—they will not approach the Executive Transition as promising candidates for career maturity. The task of the first career stage (from the early twenties through the early thirties) is the same as in pre-adolescence: to learn as much and as rapidly as possible, and to do so in a way that is ultimately perceived and respected by others.

All of the fast-trackers excelled during these early years so that those reaching their mid-thirties found themselves at the senior levels of middle-management or the junior levels of senior management, approaching career adolescence—the Executive Transition. What marked their progress during the early career phase and distinguished them from the vast majority of their peers who started along the track with them? What did this sample of fast-trackers do that caused them to be singled out as the ones who would approach and perhaps pass through the Executive Transition?

In the interview material, there are three sets of clues that hint at the answers to these questions. The first set of clues lies in spontaneous descriptions of accomplishments during these years. It is clear that the fast-trackers either did something everyone thought was impossible, or they did a job better and faster than anybody else. They were thus separated from their peers for unusual accomplishments or unprecedented speed and skill, and given special treatment. The second set of clues relates to the speed with which promotions came their way, and the apparent consistency or inconsistency of their performances. The third set of clues becomes apparent in the fast-trackers' accounts of the people who helped them or were significant to them along the way, and what, in fact, they learned from these people. In describing how they benefited from the help or colleague-ship of others, they identified the things that they needed to know in order to be the *most successful* among their peers. Each of these sets of clues clarifies the essential skills of those who speed along the fast track to the top.

ACCOMPLISHMENTS OF THE JUNIOR STARS

By and large these young men and women had challenging first jobs and met all the challenges they encountered. Many of them, however, went even further—to take on new and innovative projects, or to accomplish tasks that had not been done before. They drew upon a basic self-confidence to imagine new alternatives and to persist in accomplishing their objectives. They learned from experience, converting their learning into preparation for opportunities that came their way. They gave themselves unstintingly to their career endeavors. They were perceived as doing the impossible.

This is illustrated in the way in which a number of the fast-trackers turned ideas into realities. They did what nobody believed could be done. Rich, Hal, and Tom are among them.

Early in his career, just before career adolescence, Rich had an opportunity to use all his task- and people-oriented skills to develop a plant facility that would operate productively without a union. At the time, no one in his company believed that such a thing was possible. Managers believed that workers produced because of fear (of monetary retribution or other punishment) and this belief supported the development of unions to protect workers. The accepted management-union relationship was adversarial: managers were perceived as promoting policies detrimental to workers and unions protected the workers from this threat; and out of the ensuing negotiations and compromises of the two groups company policy was built and productivity guaranteed. In the new plant developed by Rich and his managerial team, a new set of concepts was introduced.

Rich says: "We developed a plant culture in which teams operated with the belief that if you treat people right you won't have a union. We had enormous productivity. Everyone was so happy with all of this. This was so different from the usual idea of motivation by fear. Ninety-five percent of the people will work hard if they are treated right. So then everybody wanted to follow us and do the same thing. Creating that plant was an emotional experience, very powerful."

Hal describes a succession of early-career experiences in which he, along with others, created something new. "In my first job," he begins, "they had just started to use computers to identify skills. I took this on as my project— it was a new business—and developed a program. We had a successful demonstration for the government. In my second job, I offered to install this computer system in the whole corporation. I did that and it worked. . . . In my third job, I worked at corporate headquarters with a new financial manager. . . . We had a vision and we put together a new financial organization, second to none in the company."

Tom, more briefly, describes a relatively early career accomplishment: "We put together an entirely new consumer affairs group. . . . nobody had ever heard of anything like it. . . . at this time this was a huge undertaking." Arthur describes his early positions as a succession of "taking on the impossible and bringing in clients which nobody had been able to win over before." Brian, in his third job, designed a new product introduction process and sold it to the company. This, he says, was "probably the most significant piece of work done in the division."

Finally Alec, a relative newcomer to his first organization, wrote an advertising pamphlet—on a subject with which he had had no prior experience—that established a new marketing avenue for the company. Millions of copies of this pamphlet are now distributed nationally on a regular basis. With this publication Alec came to the attention of higher executives and was placed on a super fast track.

Some of these same men mentioned above and many of the other fast-trackers made their mark by consistently being number one . . . again . . . and again.

Under Larry's management, his division and then his region came in first, over and over again. Alec increased the productivity of a product line in two successive jobs. Art's division was continually at the top of the company charts. Sandra's boss commented, "Well, you came into the division and promptly hit a home run." The same was true for Brian as well as for Sam and Hank.

Brian came out third nationally in his first company, and first nationally in his second company. Two jobs later, his unit of "malcontented people" finished first in the region, meeting 150 percent of their objectives. In his early training program, Sam finished in the top 10 percent of his class, the only trainee without an advanced degree. In the training program for his second company, he graduated number one and said, "I never worked so hard in my life . . . by comparison, college was a breeze." At the midpoint of his early career years, Hank accomplished much the same: he completely turned a whole division around and doubled business in two years.

Each of the fast-trackers did the impossible either by doing something new or by consistently being first in what one did. In this way their accomplishments, supported by their leadership characteristics, separated them from their organizational peers.

VARIABLE SPEEDS IN THE JUNIOR YEARS

The junior fast-trackers are concerned about how fast they travel up their corporate ladders. How fast one travels is another measure of "apparent" substance and is often taken as indicating merit. Yet, in reviewing the early careers of all the fast-trackers, it is apparent that some travelled quickly and some travelled slowly—and that the speed of the journey had relatively little to do with arrival at the ultimate destination.

For many aspiring to the fast track or watching from the sidelines, the fast track appears to be marked by continuous and rapid promotions. However, the travels of those on the fast track show that promotions are sometimes frequent, sometimes infrequent, and sometimes non-existent for a period of time. However, the real fast track is demarcated by consistent increases in responsibility and continued opportunities for growth and learning even in the absence of rapid promotions. Company policy and economic conditions dictate whether or not the increases in responsibility are paralleled by actual changes in level and rank.

This is evident in the early career histories of the senior men in this sample, those close to the top of their corporate ladders, who moved to the top both quickly and slowly in terms of actual promotions. Some of these men made noticeable leaps at certain times in their careers. Others made consistent upward progress at a steady pace. Some were also plateaued for a time, usually toward the end of their early career years, and these plateaus eventually became springboards for later upward movement. The speed of movement, in terms of promotions, is not as significant as continuous increases in responsibility, which are the real markers of promise along the fast track. As the fast-trackers took on more responsibility, they had more opportunities for learning, and opportunities to learn are one of the most valuable gifts a company may offer its people, because such learning is more grist for the leadership mill and opens pathways to more new opportunities.

> Some of the fast-trackers moved fast. Alec and Jon have both moved, at times, at superspeeds — Alec as a result of writing that early pamphlet which took him farther than anybody might have imagined, and Jon due to a series of unexpected and fortuitous events. Jon says, "When I went east for an interview for the next level, I wasn't sure I wanted to take it, and my wife knew I didn't want to take it. When I arrived, the man I was to work for had suddenly been fired and there was this opening two levels up. They had no one to put in the job and I was there, so they asked me to take the job, skipping the in-between grade all together. This was a big jump and an unusual one." From that point on, Jon's career moved steadily ahead.

> Some of the fast-trackers moved steadily and consistently without noticeable spurts or slowdowns. Andy is one who, with nearly thirty years in the company, has moved through a succession of developmental positions, learning the business from different angles, sometimes receiving a promotion and sometimes not. He is now being considered for the highest position in his company. He is perceived as a fast-tracker within the company, yet there were no superspeeds along the way, only steady, consistent progress.

> Many of the fast-trackers moved slowly at some point in their early careers. Much of this perception of slowness results from their impatience for new challenges and responsibility. Sometimes, but not always, this impatience prompted a job search and a move to a new company. As a result, there were eight company moves among the 17 fast-trackers during the early

years—the pre-adolescent career stage—from age 23 up to and including 35. (There were no company moves among this sample after this time.)

Tom, who *stayed* with his company, complained heartily four years into his career and describes this period as follows: "I felt sidelined but I learned about a bigger part of the business." Hank also felt a slowing down after about 10 years in his company. He was given a new job and new responsibilities, but neither the title nor the options that usually went with it. His rapid progress was, in fact, slowed down for a time. Alec, six years into his career, did not feel sidelined but rather over-supervised and took the opportunity to leave for a new venture elsewhere. After three years in the new company, he left again, for the same reasons. Sam, too, has moved twice. He is enormously impatient with slowness. . . . A few months ago, just before a recent promotion, he said, "I'm there again . . . the clock is ticking." Yet his promotion has stopped the clock, at least for a while.

Again, the apparent speed of movement may, in the end, make no difference at all. Among the most senior of the sample, Rich moved at a normal pace in his early years and a rapid pace later on; Hal moved fast, then slow for a while, and then fast again; Tom had a long plateau in the middle of his career which nevertheless was filled with challenge and excitement; Jon moved at the speed of light; and Andy went consistently along, "simply doing what was next." If there were a way to measure speed of growth and learning, this would be a truer measure of progress along the fast track than speed of promotions, titles, raises, and other visible symbols of progress in the corporation. Speed in growth and learning are the identifying marks of those moving along the fast track.

MENTORS, ALLIES AND SUPPORTERS

In describing their careers, the fast-trackers spontaneously mentioned the names of many people with and for whom they worked along the way. In all, the seventeen fast-trackers mentioned 49 names of significant bosses and co-workers in chronicling the early part of their career (an average of 2.9 apiece). Of the twelve fast-trackers who are now in or past the Executive Transition, only one referred to bosses, co-workers, or supporters who were significant to them during these mid-career years. Among the five senior people, talking about their current jobs and current senior status, 15 names were mentioned (again an average of about three per person). The numbers in themselves are interesting. In the fast-trackers' descriptions of their career history, significant co-workers are part of the fabric of their stories about the early and later career stages, but not about the middle years. (This is another signal that the middle years, the Executive Transition or career adolescence, differs in nature and kind from the stages preceding and following it.) The questions which then arise are: What people were important to the fast-trackers in their early careers? And what did the fast-trackers learn from these people that was significant?

From their early career years, the fast-trackers remember people as relating to them in four different ways. First, they frequently mention the people who hired them—often their first bosses who believed in them enough to let them try their wings. Second, they credit those people, often superiors, who taught them something that remained important throughout their careers. Third, they remember role models, people who lived out behavior they wanted to emulate. Fourth, they are appreciative of those people who were exciting and stimulating thinkers, and who led them to expand their own thinking or to see things in a new way. The fast-trackers, therefore, mention people in four roles: bosses, instructors, role models, and enthusiasts. The people who are remembered as significant may be perceived as playing one or more of these roles.

Early Bosses

The first boss is often mentioned in a mentoring capacity: for recognizing the talent of the about-to-be-fast-tracker and for creating high expectations and giving constructive feedback. Jerry says of his first boss that he "demanded and expected high performance from me and never accepted any work less than his perception of my best." Christine echoes Jerry by saying, "my first boss was truly an outstanding person because he believed in me and gave me opportunities." Sandra expresses the same sentiment: "My boss had confidence in me and gave me new responsibilities." Andrew's first boss gave him a lot of exposure to different aspects of the company, which provided a solid base for his later growth.

Jon really had two first bosses because one followed upon the other within two weeks' time. These men were of totally different characters and Jon is grateful for both. His first boss—the man who hired him—was important because his enthusiasm for the company was contagious. His second boss was not enthusiastic and much more demanding: "This man was an ex-high school principal from the northeast. He was much more structured and said I was screwing around too much, going to school and so forth, and my job was to increase market share. I almost quit but thought maybe he was right. This is when I withdrew from school . . . and began to get serious about my job. . . . He never did promote me." Jon remembers this man as pushing him toward a critical turning point in his career when he began to take his work seriously.

Two other fast-trackers remember their first bosses in their second companies. The impact of these men on their careers was similar to that of the actual first boss even though the relationship developed later in their careers. Both Art and Ken mention men who moved from their old companies to their new ones, blazing a trail that the fast-trackers would follow. They remember these men for the example that they set and also for the confidence that they instilled in the fast-trackers that they could do as well. Ken, in addition, is grateful for the protection this boss provided and says, "He kept me from doing anything stupid."

Instructors

Mentors are also remembered as teachers who provided fast-trackers with specific functional training, introduced them to important corporate perspectives, and improved their interpersonal and management skills. Ken says of an early boss who taught him everything he needed to know about marketing, "He's as good as I ever met." Christine benefitted from working for a man who, she says, gave her a "tremendous perspective on the corporation and its history." Tom learned people skills from a number of his bosses, particularly the "archaic one who needed guides to the men's room but had an unfailing sense about people." Don gives enormous weight to the input about management skills that he received from his first boss, who told him there were three different ways in which managers behaved toward their own people: "There are times when you give clues, and people can choose to do what they want with your advice; there are other times when you give counsel, and folks had better listen but for good reason may proceed in another direction; then there are times when you give commands—and they just do it without question." This was reinforced by another saying of one of Don's early bosses: "There's a time to march and a time to dance—and neither you nor your people should confuse the two."

Others remember their early bosses teaching them new ways to think or reinforcing their beliefs. Rich mentions his first boss as significant because of what he taught him: "He had a revolutionary philosophy for that time . . . he liked to analyze things and then create 'common understandings.' He brought people together to solve problems and investigate fundamental issues." Then Rich mentions a second man with whom he worked at about the same time, who read a lot and challenged all the usual assumptions. Each of these men raised new questions for Rich that were significant in his own career development.

Jerry had two bosses who helped him to see both the benefits of involving people in decisions, and the importance of communications and corporate visibility. These men also "allowed me the job freedom to take risks and try out new ideas." Andy remembers one man, especially, who demonstrated that new ways of thinking about people made a difference. "He not only told us that this is what he believed but he did it—and it endured. This was tremendously important and reinforced my own thinking."

Role Models

The fast-trackers reveal a lot about themselves in describing those they admire and choose to emulate. Alec admires one man who never did the "right" thing but "is the one I want to work for," and another who showed him "if you're a flake and *outstanding* you can succeed." Hank describes his role model as one who's good with people and who communicates well, phrases that are characteristic of his own style. Finally, Hal, a creative maverick himself, describes the man he chooses to identify with as follows: "He is a challenging, tough, hard-nosed manager with a great feel for people. He's a maverick and an entrepreneur. He helped me a lot—by his example. I think I helped him, too."

Enthusiasts

A number of the fast-trackers describe, with their own kinds of enthusiasm, the people alongside whom they were motivated to think in new ways, and to look beyond the usual. Tom describes a series of such people in his early career but says of one in particular, "We had great dreams. . . ." Jon talks at some length about a man in his company (once two levels above him, this man now works for him) and says, "He was so enthusiastic . . . early in my career we had *great* discussions." Finally, Hal describes those he worked with in developing new concepts as people who "had a tremendous impact on me." He says, more than once, "He was a great guy," "tremendously exciting," and "together, we had a vision. . . ."

From descriptions of the fast-trackers' accomplishments and of their early mentors and allies, certain generalizations emerge that suggest *why* the fast-trackers sped through their early career years to arrive at the Executive Transition. The fast-trackers *learned* many things: in terms of substance or knowledge, they learned about the business, their organization, and the people with whom they worked; in terms of style, they grew in confidence, in communication skills, and in the belief that they could in fact achieve what might be perceived as impossible. What they *did* was to continue many of the behaviors of their earlier years: they utilized their talents to the fullest, developed positive relationships with co-workers;

they created innovative products and processes; they became good—sometimes superb—at managing and motivating others; they achieved visibility for their work; and in the process actually accomplished tasks that others had thought impossible to achieve.

Much of this behavior was not new to them: for a long time they had been doing things that people did not generally believe could be accomplished. What they found out during this early career stage is that, on a grid created by others, their own ability to make things happen placed them near the top. In so doing, the fast-trackers came to the attention of their superiors and the executive levels within their companies. For giving fully of themselves, for working enormously hard, for going beyond expectations and bettering the organization, each of the fast-trackers above the age of 35 arrived at the door of the Executive Transition—where the rules are less clear and expectations change. Having accumulated as much substance as possible and with fairly well-developed styles, the fast-trackers approached the next stage of their careers. Some are still at the door, too young to enter; others have, in fact, entered and are currently negotiating the perilous course of this transition; still others have successfully passed through and are now working in management's senior ranks. In the next chapter, the fast-trackers' histories are the source for a new understanding of the middle stage of the career, the Executive Transition.

CHAPTER 6

Derailment and the Executive Transition

Reevaluation and Style

The bottom line is that I was not given the job. I had worked hard, had taken the initiative in leading the organization and I was very disappointed with the decision . . . Through some very deep soul searching, I have now recognized that I am capable but I failed to market myself properly: I lost exposure to and contact with some key people in the organization; I quit talking with some of my peers and superiors because of other business pressures; and I lost my primary mentor. I know it is my responsibility and not the responsibility of others to make things happen for me. No one else can do it . . . but I refuse to give up and fade into the background . . . I want to achieve my dreams.

SUPERINTENDENT
GENERAL MOTORS
CORPORATION

Those on the fast track in the early stage of their careers are the "whiz kids," the "young Turks," the "fair-haired boys (and girls)," and the "young stars" of the corporate world. All of these phrases indicate that at this stage the fast-trackers are still perceived as children (not grown-ups) by their superiors, and therefore are not to be taken too seriously. It is all right to be a "star" when still a junior climber up the corporate ladder; after all, the rigors of age will eventually exact their toll. The perception of youth

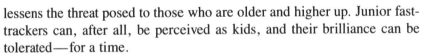

The Middle Years

SIGNIFICANT LEARNINGS

1. SUBSTANCE:
   to increase understanding of self
   to increase understanding of others
   to increase understanding of organizational expectations
   to increase understanding of organizational possibilities
   to develop a long-range viewpoint

2. STYLE:
   to accept that one is not a star but a team player
   to grow in understanding of and tolerance for diversity
   to delegate effectively to those whose skills may be lesser
   to respect the contributions of others
   to take responsibility for increasing the satisfaction of others
   to increase ability to work through and share the credit with others

IMPORTANT BEHAVIORS

Developing good partnerships
Acquiring senior mentors
Working for the team and the larger organization
Never claiming individual credit
Tolerating ambiguity
Taking a back seat and giving others the credit

lessens the threat posed to those who are older and higher up. Junior fast-trackers can, after all, be perceived as kids, and their brilliance can be tolerated—for a time.

As these young men and women approach, and move past their fortieth year (ages 36 to 43 in this sample), it becomes increasingly difficult for superiors and co-workers to see them as children or as kids. There have never been, nor will there ever be, any "middle-aged whizzes," any "aging stars," any "grey-haired men" with the same clout as "fair-haired boys" in the corporate world. The "whiz kids" grow up and begin to look, frighteningly, as if they might become serious competitors for the few positions of high influence in the company. They might not vanish into the shadowy mist surrounding the Executive Transition. They might become (and in fact replace) senior managers.

As this realization dawns on those higher up in the corporation, the insecure among the powerful begin to examine the careers of the fast-trackers more carefully: to seek out their flaws, and to look for reasons why on the basis of merit if possible (and for other reasons if not) they should be tipped off the fast track, never to be heard from again. This concern on the part of those with company seniority—this so-called "sharpening of the knives"—surfaces only at this time: as the fast-trackers begin to grow up and to enter the adolescence of their careers; and, as they are perceived for the first time as serious contenders for the crown.

To survive this transition, the fast-trackers have to learn a whole new set of rules. For years they have been used to being acknowledged, being important, being regarded as individuals of achievement. There is no such recognition during the transition; in fact, the former "stars" are ignored when possible and regarded with skepticism when recognition is unavoidable. These remain subtle undercurrents in the personal interactions of the corporate world, however, for on the surface there are company expectations about behavior, about merit, and about skill that must be met. The undercurrents are visible, however, in small unexplainable incidents that surface in the career lives of the mid-career fast-trackers—small unaccountable events that signal that something is different from before.

This response by higher-ups to the mid-career fast-tracker has not changed much over the years, nor is it going to go away. It is in many ways one of a variety of human responses to threat, to the possibility of succession, to the unavoidable recognition on the part of those more senior that they themselves are growing older. It is similar to the response of many middle-aged fathers to their adolescent sons, and middle-aged mothers to their adolescent daughters. As teenagers develop adult physiques and capabilities, while maintaining all the advantages of youth, they remind their parents that their time of supremacy is coming to an end. Parents who are less than satisfied with themselves, or concerned about their own worth and merit, can become unaccountably difficult as they watch their sons and daughters grow. Similarly, those in senior management who question their own abilities and fear the coming of their own demise, can easily be threatened by young fast-trackers growing up and emerging as contenders on the adult scene.

Unlike adolescents, however, fast-trackers really *are* adults and thus have at their command a larger number of resources with which to negotiate this transition. Their success depends in large part on their willingness to adapt and to grow, to give up the visible benefits of their earlier "star" roles, and to use this transitional period as a necessary learning experience for their career-adulthood as senior managers. It is within the Executive Transition that the junior stars must learn to give up their competitive orientation for a cooperative one, their individual stardom for a successful partnership, and their role of being mentored for the role of mentoring others. This is a tall order, and not easy to fulfill. Without the rigors provided by the Executive Transition, we might have many senior managers who were never given the opportunity to learn these essentials—and our corporations and our country would suffer for their lack.

What is it, then, that fast-trackers must learn during these perilous middle years? If they are to travel further, avoiding the potholes hidden by the shadowy mists, they must turn to the development of their interpersonal skills and not rely on the achievement-oriented skills that brought them to the door of the Executive Transition. Their emphasis on substance (knowledge and task-oriented skills) must be replaced by an emphasis on style (working through and with others effectively). In fact, they must *learn* the following things: to accept that the team is more important than the individual; that merit (substance) alone will not carry them to the top; that they must incorporate into their world views and demonstrate in their interpersonal skills (style) a tolerance for the diversity—and failings—of others; that they must take responsibility for making others comfortable by lowering their own visibility and honoring senior members of the company; that they must work effectively and share credit with others; and that some of the best leadership occurs behind the scenes.

As they turn from substance to style, from being first to being behind-the-scenes, they will benefit from *doing* the following: maintaining good partnerships; acquiring new mentors; consciously working for the team and making oneself an essential member of that team; and sharing credit with others. During this time of transition, they are helped by remembering that the uncertainty prevalent during this time only lasts eight years or so and that the die is cast one way or another at the end of this time—and that once one is derailed for certain, the uncertainty of this period may become much more attractive.

More about the Executive Transition may be learned from the stories of those who have been there and those who are now crossing the bridge between the junior and senior years. From the seniors, and from their career histories, we can see that this transition may be passed through with difficulty or more easily, and the difference may have to do with external conditions but also with the expectations one holds about how high, how far, and how fast one must go in order to measure up inside one's own head.

SURVIVORS OF THE EXECUTIVE TRANSITION

Some clues to successful passage through this transition may be gleaned from the accounts of the senior managers in this sample as they review this period of their career histories.

Tom, for example, went approximately 15 years without a promotion, and even though he acquired more and more responsibility and went on to create organizations on a larger scale, he did not receive the usual company recognition surrounding such an accomplishment. This may in fact have been a bonus, because a non-promoted executive in transition is of little threat to those above him. In fact, Tom says of these years, he never needed much lightning protection (that is, bolts of lightning from on high were not likely to take him out of the running). It was during these years too that Tom came to "love my company," so that now his efforts are designed to better his organization regardless of his personal fate in the corporate ranks. He says, "I could never leave," which is a sentiment expressed by the fast-trackers only after the transition is in the past.

The consistent, steady pace of Andy's career moves during these years (with more lateral than upward moves) also suggests that he was perceived as posing little threat to those above him. Andy mentions no times of superfast movement during the early or middle part of his career, and no times of particular difficulty. In addition to the consistent career pace, Andy's toned-down modest demeanor would also deflect any stray use of his position as a target for sharpshooters.

Similarly, Rich also attained high levels of visibility only after the Executive Transition was behind him. In the last eight years as a senior manager, he has been perceived throughout his company as moving on the fast track. The perceptions of his success were formed after he passed through the mid-stages of career and emerged as a senior statesman.

CURRENTLY IN TRANSITION

From those fast-trackers in this sample now negotiating this transition we learn lessons of a different order. Two, perhaps three of the seven fast-trackers in this career stage have been in serious trouble with the company and have survived. They have learned the lessons that will guide them through the next several years. None of this group has yet fallen off the track during the perils of career adolescence. Some, however, have teetered very close to the edge.

Hank spent more time than the other fast-trackers outlining the difficulties he confronted and conquered during this time. Another story, by an academic fast-tracker (not part of this sample), is very like Hank's but results in actual derailment. The similarities and differences in the two stories highlight the often subtle distinctions in perceptions of self, others, and in actual behavior that lead to survival or defeat in the journey up the fast track. Bill is very much like Hank in age, in general appearance, and in accomplishments. His career in the academic world has many parallels with those of the corporate fast-trackers but spells out more clearly the perils of the middle-career years as well as the outcome that may in fact await many on the fast track—although not the fast-trackers in this sample, at least not yet.

> Bill was a young star who came to a major university as a junior faculty member with very good credentials. Once in his job, he followed one accomplishment with another, meeting all the expectations for eventual promotion—and then some. In his work he was helped by a senior colleague (one who was in the perilous transition years), and they collaborated together on research and articles (the number and quality of which are the measure of achievement in the academic world). As the time came for Bill to move into the transition years himself, and for his more senior colleague to move out of them, both were made somewhat anxious, preoccupied, and tense by upcoming evaluations of this work that accompany the promotion process. Both wanted to move up, the senior man a step ahead of the junior man. As a consequence, Bill began to emphasize what he perceived was his rightful share of the credit for their work together. He was afraid that if he was not perceived as a super-achiever on an individual basis, he would not reach the next step.
>
> At this point, Bill was in his early thirties, and there were signs that he was heading for the shoals—but he paid no attention. He did not notice that his senior colleague was becoming more distant and he did nothing to alleviate tensions that were growing between the two of them. A few months later, when the time for formal evaluations arrived (the process takes about a year), Bill's colleague was a member of the committee considering Bill's promotion. In the promotion meetings, he denounced Bill for claiming too much of the credit, casting aspersions on Bill's system of ethics. Others who did not know Bill personally, but had worked for a long time with his colleague, then began to think of other incidents (which they had observed or heard about) that could be interpreted as indicating that Bill's ethical system slipped when his individual future was at stake. Although Bill was and is an excellent teacher, respected by his students, his teaching was devalued and he was accused of misusing student work to further his own aims. Bill's promotion was denied. (It was no solace to him that his colleague's was as well.)
>
> Bill was angry at the injustice of these actions. With many offers available from other universities, he left to take a new job. After his departure, the stories about Bill multiplied, and he was used as a scapegoat for a variety of other problems at his "home" university. Bill later chose to return to his original university, where, in his absence he had actually been promoted. At this point, Bill (now 36) found himself facing the difficult mid-years of his career under bad omens.
>
> Since that time Bill has continued to do superb research valued by colleagues at other universities and by professional associations; enjoyed

considerable success as a teacher, developing a strong contingent of students who claim him as their mentor; and has developed an academic record that looks strong—almost brilliant—to those who view him from outside the university. Yet colleagues at his university still tell stories, and the stories become so exaggerated that senior administrators within the university have come to believe that not only are his ethics suspect but his research as well. He has been turned down for further promotion three times, and each request for promotion has given his senior colleagues the opportunity to pass stories of his mis-doing on to the next generation, so that "everybody knows . . . that Bill is the kind of person who is only out for himself."

Bill was not perceived as demonstrating the virtues of saintly behavior or working solely for the good of others. He has never acquired a new mentor, or new allies (because he is still carrying within himself the sense of injustice about those who did him in). There is no one in high circles who is in his corner and can correct the misinformation about his career before it mushrooms into an all-encompassing cloud. He has no protection from the lightning that frequently strikes down fast-trackers in the middle of their careers. He is still operating solely as an individual, with some humor and resignation at this point, and protesting the injustice of the system.

Hank's story is very similar, but the lessons learned and the resulting outcomes are positive instead of negative.

Speeding along with rapid early promotions (which are not available in the academic world, where the timeframe for feedback and upward movement is very much attenuated), Hank was approaching the years of the Executive Transition in his early thirties. At this time, some small incidents occurred that appeared strange to him, and that he did not fully understand. He was given a new job, a high level job, but without the full title and without the bonuses that this job usually carried. He assumed at the time that this was because of the current recession. He wondered if this were a sign, a clue, that the organizational undercurrents were no longer flowing in his favor. (Now, he says, this is often done in promotions: to promote people half-way and let them earn full credits, but he did not know this at the time.) Nonetheless, he continued to excel, to better his organization, and to polish his own record as he had done in the past.

Still shy of the transition years and in the last months of his early-career phase, Hank was promoted again. The promotion was based on merit, but this time he was denied the salary that usually came with the promotion. Placating reasons for this were passed along from corporate headquarters, which made little sense to Hank. He protested, but not for long. At age 36, another promotion was in the offing, this one in the South American office.

Before this new job was finalized, however, there were unaccountable delays: superiors in the company didn't know where the base of operations was to be; they didn't know when the job would begin; they weren't really sure what the job entailed; they did not know what span of time would be involved in carrying out the job; and, finally, they said, "his wife was too independent to live in the South American culture." With this, the corporation fell silent.

(When merit cannot be attacked, other reasons will be found if the knives are sharp enough. With Bill, administrators cast aspersions on unassailable research and teaching. With Hank, others in the company took aim at his family.)

With the South American job on hold, Hank was moved to a new office in his former location. He was given no work to do. He did not have a secretary. He wrote letters that were not answered. He called Personnel Headquarters, which did not respond. The wave of support he received, however, from former subordinates and co-workers kept him going.

Sitting idle in what seemed like outer Siberia, Hank considered his options, which basically boiled down to flight or fight. He could flee and find another job or he could fight the injustices of the system. However, as in his difficult elementary school years, good advice came from people on the sidelines who were watching his non-progress. "Do neither of those things," they counseled, "just sit tight." "We can take the company to the cleaners," said a lawyer friend, "but you will never work in the industry again." "Hang in there," they said. So Hank hung in there and kept his mouth shut, and he went to the office and he sat there, and he nodded and smiled at those he passed in the hallway who often passed as if they did not notice him. Then he went on his customary vacation with his wife.

In the middle of this vacation he was called back, notified of a corporate shake-up and a new man in charge, and Hank was promoted to a full vice-presidency as head of his division. The one senior manager (Mark) whom Hank had most threatened had now moved out to another company; it turned out that Mark had been using his "essentialness" to the home company as a means of leveraging up his new salary. Hank's skills, if visible, would have threatened Mark's essentialness, would have shown others in the company that Mark was not, in fact, absolutely necessary, and thus would have diminished the leverage that Mark was bringing to bear in negotiations with his new company. In Mark's career moves, Hank was only a pawn in the game.

It was a year or two before Hank learned the full story, but he has never protested, never said a word, and has continued to do his work well. After being "out in the cold"—a period of solitude and reevaluation—he is well on his way to being a team player, an achiever for the good of the organization, and a support to the senior managers whose ranks he will, most likely, soon join.

Hank learned the critical lesson. He learned to slow down and let the other guy win, turning in his prior competitive mind-set for the cooperative one that is essential in order to move forward again. Currently, he is cultivating mentors and allies, and has a wry sense of humor about "when the game turns against you." He holds no animosity for those who stood aside and let this happen. He has also learned, however, to keep external options open so that he maintains a range of choices should the game go sour again. It is unlikely that he will need those options.

Hank, unlike Bill, was willing to shed his earlier behavior patterns and go through the difficult process of learning new ones. This meant developing a new tolerance for uncertainty and a willingness to walk through shadowy areas that had seemed clearly lit before. Bill has not yet learned that lesson.

Several of the other fast-trackers mention incidents from this period which suggest that they, too, spent some time in isolation, learning the lessons in store for all managers passing through the Executive Transition. Art speaks of a recent period during which he was "totally frustrated—I had absolutely no impact on anything that mattered." Jerry has recently had a downgrade in his title though his responsibilities have increased. Only time will tell whether this is one of the signals of new undercurrents or simply another step in career development. Larry is the only other fast-tracker who briefly discussed this time of transition.

> At the beginning of the Executive Transition, Larry was sent to a position on the periphery of the organization. He describes the job, with some anger, as a "rip-off." He says of this time, "I resented it but put up with it; I was really on the verge of leaving. But I did get a chance to work with a lot of really competent people." Partly because everyone thought he was leaving, he says, he got a new assignment in research. This job turned out to be a bonanza for him because he became acquainted with areas of the company that previously had been total unknowns to him. "This was the learningest job I ever had," he exclaims. Three years of learning, resulting in his increasing corporate profits, brought him to his present position as president of the company's newest and prestigious subsidiary, situated right on the leading edge of technology.

Larry provides a key to understanding what constitutes a successful passage of this career phase. This is a time to learn, not a time to do. Those managers who can see in potential defeat or potential derailment an opportunity to slow down; to do less; and to learn more about themselves, others, and the organization are those with the highest chances of survival. Even during this difficult time—what one advisor told Hank would be the "worst time of his career"—those on the fast track have turned perceived defeats into opportunities. They have taken the opportunity to unlearn old behaviors and to begin to learn new ones. They have learned to put others first, to cooperate, and to become team players. These are new rules, and only those with the flexibility to learn anew will climb any further up the ladder of corporate success.

In addition to changes in the rules during the Executive Transition, there are changes in the relationships that one has with others. Despite the brevity with which the fast-trackers speak of this time, it is notable that they do not mention people in their work environment during this time, as they do when they talk of both the junior and senior years. In their descriptions of the years on either side of the Executive Transition, all of the fast-trackers each interject an average of three names of people who were significant to them in their work lives; the mention of no names (with one exception) in the middle years is striking. This suggests that the middle career years, the transition years, are a no-man's land in which individuals are left on their own—without rules and without guides—to find their way through a thicket of contradictory signals.

SURVIVING THE EXECUTIVE TRANSITION

The survivors of this period are but a small percentage of those who enter. Briefly, the fast-trackers refer to others—peers and bosses—who did not make it through the transition maze. One senior manager refers to a former boss (who now reports to him) and says that he got stopped because he did not learn to take responsibility for new directions, spending too much time keeping people happy. A mid-level manager speaks of all his bosses who are gone now: "They're out!" In fact, one of the consequences of the great weeding-out of this time of mid-career is that many of these fast-trackers lose their former mentors and allies. The survivors must establish new ties as senior managers among each other and among those with promise, still junior, who are on the other side of the Executive Transition.

Thus, not only do the rules change, but all the guides and mentors change as well. The transition to a cooperative, people-oriented attitude occurs when in fact the individual is most alone. The solitude allows some to develop a new appreciation of others. For some, however, the solitude becomes a program for derailment, which results in a "merely competent" conclusion to a potentially brilliant career.

EVALUATING THE EXECUTIVE TRANSITION

There is a clarity of expectations for those in the childhood and adulthood of the career timeline that cannot be found during the more turbulent career adolescence. During this time, the rules are less well-defined and support groups often disintegrate. Are we in fact programming the brightest and best for derailment during this time by expecting first one thing and then another? Or are we providing for the talented among us an appropriate testing ground for those who may assume significant leadership positions in our culture?

It is possible in fact that the Executive Transition does provide an appropriate test of fortitude, patience, and humility between the realms of junior and senior management, because great changes in manner, style, and approach are necessary to travel from junior stardom to senior statesmanship. The behaviors for which junior corporate stars—the "whiz kids"—are rewarded are not the same behaviors that will carry them to the top. The behaviors for which the young earn praise will not bring plaudits to those who are more senior in years and who are responsible for the direction taken by the entire corporation. Rather, the behaviors for junior "stars" and for senior "statesmen" are quite different from each other.

During this transition, some fail to adapt and persist in the patterns of their youth. These do not then pass any higher up on the fast track to the top but are shuttled from the uncertain world of the transition years to the corporate periphery, where they may continue to work, competently to be sure, but without any prospects of real advancement for the remainder of their careers. In effect, they have failed to jettison the baggage of their junior years (strong individual achievement orientations) and have returned to earth to move along with most of their former peers. They have lost their chance at the moon.

Those who traverse the Executive Transition, however, become the true adults of the corporate world and trade in their early competitive orientation for a cooperative one in which the organizational good supersedes individual priorities as the focus of their efforts. They forego the guidance of their mentors, remember that it is all right for the world to stop saying "thank you," and turn instead to helping those who are following in their footsteps and climbing the ladder behind them. They assume responsibility for a multitude of others, and realize that no longer does another assume responsibility for them. Power and influence, albeit diluted by the recognition of uncontrollable factors attending any large-scale undertaking, now lie in their hands, and so too the responsibility and accountability that accompany the use of power.

It may be, in fact, that the only, or the best, route to the cooperative, partnership, teamwork orientation of senior management lies through the competitive, individualized path of the junior levels of the corporate hierarchy. It may be that only in taking care of oneself first that one learns to genuinely respect the opinions and actions of others. Moreover, if adaptability is a priority in those who run our corporations, they have been trained well: for they must be first one way and then another, and only those who have succeeded in living out this paradox and making this about-face may have the flexibility to set the markers for the rest to follow.

In fact, how one judges the contradictory demands placed on executives in their junior and senior years rests at bottom on the measuring stick used for judgment. If the measuring stick is one that values and assesses comfort, ease, and lack of surprises, then our senior managers have been subjected to an unfortunate set of demands. If the measuring stick, instead, assesses the degree of strength exhibited in the face of conflict, then our senior managers have run a gauntlet appropriate for their task.

Human beings often disagree with each other because they choose different measuring sticks, have different sets of values, and, therefore, arrive at different judgments about what is wise and unwise, right and wrong. Some people use measuring sticks that rate positively certain levels of conflict—or contradictory demands—because of the value placed on the psychological strength and resilence that emerges in the face of conflict; others have different measuring sticks that rate negatively conflictual situations and contradictory demands because of the value placed on psychological serenity and contentment. However, psychologists have pointed out that a degree of conflict promotes human growth. The question may be then: What is the right degree of conflict? And are the benefits worth the cost?

In other words, the questions may be phrased in terms of the collective level of managerial competence in an organization. Do the challenges that promote strength in some, lead to disappointment and defeat in so many more that the collective level of managerial competence in an organization is diminished? Or is the amount of disappointment and defeat more than counterbalanced by the resulting strength? The answers to these questions are undoubtedly specific to individuals or to companies. Yet, everyone might profit from greater understanding of the arduous course of career development along the fast track and choose, for oneself, to either undergo the rigors of this path with clear insight and acceptance of its difficulties; or equally well, to choose to stop along the way in a place that best suits one's individual talents and aspirations. On either course, travelers would make individual decisions based on knowledge of the paradox of leadership: that the road to the top passes first one way and then another, and only those who can be competitive individually and then shed the mantle of competition can move to the highest seats of power, thus continuing the journey upward on the fast track to the top.

CHAPTER 7

A View from the Top
The Integration of Substance and Style

. . . the executive must develop his own human skill, rather than lean on the advice of others. To be effective, he must develop his own personal point of view toward human activity, so that he will (a) recognize the feelings and sentiments which he brings to a situation; (b) have an attitude about his own experiences which will enable him to re-evaluate and learn from them; (c) develop ability in understanding what others by their actions and words (explicit or implicit) are trying to communicate to him; and (d) develop ability in successfully communicating his ideas and attitudes to others.

ROBERT L. KATZ
"SKILLS OF AN EFFECTIVE
ADMINISTRATOR"

Those who successfully negotiate the Executive Transition continue to grow and learn, moving into the "adulthood" of their career lifetime. They become senior managers and elder statesmen guiding the organization and its people with the wisdom that they have drawn from their earlier experiences. The senior years are in some ways as well defined as the junior years; and both clearly contrast with the nebulous transition in between. Those now of senior rank talk as enthusiastically about their current jobs as they do in remembering their junior ones. The same enthusiasm is not present in detailing the years of the Executive Transition.

The parallels between the junior and senior years reside in the clarity

The Senior Years

SIGNIFICANT LEARNINGS

SUBSTANCE + STYLE
to work with and through others to accomplish company goals
to integrate doing into the context of a bigger picture
to place others and their welfare first
to grow comfortable with the lessened control over actual events
to define long-term strategy and short-term objectives

IMPORTANT BEHAVIORS

Formulating a philosophy about life, organizations, and management
Establishing priorities and communicating them
Being clear about oneself, others and the organization
Setting directions for the organization
Demonstrating concern for the welfare of others

with which we may speak of either, not in the content of those years. It is easy to define what is expected in the first and last stages of the career track. The content of the two stages is quite different—contradictory, paradoxical—but the ease with which the different expectations of each stage may be defined is in marked contrast with the more nebulous experience of the mid-career years, the Executive Transition.

It is clear, for example, that the emphasis is on individual achievement in the junior years; whereas, the emphasis is on terms and partners in the senior years. In the junior years, visions of what-is-to-come take the form of time-bound objectives that can be accomplished primarily by individual effort. In the senior years, visions of the future are more open-ended and can only be enacted through the efforts of many, many people. In the junior years, influence is less, but control over what matters is greater. In the senior years, influence is greater but control over what matters—those events affecting expected outcomes—is much less.

For example, Alec, who is a particularly innovative junior manager, has reshaped the images of different product lines in previous companies. In doing this, he worked with two or three subordinates. The impact on the company's marketing strategy was considerable: He reshaped the message that was given out. He did not, however, reshape the way of doing business nor the processes by which salespeople worked. Rich, on the other hand, another innovative but senior manager, has reshaped the very processes by which individuals transact business—first in operations, then in divisions, and finally in structuring the "world of tomorrow" in a new division that may set the pace for the entire organization. All told, thousands of people have reported up the line to Rich, and have had their daily lives affected by the innovations he and his team of the moment have brought about. Rich's influence is considerably greater than Alec's.

Yet, in terms of accomplishing the goals that each has established, Alec was able, in his previous positions, to maintain greater control. He met face-to-face with everybody who reported to him on a daily basis. He was able to monitor their work, to give direct supervision, and to see that what he wanted to happen indeed did happen. He had the opportunity to direct and motivate his employees on a one-to-one basis. Rich, in contrast, is currently in charge of about 3,000 people who believe that they are creating a new way of doing business. He was stalled in accomplishing his own objectives over a period of several months because of factors that developed within his workers, people with whom he would normally not be in daily contact. Among these groups, over time, Rich again built a "common understanding" by spending time encouraging communication among all the individuals involved. Now on the move again, his company is responding to new turbulence in the external business environment, which requires those in the company to realign their immediate objectives. Through all of this he is persevering in directing what he calls the "grand experiment." However, the control he alone exercises in meeting objectives is much less than that of Alec. His influence is indeed greater, his control less.

In the junior years, young managers will move on to other companies if things don't go their way; in the senior years, they are committed to their companies, no matter what. Success in the junior years may be achieved by persistence, willingness to go up against heavy odds, assertiveness, and individual initiative. Success in the senior years is achieved only if large numbers of people can be motivated and inspired to face in the same direction and pursue common goals.

The patterns necessary for success at junior and senior levels of the management hierarchy are very different from each other but alike in the clarity of their definition. They contrast with the more ambiguous realm of the Executive Transition. The concerns of the senior statesmen are a modified version of those of the junior stars; the concerns are somewhat alike but the activities that they generate are different for the stars and the statesmen.

These concerns may be phrased as questions: What guides the actions of the best among those at senior management? Are there any clues as to how they have negotiated the transition that brought them to this point? Are there any guidelines that they would offer to those still on the trail, and still in danger of being swallowed up by the adolescence of their career, the Executive Transition? The answers given by the senior statesmen are more complicated than those offered by the junior stars. For one thing, what they do is more inextricably entwined with who they know and what they *think*, and these factors cannot be separated from each other. For another thing, speed is less of a factor than at junior levels. Speed becomes important when the direction is determined, and for most of the junior stars, the direction is up, and the question is "How fast?" However, direction, not speed, is the question at senior levels, and "Where next?" replaces "How fast?" as the important question to be answered. These questions provide two categories for reviewing the histories of the senior fast-trackers: how they perceive what is going on now and how they guess at what will happen next.

THE WHAT, WHO, AND WHY OF ACCOMPLISHMENT FOR SENIOR STATESMEN

What the senior managers *do*, by and large, is provide guidance and direction for hundreds or thousands of people within their companies. In the process of doing this, they operate with more influence and, in many ways, less actual control than do those beneath them on the corporate ladder. They do not talk of influence and control directly. Rather they hint at this dimension by saying, "Of course, there is more political maneuvering at each level." What they seem to mean is that more people are involved in making every decision, and in implementing these decisions. With increases in the number of people involved, individual control necessarily decreases. It is, therefore, more difficult for these senior statesmen to enumerate individual accomplishments now than in the early part of their career.

Who they know, however, is equally important to them. Just as the junior people, often enthusiastically, mention their mentors and bosses, these senior people mention their allies and those working for them. The number of times that others are mentioned in describing the work history of the senior years is exactly the same as in the junior years—and completely different from the middle years (in which no other people are mentioned by any, except one, of the sample). However, during those middle years of the Executive Transition, the successful fast-trackers have shifted their attention from others above them, to others at their side and below. Although the focus has shifted, a strong concern about others is charactersitic of both the junior and senior career phases.

What the senior managers *think*, moreover, is also characteristic of their descriptions of their work life at the top of the corporate ladder. For the senior fast-trackers, action is paired with philosophy, which is set within the context of the welfare of the organization. Why they do something is as important as what they are doing, and action takes place in the context of a philosophical framework that encompasses the welfare of large groups of people.

Hal, for example, describes himself as an "architect for change;" Tom views his actions in terms of a lifetime "destiny" that is to empower others; Rich describes his work in terms of making a dream, an experiment, and a reality, and in terms of bringing satisfaction and an emotional high to others. This language and these descriptions are totally absent in the interviews of the junior people and only creep into the language of some of the more senior middle people. The large-scale thinking of those who work at the top provides a context in which to make choices, an anchor in an uncertain world, and gives meaning to their work. And, since they are leaders of many, this meaning is passed along in communication to others in the company so that many or most employees know that they are working for a purpose that exists outside of themselves. The frameworks that these men operate in are philosophical in an applied—not necessarily abstract—sense and imbue their world and the worlds of many, many others with meaning. This is, according to some popular gurus of organization development, the core of leadership.[1]

In short, all of the senior statesmen set directions for their company or division, are strongly committed to their people, and have a philosophical framework that guides their actions. The creators and contributors among these senior managers, however, differ from each other along another dimension. The creators among them define their responsibilities to the company in terms of change, whereas the contributors define their work in terms of effectiveness. The creators are more often working in positions or entire divisions in which "making things different" is part of their mandate. On the other hand, the contributors are working in the mainstream of the corporate hierarchy where "making it better" is the charge. As the senior managers talk about what they do, who they know, and what they think, the two different perspectives of creators and contributors emerge. The stories of the creators, Rich, Hal, and Tom, precede those of the contributors, Andrew and Jon.

Rich's emphasis throughout his description of his senior management career is on the people with whom he works and on his thinking about the organization. Together, for him, these coalesce into an emphasis on *strategic planning* in order to create change. His emphasis on planning, however, grew through several stages and through a series of different leadership positions.

As the manager of a small division, he supervised the merger with a larger division and then moved to the top of the division as a whole. In the smaller division, he loved being able to be close to the people. He appreciated the business knowledge of those who worked with him and he began to learn about strategic planning. He says: "In order to bring about the merger we needed a strategic business plan. . . . It became even clearer to me how important the strategic planning process was to the whole transformation. What I mean by a strategic business plan is really using long-range goals as an incentive for personal growth and development. This is a process that produces amazing results. The plan involves all the people and also provides a link to top management. It pulls the organization together around some common goals. It provides a common language—and this is a critical success factor." In his next job, as head of an even larger division, he came to see even more clearly than before the importance of planning and strategy. "It is important to have a direction, to encourage others to take ownership of that direction through communication. We got a lot of cooperation. This is powerful stuff."

In his current position, Rich heads up a very big experimental division of a megacompany. Again he talks about his job in terms of strategy: "My job focuses on what the mission is all about. We are challenging current thinking by introducing alternative strategies and different styles. We're supposed to initiate change. Even our people are resistant to this and have a 'can't do' attitude. I think we broke through this recently and are creating new opportunities . . . There have been difficulties in the last few months. People are upset with different ways of managing and believe we are not doing what we do very well . . . We are working on this by going back, in part, to strategic planning and getting them to help us look at what will be happening five to ten years down the road and not just today . . . We're generating a lot of new options . . ."

In reviewing his recent history, Rich mentioned two people who worked *for* him who knew the business, and two who worked *with* him and helped him develop the notion of strategic planning. How he operates now is integrally related to those who facilitated his learning process and contributed to his philosophical stance. In talking about the process of implementation as well, his emphasis is again on those with whom he works: "In this job I have to work with others who can teach the people how we are going to run this operation—I cannot do this alone." Rich's job involves thousands and thousands of others, and their involvement has been critical at each step along the way.

In his last few years as a senior manager, Hal has been part of the senior management team at his corporate headquarters. As he describes his work, the same three emphases, apparent in Rich's story, emerge: Hal talks about *people* individually and collectively as the potential of the company; he talks about *thinking* in describing himself as the architect of change, outlining the specific organizational functions that must undergo transformation; and throughout, more clearly than almost any other, Hal talks about *change*.

He has been instrumental in redesigning the organization as a whole, and in reshuffling the divisions, in order to strengthen the company "for the long-term haul." In the process he has institutionalized many practices that have gradually led to the infusion of a new management style among many at the top, and provided the means for the new approaches to reach down through the ranks. He has worked with others to increase the effectiveness of the company, and helped to shut down operations that did not respond to the new expectations.

Currently, he works most closely with the other two or three men at the top of the hierarchy to create company-wide change, to "move the mountain without the mountain knowing it is moving." He says: "My job is to be architect for change in this company — in a well-ordered, consistent way. The company is unbelievable in its potential if we can just learn how to manage it. I am involved now with two colleagues in creating plans that include structure, decision-making process, top management capabilities, incentive systems, and changing the culture. We've come a long way and have a long way to go. It is just fascinating." And later, he goes over his objectives again and says: "We will do more with less. There is tough competition out there and we must take action now. . . . We are emphasizing a five-year time frame with a big emphasis on knowing our competitors and knowing what they're doing. We need to manage differently. . . ."

Elsewhere in his descriptions of his responsibilities, Rich has placed the same emphasis as Hal on devising strategies for the present that take account of tough competition. Both men, from different relative positions in different corporate hierarchies, emphasize the need to manage differently. Hal puts this in a context defined by how he thinks: "I always had a *vision* of the great, well-managed company we could be. We're getting there but it could be better than it is. In order to be that company we have to shed our old style and change peoples' attitudes. My colleague and I together now have a vision of how this company could change."

Tom also describes his career as a senior manager in terms of dreams and destiny. Dreams and destiny, for him, reflect his sense of working for the *people* and creating *change*. However, more clearly in what follows below than elsewhere, Tom emphasizes his thinking about change, and the characteristics essential for bringing change about.

Tom's first move as a senior manager was a lateral move to corporate headquarters. His move occurred at a time of major transition for this huge company amidst very unsettling circumstances. He says, "This was a living hell. One morning I was called into a meeting and told, without question, that I had to shut down the business I had just created. It was like giving up my children, but I did it. The company was in no sense ready to do anything, much less do it well. There was setback after setback. . . . Two years later, there was a growing clarity in my part of the business about the consequences of potential failure: namely, an exit from the marketplace. Then, there was a major management change . . . followed by a remarkable turnaround . . . we are beginning to break even.

"What happened is that for the last three years, we cleaned house. People decided to identify the problems and do something about it. This was very exciting. . . . The change took clarity and discipline and *attention to making it happen* and an unfailing commitment on the part of the senior management team.

"In the last year, I have been working for a new boss, absolutely top drawer. I knew the minute I met him that he was the one who could complete this change. . . . I never spent an hour with him when I didn't learn at least three things. Four months after his arrival, with everybody working 16–18 hours a day, there was a complete turnaround in manufacturing, research and development, marketing and sales. He and I had a partnership for four to six months. These people are my family. . . . This is why I came here: to realize my dream and empower the people. This again is a feeling not easily put in words."

Tom's thinking hinges on words like partnership and destiny. Elsewhere he says, "I always felt like I had partnerships with the people I work with. That's what I've been trying to do with my whole life. . . ."

These three men, all senior creators, consistently emphasize people, thought, and change. They care about people—they think about what they are doing and why they are doing it—and they want things to be different because they believe that *different* means *better*. The two contributors, Andrew and Jon, have the same emphasis on people and thinking. They are briefer in their descriptions than the creators and, as Andrew says more than once, matter-of-fact. For these two men, the goal is to make things better, but better is not necessarily equated with different.

Andrew describes a series of moves into wholly different environments— different geographic locations, and functional areas as well—since he entered the senior management stage of his career. In recounting the story of the last eight years, he lists his jobs, cites his boss along the way "who is a leader," and uses words like "delightful" and phrases like "getting to know the whole organization" with some frequency. An important assignment for him, though of short duration, was his work on a corporate committee that determined a major reorganization of this huge company and "rethought the corporation." Currently, Andy is still new in his job and is feeling his way. He doesn't yet know whether it will be "delightful" or not . . . He is waiting to see. He is clear, however, on his approach to management: "It helps to focus on the team player concept and what is best for the organization. I like working it out and the challenge posed by a problem. . . . I love it when a plan comes down. . . . I do it because it's there. I never had any slack time. I'm very matter-of-fact."

Jon describes the rapid increase of his responsibilities over the last five years with the same brevity that Andrew uses. He spends more time, however, explaining basic principles that have worked well for him in the management of a huge organization. He says, more than once and in different words, that it is necessary to point the ship in the right direction and explain things to the people. "I tell them they are here to increase market share. I explain why. They love it."

In his current job, Jon has world-wide responsiblities and spends over one-third of his time travelling. In each of his visits to different parts of the world he emphasizes the direction the company has set . . . where they are going and what everybody has to do to get there. One suspects that in all the different countries abroad, as at home, the people appreciate the clarity and the communication and that, in fact, "they love it."

Andrew and Jon are not given to telling long stories about their work. Andrew elaborates on a point only once, and that is when he mentions his grandmother. "Oh, golly!" he exclaims, "she was a live wire!" Jon tells a few more stories about his work than Andrew but his most interesting stories are about his wife, the children they are just having in mid-life, and their adventures in the housing market. In his descriptions of his non-work life, Jon shows the same enthusiasm and excitement seen in the creators when describing their work. In regard to houses, not work, he uses the word "vision." In regard to houses, not work, he talks about the processes of "building" and "creating."

Yet both men clearly care about the people they work with and those who have helped them along the way. They mention the names of other co-workers as frequently as do the creators. They are also clear, but brief, about their philosophy of work. For Andrew, the team is important; for Jon it is the direction. In substance, these contributors differ from the creators only in the absence of any mention of the word "change" or its synonyms. The implication is, however, that they make things work, they make things work very well, and they increase the effectiveness and profitability of any unit that they run.

It is important to note that both of these contributors are in the mainstream of corporate management. Both are likely successors to the top executive seat in their corporation. They are not, as is the case with the creators, running experimental divisions, nor were they hired to create change in the company. They are where they are because they know, on a grand scale, how to make things work. For them, making it better does not necessarily include making it different. And they feel less need to expound upon their principles, their histories, and their belief systems. Their belief systems are, to a large extent, those of the corporation for which they work, and which they will very likely run in the near future. Their principles are public policy.

FUTURE DIRECTIONS

The junior stars want to know how fast they're going. The senior statesmen want to know where they're going. At the junior level, an upward direction is assumed and the distinguishing factor is how fast they travel. At the senior level, up is *not* assumed (they *are* up, at least in terms of all of their aspiration). So they ask, "Where to next?"

None of the creators really owns up to the possibility that he may very well run his company in the next few years. Instead all of them emphasize the importance of their current jobs, and the futility of concentrating on possibilities that are not yet in the immediate offing. Some are clearer about this than others. Some, too, talk about retirement although they agree, when asked, that any idleness on their part is unlikely. They speculate on what other non-corporate possibilities might exist.

> Rich emphasizes the likelihood and importance of staying in his current position, and does not look to other possibilities: "I expect to stay here. There's a need for commitment in this job, a willingness to see it through. I wouldn't mind retiring here . . . There's a lot of excitment here. What motivates me is the feeling I have for the people. I don't want to be at the top of the whole company. . . ."
>
> Hal at first says, "I think I will retire. It will take three to four years to manage this change and see results. I will have done what I set out to do. I do not want to go to another big corporation—it would be doing more of what I have already done." Then he enumerates his outside interests and the number of business ventures he and his wife have generated, all of which will need consistent management. And then he notes that the continuing question is, "Will I be challenged?" His wife worries about this and so he thinks: "Maybe I'll have to go to Washington. . . . I'm doing what I've always wanted to do. I believe in continually creating change in your own life. I have done that within the confines of this company. What next? . . . Washington?" Talking about retirement for Hal is only a starting point for exploring other options, which might provide the challenges to which he is accustomed as part of his regular routine.

Tom, slightly more junior in status than Rich and Hal, oscillates between possibilities of moving up another notch to the division presidency and retiring. He says: "I want more balance. I like to cook, have a great garden. I am not very good at raising children and want to be better." And later, he says, "I want to manage a restaurant with my wife in an old New England Inn, but we cooled down on this idea when we visited one we wanted, and learned that the couple who owned it had been murdered and their house had been burned down. We're not so interested in this idea right now." Then, later, he mentions consulting. Rather like Rich and Hal, the key ingredient for Tom is challenge. He yearns for more balance in his life but so far has not built this in. Each of these men are looking at a variety of options for continuing to love their work and to pursue their dreams on yet another scale.

The contributors, Jon and Andrew, on the other hand, are more matter-of-fact about their jobs, and more crisp about their possible options. Both of them are planning to stay within the company, and move on to the next slot. Their responses have quite a different flavor from those of Rich, Hal, and Tom.

Andrew sees that he might become a Vice-President of a different group, or that he might acquire new operations in his current job. He chooses not to expand upon his options and says clearly: "I have never concerned myself with what's next. I am already *much* higher than I ever imagined I would be. I have no burning desire to be the President or the Chairman. I want to be a *positive contributor* rather than top dog." In this phrase, he selects the term used for his orientation throughout the book, that of contributor, and expresses the orientation that may in fact take him right into the chairs held by the President or the Chairman. He goes on to say that "In my career, my job positions have moved back and forth between project management and more general management responsibilities, between being responsible for my own talents and output and helping others to do the same. Each time I have moved back and forth it has been to put in place what I know or have experienced—at a higher level with a greater degree of politics." With this, he sums up his own career, and comes back to a phrase that lights up his face: in whatever capacity, he loves it "when a plan comes down."

Jon has nowhere else to go in his company but straight to the top and he regards this as a definite possibility. For him, the alternative is to become chairman of another company, but he has already had the chance to turn down one such opportunity. This was a job offered to him by a competitor in another country, one-half the size of his current company, along with an outrageous salary, outrageous options, and all the privileges associated with the European ruling classes. This is the job to which his wife objected on the grounds that their search for an American chairman said too little about the value of their own culture for her to look at it favorably as a setting for raising their very small children. Jon is comfortable with refusing this opportunity. There will be others. But the most likely position is at the head of his current company in the not-too-distant future.

The senior creators are looking to other arenas for new opportunities to create and to build. They are not heading for the very top of their corporations and they are searching for larger contexts in which to bring change. The academic world may in fact offer them a springboard, but the only viable landing place is in the national arena, the federal government, and positions of influence in Washington, D.C. They alternate, stretching believability, between such scenarios and the thought of retiring and tending their gardens. There is, indeed, no viable option in between.

Very different are the expectations of the two senior contributors. If there is only one seat left in their company, they expect to move into it. If there is a circle of musical chairs before the leap to the top, they expect to move around this circle, always having a seat, until and if they move to the top. They are, in the best sense, company men.

What does this tell us about life at the top? What are the guidelines we might extract for those who are following? What one does, with whom one works, and what one thinks are inextricably bound together. It becomes more difficult to speak of discrete incidents, specific accomplishments. In addition, the opportunity to influence the lives of thousands is accompanied by a corresponding decrease in the amount of control exercised over immediate events and short-range objectives. At the top, these men are more influenced by things that they do not control. There are no buffers between them and the events transpiring outside of their worlds. For each of them, moreover, people are of primary importance—not necessarily people on a one-to-one basis, but rather people on a large scale, the welfare of the many. Words like team and partnership are very frequent in their stories. They know that they are there to serve many, but also that their ascent to the top was the result of many efforts besides their own.

They are also clear about what they *think* and have developed a conceptual framework that gives meaning to their work. These conceptual frameworks take on the characteristics of philosophies—clear and well-defined for each of them: for Rich, it is strategy; for Hal, quiet and consistent change; for Tom, it is destiny. Andrew says it is the team, but his face expresses delight when he talks about planning. Jon has found a key for himself in clearly setting a direction and then communicating, communicating, communicating. This clarity in philosophic orientation is not apparent at the junior levels and is only beginning to be heard at the middle levels. In this, above all, the senior fast-trackers distinguish themselves from the juniors.

They have also defined their *orientation toward change* and are in positions that suit their individual set of beliefs. What typifies these senior men as a whole, then, and sets them apart from the junior "stars" is their clarity on their own orientation. They know who they are and what they do well. They do not shape themselves to fit a niche that does not match their orientation, not do they try to bend the world to fit their perceptions. They are also willing to accept what is, and if it is not what they might desire it to be, then so be it. Their clarity about themselves, in all five men, is the foundation of their uniqueness—and also the most marked commonality among them.

The lives of the senior fast-trackers illustrate the importance of accepting ambiguities in life, the lesser control that comes with greater influence, the continued importance of people, the distinct necessity of having worked out a philosophical framework, and the importance of clarity about self and the world. These senior statesmen demonstrate the integration that occurs from *knowing oneself and others* and *being oneself with others*. Near the top of their corporate pyramids, they demonstrate the leadership that results from integrating high levels of substance and style.

PART III

Growing Up in Families

The Origins and Effects of Style

Management is a highly individualized art. What style works well for one manager in a particular situation may not produce the desired results for another manager in a similar situation . . . Every manager . . . must develop his own natural style and follow practices that are consistent with his own personality.
J.S. LIVINGSTON
"MYTH OF THE WELL-
EDUCATED MANAGER"

Some distinguished conductors have been petty tyrants; others play poker with their musicians and become godfathers to their babies. These matters are essentially irrelevant . . . no one can become a Toscanini by imitating his mannerisms.
W.C.H. PRENTICE
"UNDERSTANDING LEADERSHIP"

The Origins and Effects of Style

STYLE
_____

..... COMMUNICATION
.... CONFIDENCE
.... COMMITMENT
.... BEING YOURSELF
_____

ORIGINS OF STYLE ARE SEEN IN THE:	EFFECTS OF STYLE ARE SEEN IN THE:
Balance of parental input	Timing of career entry
Number and achievement orientation of siblings	Timing of marriage and children

As we have seen, the styles of the fast-trackers range across a variety of dimensions, illustrating with bolder strokes than usual what many of us observe in our everyday routines. There are those who are fast and those who are slow, there are the noisy and the quiet, the enthusiastic and the solemn. The variety of styles of all the fast-trackers is evident in initial meetings, in the settings in which they work, in their language, the stories they tell about work, and those they tell about their personal lives.

Style is one of the essential components of leadership. Style refers to the confidence in self, the manner of communication, and the strength of commitment to various purposes. It is this combination of elements that commands attention and elicits commitment from others so that they listen, consider what is discussed on its merits, and are willing to buy in. Style is basically caring: caring about others and about what happens, caring enough to stand up for issues and to communicate clearly. Style is acting out of one's own center in order to make connections in the family, the community, the organization. Style is how people relate themselves to the larger networks in which they exist and operate.

The styles of the fast-trackers are varied, each style expressing the unique orientation of the individual. In Chapter 3, the styles of the fast-trackers were grouped into two major categories: creators and contributors.

Styles were also classified as cooperative or competitive and this distinction cut across the ranks of both creators and competitors. The styles of the fast-trackers affected their approach to their work and their choice of positions in the mainstream of the corporation or in the more experimental areas.

The styles of the fast-trackers are also evident in examining their personal lives. In fact, aspects of the early family experience of the fast-trackers fall into relatively clear patterns when creators are contrasted with contributors and when cooperators are contrasted with competitors. Further, the adult family patterns—the timing of career entry, of marriage and of childbirth—also become more distinct when style is used as a distinguishing factor and creators are contrasted with contributors. It would appear then that style affects the overarching patterns of adult life—the balance of career and family concerns—and that the roots of style reach far back into early childhood. Thus, the past and current family settings of the fast-trackers reflect both the origins and effects of style.

This is not as surprising as it may seem at first. Style is the way that we communicate with and relate to others. In fact, style develops in interaction with others. In the personal sphere, how one relates to other people is of prime importance, and getting things done, accomplishing tasks, is important but secondary. On the other hand, in the work sphere, getting things done is critical, and how one relates to other people is important, but perceived as secondary. It is perhaps to be expected then that the strong evidences of differences in style among the fast-trackers are paralleled by differences in the early family, in young adulthood, and in the nature and timing of major life decisions.

The next chapters focus on the origins and effects of style in the personal sphere of life. Just as we refine and develop our style while growing up in organizations, we first establish this style when we grow up in families. Style reflects our most basic sense of self, our integrity, standards, and beliefs. Individuals with well-developed styles *are* themselves; they are not attempting to be somebody else. It is style as much as substance that carries them up the ladder along the fast track to the top.

In the next chapters, therefore, these differences in style among the fast-trackers are identified, and the development and consequences of style are traced through their personal histories, concluding with a summary of how both family and organizational factors affect the development of substance and style, the two components of leadership.

CHAPTER 8

Impressions of Families

The Development of Style

*Leadership style is essentially the outcome of the
developmental process and can be defined . . . as
the patterned modes of behavior with which an
individual relates to external reality and to internal
dispositions.*
ABRAHAM ZALEZNIK
"MANAGEMENT OF
DISAPPOINTMENT"

*Those relationships [in the family] which affirm the
self, can survive conflict, and allow expression of the
whole self are an enormous help in supplying
comfort, meaning, pleasure, gratification, anchors
for the self. People have not drastically let that
reality slip or lost track of that core area of
significance.*
ELIZABETH DOUVAN
"THE MARRIAGE ROLE:
1957-1976"

In considering the sources of their success, the fast-trackers refer
more often to their early background than they do to their work history. The
people who affected their career decisions were more often family members than people in their work setting; the people who helped shape their
values and beliefs were almost always the parents or other close relatives.
What was it about the family setting and/or early educational experience
that put these fast-trackers on the road to success? What were the significant factors that led them to focus their energies on the business environ-

---

Composition, Perceptions and Interpretations of the Family

GROUP	COMMON PERCEPTION	INTERPRETATION
ALL FAST-TRACKERS	• Small or moderate family size • Mentors or role models in family • Occasional mentors or role models at school or work • Occupied position of oldest child • Saw self as successful in childhood	Received considerable adult attention and support
COOPERATORS	• Smaller families with mostly brothers and moderate college attendance among siblings	Little competition in areas of interest
COMPETITORS	• Larger families with many sisters and high college attendance among siblings	Strong competition in areas of interest

---

ment and predisposed them to rise to the top? Finally, did factors in their childhood influence the development of their current style as cooperators or competitors, creators or contributors?

PORTRAYING THE SIMILARITIES

The similarities in the early backgrounds of the fast-trackers are more striking than the differences. The ways in which they are alike, taken together, may be predictive of future success in the business world. The differences, on the other hand, can be interpreted as encouraging the development of different styles and orientations. The similarities shall be presented first in the fictional portrayal of Barry, a typical fast-tracker who is a composite of many of the characteristics of the people in this sample. Toward the end of the chapter, the differences will be examined in terms of the development of different styles.

Barry was the oldest of three brothers born as his parents, Jim and Myra, approached their thirties. Barry grew up, as had his parents before him, in a small town in the Midwest where farming was the major occupation.

Jim and Myra, themselves, had each grown up on a farm and knew what it meant to work long hours. They married out of high school and went to work for other people. Soon they had accumulated enough capital to pursue their shared dream. They quit their jobs and opened a small printing business. It was several years before the business took hold, becoming a center of activity and well-utilized resource in town. Jim and Myra each took a brother into partnership with them as the business grew. With all the work at hand, they delayed having children until Jim was 30 and Myra 29. Even with children (first Barry, and three and seven years later, two more boys), Jim continued to work a 16-hour day and Myra tapered off only slightly. She had always done the books for the business and now she did these at home so she could be with the children—but often she took the children to work with her. They were given small jobs to do very early, and as they got older were given more and more responsibility.

As a matter of course, it was expected that one of the three children would take over the family business. All three were involved in its daily operations. Somewhere between the ages of 10 to 12, each was earning his own salary and paying all his expenses outside of the house. Jim clearly had high expectations for his boys and he did not let them off the hook when they complained about working hard. He gave them lectures on the work ethic and on integrity, and always putting the customer first. Myra was very supportive of her boys: she thought they were wonderful and could do anything they wanted to do, and she let them know this. In fact, she often told them to be open about their feelings and helped them share their thoughts with others. By example, too, she showed them that hard work was an integral part of life, and that it paid off when one kept one's head, remembered that people mattered, and was honest with oneself and others.

Barry liked the print shop with its constant noise, activity, and flow of customers. In contrast, he was often bored and restless in the slower pace of the classroom. The other kids thought he was an oddball. However, in third grade and again in sixth grade, two teachers singled him out and said he had a lot of spunk and leadership ability. They realized he occasionally got into trouble only because he was bored, and encouraged him to get more involved in school activities. Consequently, by seventh grade, Barry was involved in every school activity that fit his own interests: he played all sports (was especially good in track), he ran the yearbook, he was in the drama club and acted in school plays, and served on the Student Council, later becoming junior class president, and, finally, Student Body President his senior year. He graduated with a B + average.

All this time, he had continued to work evenings, weekends, and summers for his parents' business. But Myra and Jim had begun to think that Barry was the one family member who, for sure, could go on to do other things. Consequently, they decided during his junior year in high school that he would go to college (Myra and Jim had not had the chance to go and wanted this for their children). Barry thus applied to a variety of nearby schools and was accepted on a track scholarship to a small, private school in an adjoining state. His entire family accompanied him on the trip to college, each one cheering him on and wishing him well. They were all very proud of their college son.

Barry's first year away from home was difficult but he had lots of help from his fellow students in learning how to study, and how to get along in the school. He was not a star on the track team but was a solid contributor to that team. He majored in economics after a brief excursion into psychology, and spent a lot of his time studying. In the evenings and summers he worked part-time jobs to supplement his track scholarship; he worked at the college and also for a local printer, an associate of his parents. He had less time for additional activities than in high school, but he was an officer in his fraternity. He didn't date much because, he said, "I was very shy." With no interruptions, he finished promptly in four years.

By that time, it was clear that his next oldest brother wanted to work in the family business, and that the youngest was probably going on to college, maybe to be a teacher of some sort. Thus, Barry did not return home but interviewed for jobs and took an entry-level business position with a large corporation in another state. His parents thought he was wonderful, and Barry knew he could never disappoint them no matter what happened.

Barry has characteristics drawn from the early personal histories of all of the fast-trackers. His story illustrates many of the points the fast-trackers have in common and provides a backdrop against which to examine some of the differences. It is important to remember that all of the fast-trackers deviated from the common pattern to some extent. The similarities and differences are explored below.

PERCEPTIONS OF FAMILIES, ROLE MODELS, AND MENTORS

The fast-trackers have much to say about their families: their parents, their brothers, and their sisters. Some of what they say can be converted into numerical data: ages of parents and children, number of brothers and sisters. This information is treated as factual and presented in the tables below. Much, however, of what they say is clearly *their* perception of their family members, which represents another type of information. This is qualitative information that, in fact, illuminates the perceptual framework of the fast-trackers. This tells us what they think about themselves and others. This information *is significant in terms of who the fast-trackers are, what they think, and what they remember*. Similarities among the fast-trackers in *perceptions*, however, suggest a certain "mind-set" or perceptual framework that may be correlated with survival along the fast track.

The fast-trackers' perceptions may or may not actually accord with the reality of their family lives as perceived by others, including their brothers and sisters. In this context, the fast-trackers' perceptions are also treated as factual information, which illuminate the framework from which fast-trackers approach the world.

Finally, marked similarities and differences in these two different kinds of information, numerical and qualitative, are subject to interpretation based on other research information and "common psychological understandings." The interpretations suggest areas for future research and point the way toward what might be interesting and provocative conclusions. Considering the size of the sample, and the perceptual nature of much of the information, these interpretations may not be considered conclusions in themselves. (A more detailed description of this approach appears in Appendix B.) We turn now to a description of the ways in which the fast-trackers are like each other.

Family Size

Nine of the seventeen fast-trackers grew up in relatively small families of three children or less. Seven were in families of moderate size with four to six children. Only one, Pete's, was very large with ten children. In addition, five of the seventeen sets of parents waited until their mid-thirties or later to have children, indicating that other interests may have previously predominated in their lives.

Parents as Role Models

Many of the parents of these fast-trackers had small businesses of their own; a majority of the parents, including these small business owners, had jobs that both allowed them to control their own time and encouraged them to work far beyond the usual eight-to-five working day. Twelve of the seventeen fast-trackers were exposed to family situations in which the working parent or parents did not report to an immediate boss and where the demands of the vocation took them long beyond an eight-hour day.[1] For any random sample this would be a rather high percentage.

In addition, a surprising number of mothers worked. Three worked regularly in family businesses while one worked there only during periods of necessity; three mothers worked (at least part-time) in blue-collar jobs; one was a professional. Again, eight—nearly half of the fast-trackers—had at least occasionally working mothers.

All of this may be taken as illustrative of the high value placed on hard and demanding work in the backgrounds of the fast-trackers. It seems clear that all the children raised in these families recognized the value of hard work.

Parents as Mentors

Almost all of the fast-trackers refer to their families as the primary source of their success. Within their families they (1) found role models who demonstrated the value of hard work and integrity; (2) received advice and instruction on how to live their lives; and (3) were offered support in meeting their parents' expectations.

For many of the fast-trackers, their parents have remained lifelong sources of inspiration. Hal, who thinks of himself and is thought of by others as very creative, says of his father, "He had very creative ideas and liked to change things." Larry learned to be what he calls an "opportunist" from living and working with his father: "He follows rules but stretches them; he takes advantage of the situation." Christine learned from both her grandmother and her father. Her grandmother, a businesswoman, was a pioneer among women—after her husband's death she sustained and expanded his business. Her father, a doctor, was an individual committed to helping; he valued learning new things and finding better ways of doing something. Christine herself is also a pioneer, one of very few women at her level of management, and defines her job role in a way that emphasizes her skills in helping others.

Often the parents of the fast-trackers verbalized their points of view, and expressed them directly to their children. Brian's father told his children to "always do what you believe is right," and "be sure and leave the world a better place than you found it." Sam's parents told him always to "remember who you are" (which meant upright, ethical, honest). Sam reports that all through his life, when he's thought of doing something outside of the straight and narrow path, he has heard his mother's voice in his head saying, "remember who you are." While this hasn't always prevented him from acting, it has resulted in his thinking twice about what he was about to do. Christine's father, much like Brian's, told his children that they were supposed to contribute to the good of society, to grow, to adapt, to learn and never to be afraid of anything just because it was new. The messages from almost all of the parents not only emphasized hard work, but self-reliance, integrity, and the importance of making a contribution to others.

The fast-trackers were supported by their families; their parents, and sometimes other relatives, believed that these young people could fulfill all the expectations the family had for them. However, the parents were often perceived as being more supportive of achievement-oriented activities "than just plain loving." Hal's father is typical. He told Hal, "You can do anything you want to do, just depend on yourself and not on others." Hal's mother, too, encouraged him strongly. Hal says, "She was strong and ambitious for me and pushed me in all sorts of areas." Jon's father too "encouraged me to do the best I could" and to go on and do the things that he had not done. Brian says, "My parents were very supportive," and goes on to say, "enthusiastic on achievement but not 'loving.' "

By and large, the fast-trackers were liked by and, in return, liked their parents very much. Pete says, "They thought we were pretty good." And Larry says of his parents, "Between the two of them, it's pretty good," and he means good for the family as a whole. The attachment to and appreciation of their parents is often continued into their current lives, and many fast-trackers regularly talk with both parents or, for some, with a widowed parent. Hal spends time with his father, Hank's mother visits often, and Pete calls his mother to drop in for breakfast and to "tell her I love her."

Mentors and Role Models at School

Fast-trackers do not, as a rule, mention as significant the help they received from teachers and instructors during their educational career. However, for the one who didn't have a father or, in another case, did not relate well to his father, and in two cases where the fathers were often absent from home due to work obligations, teachers made significant contributions to the early thinking of these young people.

Brian, whose father was often away, received much help from his parents but also from his teachers. He feels that they took him under their wing—"I was always lucky," he says—and showed him that he could be a leader. Their support led to his strong involvement in school activities, and to a change from poor citizenship grades to excellent ones. He remembers two or three teachers in elementary school specifically, and also his coaches in high school. Brian's energy could have been used to cause trouble or to lead. His teachers helped him select the leadership route.

Finally, Art, the one fast-tracker who grew up without a father figure in his early life, whose mother was on welfare, and whose opportunities in life generally looked dim, credits the school atmosphere in general, and one instructor in particular, for helping him to get on quite a different track. He first came into his own due to peer pressure within the school, beginning his senior year in high school. For the first time, he decided to give school a try. He was able to improve his grades enough to just get into community college. In his first semester there, he had an instructor who prodded him to think and this proved to be a catalyst in his life. From then on, he worked hard and graduated on the dean's list.[2]

The school environment sometimes reinforced, and sometimes compensated for, factors in the home environment and gave a much needed push to several of the fast-trackers.

Mentors in Early Work Experiences

All the fast-trackers worked part-time and summers, most of them all through junior high and high school as well as college. Their work experience was critical for a few. Sam believes the woman who ran his tennis club was an inspiration to him: "She was strong, hardhitting and very capable and believed that the customer was the most important thing." Rich credits his boss at the drugstore with bringing him out of his shell. Both of these two men were not exposed directly in their homes to business environments, so they borrowed examples from outside.

> Rich describes his high school work experience: "I didn't do sports or other high school activities. I had a functional heart murmur and at this time doctors thought that activity should be restricted. So I worked at the drugstore as a drug clerk. I came out of my shell there. I worked hard until 9:00 at night every night. At that time I was very shy, petrified, did not want to talk to anybody. When I started, the pharmacist had me work in the back room, organizing stock. After one week, he said, "Well, I guess there isn't any more to do back here. You'll have to come up to the front." I went out and had my first customer, a woman who argued with me about the bill—she thought it was $.63 instead of $.65. She was wrong, but I gave her two cents. The pharmacist was helpful. He said, 'You did the right thing. A customer's good will is always worth more than two cents.' I learned a lot from Mr. X and I became better with people."

This was the same drugstore in which Rich first learned about ethics by sweeping out the store in order to pay for the comic book he had stolen (see story in Chapter 2). The drugstore owner was a long-term and significant figure in his early learning.

PERCEPTIONS OF SELF IN RELATION TO BROTHERS AND SISTERS

The fast-trackers *remember* thinking well of themselves and being well-regarded by others. Their perceptions suggest, in fact, that they assumed the place of oldest child in the family, whether or not this was so, and that they in many cases are the "star" of the family. These perceptions clearly guide their own behavior. Whether or not these perceptions would agree with those of their parents, or with those of their brothers and sisters, is not explored. The perceptions that they do have tell us about themselves, not necessarily about their family members. What the fast-trackers think, however, is vital in understanding what they do and how they have arrived at their current position.

Perceived as Oldest or Only Child

The conventional wisdom is that oldest or only children achieve more than others, because these children spend more time with adults, receiving more adult attention and support. Initially, it was therefore a surprise to find that nine of the seventeen fast-trackers were not first-born—eight of these were second children and Pete was a fourth child—while eight were first or only children. Yet when this is examined more closely, it becomes apparent that almost all the fast-trackers, in one way or another, occupied the *position* of first child and were the focus of parental expectations generally directed at first children.

Of the nine fast-trackers with older brothers and sisters, *five* had brothers or sisters who are perceived by the fast-trackers as "dropping out" of the establishment, forfeiting in their parents' eyes their place as oldest child. The four who had achieving older brothers and sisters were Alec and Christine with achieving older sisters, and Don and Pete with achieving older brothers. In effect, there were 13 fast-trackers among the seventeen who perceived themselves as assuming the position of first-born child.

Perceptions of Success in Early Childhood

The fast-trackers as a whole perceived themselves as having been successful early in childhood—sometimes more successful than their siblings, sometimes as successful. None of them mentioned being less successful or less able than others in their families. Tom says of his childhood, "I knew somehow I was doing OK—I thought that I was all right."

All of the fast-trackers with *older* brothers and sisters, with the exception of Christine and Pete, perceived themselves on one measure or another as more successful than their older siblings. Six of these fast-trackers question why they grew up so differently from their older brothers and sisters, and examine their pasts to see if differences in environment are discernible. Two of them display a bewildered amusement, mixed with concern, in describing their brothers who joined motorcycle gangs. Both of these fast-trackers might have said something like the following:

My brother, Joe, is still living in the sixties. He is bright but flaky, reckless and irresponsible. He was supposed to take over Dad's business but dropped out of college at the last minute, got a job in the factory, and rode with a motorcycle gang. He went with whatever the flow was. He's been in prison for dealing drugs, he's been rehabilitated, he's been separated from his wife and now he's back again. He looked on me as the college boy but . . . we did things together. We had some weird times as teenagers when I went along with his gang.

More concern is shown by another fast-tracker about a less exotic older brother who also failed to measure up to expectations. This fast-tracker says:

My dad and I still wonder why I *did* things and John did not. He never had any initiative, never seemed to strive for anything. Dad feels he treated us the same. But if ever there was a reward for work, my brother never wanted it enough to do the work. I always pitched in. This still bothers my dad.

Even more concern is shown by two other fast-trackers for the two older sisters who have been in trouble, both of them living on welfare. For one fast-tracker, there is now hope that his older sister may get her head together, for another there is anger mixed with the concern:

The first describes his sister as follows: "She left home at 16, married, had children who are now all screwed up and in jail. I want her to get a new start in life. She has finally met a man who is a stable human being. . . ."

The second, slightly younger, is puzzled, concerned and *angry*: "She is totally different from me. She did terribly in school. She hated it. She was very independent. She fought with my mother a lot. Why was she like that? . . . My sister did marry a stable guy, older, a homebody. She had five kids right away. Her husband loved the kids. He was closer to them than my sister. (It was like I had five little brothers and sisters.) He died of a pulmonary embolism at 42 when the oldest child was about 12. My sister just lived on welfare after that and never want back to work—and sometimes didn't even take care of the kids. Now one of the kids who was doing okay, got married, had a baby, and her husband died and *she's* living on Social Security . . . The same story all over again. My mother wonders why all this has happened. . . ."

The fast-trackers spend less time talking about their younger siblings, who are by and large living productive lives, than those who were older than they. In some cases, again, they perceive themselves as more successful than these other brothers and sisters. However, these differences often exist in their own perceptions and are not a direct reflection of social standing as usually assessed. Two of the male fast-trackers, for example, note the differences between themselves and their next younger brothers, both of whom are close to them in age, and both of whom also have Ph.Ds. These siblings have succeeded according to the standards of many, but fare less well in the perceptions of their brothers. Each of these fast-trackers spontaneously volunteered almost identical remarks about these brothers:

> Says one about his brother, "He is the mirror image of myself, he didn't have a lot of ambition. My parents always worried about him."
>
> The other says more bluntly, "I don't like him. He is the antithesis of me. I just spent a week with him and his wife and was bored out of my mind. He never gets excited about anything. From the time I can remember, I always was so successful and he was not."

Some of the fast-trackers clearly refer to their siblings with both warmth and humor, even as they distinguish themselves from these siblings. Alec is fond and admiring of his "perfect" older sister (he is the one white male with an achieving older sister) of whom he says, "We always got along well." Larry speaks with warmth of his next youngest brother, of whom he yet says, "He would never make it in a real corporation—he has too many idiosyncrasies," but who is nonetheless a vice-president of a relatively substantial firm. Pete, the black male, feels close to his successful older brother ("Who is in the public not the private sector"), and speaks warmly of all his many sisters. Yet, in the interview sessions, the fast-trackers' attention focused more often on the behavior of those siblings who were *different* and whose behavior concerned both them and their parents.

ORIGINS OF COOPERATIVE AND COMPETITIVE STYLES

To explore the assumption that differences in *style* begin in the family, differences in early family composition were compared between creators and contributors, cooperators and competitors. Some differences did emerge from these analyses in relationship to competitive and cooperative orientations: *competitors came from larger families with more sisters and indications of a higher achievement-orientation among siblings.* The possible significance of these differences is explored after presenting the numerical data in the tables that follow.

The average number of brothers and sisters for competitors and cooperators show competitors to have slightly more siblings on the average and markedly more sisters. However, these averages disguise the real significance of individual differences: four of the ten male cooperators

(Hal, Don, Hank, and Brian) have one sister apiece and three of these sisters are younger; whereas *all* five of the male competitors were born into families with sisters.

————••◦◦◦••————

Siblings of Fast-Trackers

	Average Number of:		
	Brothers	Sisters	Siblings
Cooperators: Rich, Andrew, Hal, Tom, Jon, Hank, Ken, Don, Jerry, Christine, Brian	1.3	.5	1.7
Competitors: Art, Larry, Sandra, Alec, Pete, Sam	1.3 (1.4)	2.7 (1.6)	4.0 (3.0)

( ) Excluding Pete's unusually large family

————••◦◦◦••————

Further, on the assumption that a college education is one mark of an achievement orientation, there are continuing contrasts between cooperators and competitors. Among the siblings of the cooperators, six brothers and one sister (Christine's) went to college, with two of the brothers and the sister earning Ph.Ds. Among the siblings of the competitors, on the other hand, six brothers and seven sisters completed a four-year degree (still five brothers and six sisters without Pete's large family), with three brothers and two sisters earning advanced degrees. Not only do the competitors have more sisters than the cooperators but strikingly more sisters who demonstrate behavior likely to be associated with a strong achievement orientation.

————••◦◦◦••————

College Education of Fast-Trackers' Siblings

	% Brothers w/degrees	% Sisters w/degrees	% Siblings w/degrees
Cooperators: Rich, Andrew, Hal, Tom, Jon, Hank, Ken, Don, Jerry, Christine, Brian	43	20	37

Competitors:
  Art, Larry, Sandra,
  Alec, Pete, Sam   75 (71)   44 (75)   54 (73)

( ) Excluding Pete's unusually large family

Interpretations of this data are hypotheses at best because the sample is small and differences are occasionally slight. However, there *are* differences in the number and achievement-orientation of the siblings of the two groups of creators and competitors. How might these differences be understood? First, the difference is not due to social class nor educational background in the family because occupational status and family educational background is approximately the same for both groups. Second, the competitors differ in average age from the cooperators and grew up in a culture in which many more individuals attended college. The fact that more of their siblings received degrees is, in large part, a result of the changes in the larger culture. Nonetheless, this still provides a difference in family context between the two groups.

Third, there is no explanation outside of chance occurrence for the larger numbers of sisters in the families of the competitors, which, when combined with the larger proportion of siblings in college, means that the competitors had not only a larger number of sisters but achievement-orientated sisters at that. The result may well be, in these families, that a more competitive orientation is developed by competing with siblings — and most particularly with sisters who were pursuing their own dreams. (One has the sense that sisters who are less likely to be raised according to the rules of team sports may, in fact, represent a more individual threat than brothers who learn earlier, "All for one and one for all" on the sports field.) As Alec said more than once, "I just wanted to be better than . . . or as good as . . . my older sister." No fast-tracker made such a remark about brothers.

Regardless of the origin of the differences, it seems clear that the small group of competitors grew up in a different family setting than the cooperators. The competitors came from larger families with more sisters, a significant proportion of whom were achievers in their own right. It could be then that the competitive and cooperative orientations are not solely age-related (as suggested in the previous chapter) but also forged in the crucible of family life. It is possible, in fact, that the cooperators were more clearly the "stars" of their families, with much of the family "cooperating" in their success, whereas the competitors had to "compete" to earn this position and, moreover, to compete against their sisters. For the competitors, it is possible that competition was an early part of the family scene and influenced their later orientation. It may, in fact, be more difficult for these young fast-trackers to give up their competitive orientation as they move into the senior ranks.

In summary, the fast-trackers as a whole are oldest children or were perceived as oldest children in small- to moderate-sized families, in which parents worked long and hard on their own initiative and were not beholden to others. In these settings, the fast-trackers grew to value hard work, and felt capable of meeting the high expectations of their parents. Many of the lessons learned by the fast-trackers have their origins in early family life. By observing their parents, from listening to their advice, and as a result of the support they received at home (as well as at work and school), these young people learned to manage their time, focus their energy, work long and hard, be honest and straightforward, and value their connectedness with others. From experiences with their families, they learned too that problems are really opportunities and that perceived failures are only springboards to later success. The career of the fast-tracker thus seems to begin in the very early years.

CHAPTER 9

Career Timing and the Family

A Reflection of Style

. . . the earliest period of a man's life . . . is never long enough to allow full use to be made of it and its importance is such that constant vigilance must be exercised. That is why I have placed such emphasis on the art of prolonging it.

JEAN JACQUES ROUSSEAU
EMILE

In a society in which no one will be forced into a premature adulthood, many people will remain adolescent all their lives, following a vision that is not yet clear, puzzling over a theory that is not yet fully formulated, attempting to create in sound or in color, in meditation or in prayer, in the laboratory or in the library, in the halls of government or in the councils of the nations something as yet unknown.

MARGARET MEAD
FAMILY

People in our society assess the maturity and responsibility of young adults in different ways, in effect using one of two measuring sticks. The traditional viewpoint, figuratively one yardstick of maturity, is that the early assumption of responsibility and commitment to a life course best represents the maturity of the young adult. Students in college reflect the prevalence of this point of view by incorporating it into their own thinking and believing that the decisions they make upon graduation will (in fact, *should*) determine irrevocably the direction of the rest of their lives. The second viewpoint, which has been voiced periodically throughout history,

---

Relationship of Family Information and Career Timing

STYLE	INFORMATION	RELATED INFORMATION	INTERPRETATION
CONTRIBUTORS	Entered careers immediately after college and majored in business-related subjects	Fathers markedly older than mothers	More input from fathers resulting in focused interests
CREATORS	Delayed career entry and variety of majors in college	Parents about same age	More input from mothers resulting in diverse interests

---

is that delaying major commitments may allow for the greater development of diverse interests in young adults and ultimately result in the assumption of higher levels of responsibility and commitments of greater breadth and depth. Clearly, each viewpoint has been developed in response to actual choices made by young adults throughout history—and each represents a viable path into mature adulthood.

The early immersion in work is the traditional and more accepted route to pass from adolescence into adulthood. The postponement of long-term work commitments, on the other hand, is a route that has been viewed by social scientists as offering greater possibilities for both failure and success. Those who delay "adult" commitments may, in fact, fail to assume these commitments at any time in their lives, or they may utilize an extended learning period to bring a more complex experience and deeper understanding to these commitments at a later time.

Some of the fast-trackers have chosen each of the two routes to success: some have plunged into work after college and some have put off ultimate work decisions for a time. As the timing of career entry is analyzed, these early adult decisions turn out to be a reflection of *style*, with origins again in the early family setting.

FAST-STARTERS AND SLOW-STARTERS

With the completion of their undergraduate degrees at age 22, Brian and Sam leapt onto the fast track in two different companies. Each of them was promoted quickly, but impatient with the slowness of relatively rapid promotions or dismayed by a certain perceived dimming of future possibilities, they jumped tracks without losing speed, moving along swiftly in yet two more companies. In a similar fashion, after completing a five-year "co-op program"—half work and half study—Andy, Jerry, and Hank (with a Master's degree also under his belt) stepped at age 23 onto the fast track in another company, one which Hank left a few years later for a new track with even greater potential for a swift climb to the top. At the same age, Pete entered his career track having finished a four-year college degree—and having worked 70 hours a week at his job to support both his education and his new wife. All of these individuals made a fast start toward a perceived destination—some spot up the track far off in the distance. They were joined within a relatively short period of time by Christine, Sandra, and Jon, the oldest of the fast starters, who summed up the philosophy of this entire contigent: "I am going to do as much as I can as fast as I can."

In contrast, another group of fast-trackers dallied in the pastures along the track or started off in another direction altogether before heading for the top. Rich and Tom both had four-year stints of military service first which, for quite different reasons, they described as one of the best experiences of their lives, and times of "tremendous learning." Ken created a new graduate program for himself and other students, and then opened a college-town restaurant to which he devoted a minimum of eighteen hours a day for three years. Larry was thrown out of college, went to work, and finally returned to school, carrying newly acquired obligations to a wife and their economic survival. Art, with a technical degree from a junior college, went to work, decided he hated it, took classes at night, and then entered and graduated from a full college program. Alec went abroad on an extended honeymoon with his new wife before they both returned to graduate school. Then, sometime between 24 and 30, each of these individuals leapt onto the fast track in various corporations, three of them jumping tracks when the going was slow. By and large, they eventually caught up with their earlier starting peers. These men were the slow starters among the fast-trackers.

The more diverse the interests and the wider-ranging the dreams of these young people, the slower were some to begin a swift ascent to the top of five different corporations. It is not particularly surprising, at this point, to realize that the fast starters are the *contributors* and the slow starters are the *creators*. There are differences between cooperators and competitors as well within the creator orientation, but not in that of contributor.

————◦◦◦————

Fast-Trackers' Age at Career Entrance

Orientation		Average age of entering managerial career track
Creators:		26
Cooperative:	Rich, Hal, Tom, Ken, Don	27
Competitive:	Art, Larry, Alec	24
Contributors:		23
Cooperative:	Andrew, Jon, Hank, Jerry, Chris, Brian	23
Competitive:	Sandra, Pete, Sam	23

————◦◦◦————

The ages at which creators and contributors began their careers are different enough to prompt inquiry into their origin. Why is one group slower and the other faster in starting up the track to the top? Working backwards in time, differences in early adult experiences, college majors, and family background all contribute to an answer to these questions. The focus of this exploration is on the creators who chose, or drifted into, the less traditional route into adulthood.

EARLY ADULT EXPERIENCES

Many of the early adult (after 21) experiences of the contributors took place in the business world, where a series of rapid promotions occurred for this entire group once they were on their respective career tracks. What, on the other hand, were the creators doing at this time in their lives? A partial answer has already been suggested, but we shall explore this further in the words of the fast-trackers themselves. We might ask as well if the slow-starters, the creators, perceived their post-college and extended-college experiences as benefiting them in their eventual journey up the fast track.

The senior fast-trackers speak for many of the creators who spent time out of the business world in their twenties and learned from that experience.

Rich, like many of the fast-trackers of his age or those just younger, faced the choice of either being drafted into the service or volunteering for Officer Candidate School upon leaving the deferred student status of his college years. He made the same decision as Tom, joining the company of his choice for a few months, then left his job for Officer Candidate School and four years of military services. He describes those years as follows:

My wife and I spent four years in Japan. She is very interested in "culture" and insisted that we live off base with the Japanese. It was a remarkable experience. I developed a respect for the tradition and the history, and I was impressed with the permanency of what they create. I also respected their calmness and simplicity. We spent as much time in the country, in out-of-the-way places as we could. On the weekends, we would take our '56 Chevy and go into the mountains to little villages and inns. The beauty was unbelievable.

On his return to the United States, and the job he had left, Rich was shocked by the misperceptions Americans held of the Japanese culture. "I felt I was living in a time warp!" His understanding of the importance of different perceptions, and the frequent disparity between perception and reality, has stood him in good stead in his career ("We're really talking about perceptions here, not fact," he insists) as has his knowledge of the Japanese culture itself.

Tom spent his four years of military service in charge of a stateside port facility and says it was excellent management training: "This was a tremendous opportunity to have a non-threatening, low-risk situation in which to develop and test management skills." In addition, he joined Toastmasters there, and presented a speech twice a week during the entire four years. This too he saw as a tremendous opportunity: "I learned how to present orally, two times every week with a critique; I could write like a bandit but I needed to learn how to speak."

Hal, in contrast, spent his in-between years in graduate school preparing for a career as a clinical psychologist. He took time out from his degree to take his first career-oriented job, planning to return to school, but he has never left the company he joined on his "time out." He says of this time in his life that he had questioned continuing "because it seemed to me that the people who were planning to help people needed a whole lot of help themselves," and this led him to reevaluate his own directions. His time-out experience turned to be the most exciting time of his life, excitement that continued for the next 24 years. He says, however, of his clinical training, "This whole learning experience was incredibly important to me. The learning about people was the foundation of my career."

Rich, Tom, and Hal each had the opportunity after completing a college degree to learn from varied experiences that later were very relevant to their specific career interests. Much of their management training, in fact, occurred after and not during college. Two of the mid-level creators got off to slow starts for quite different reasons: both of them experienced delays in getting their initial college degrees.

> Art did poorly in high school: "I never thought much about schooling and felt peer pressure *not* to do well. I was very insecure, had poor self-esteem, and acted in accord with that. I scored well in mathematics. At least in math, I could study for three hours and get an A. There was a specific answer. In social studies, you can study for three hours and still get an F. That didn't interest me. Senior year, however, I began to come out of this. I met some new people and got involved in sports. I graduated with a C average (much better in math) and decided to on to junior college. There I made the Dean's list." With an Associate's degree Art got a technical job in a big company and hated it. He kept at it for four years while he took more courses at night so that he could get into a four-year college. When he was ready, he went to a local college and in three years earned a bachelor's degree. At that point, with the help of his wife, he located a job in the same company that had career potential for him. Outstanding achievements led to rapid promotions and, later, a change of company. With a slow start, Art is now very close to the top.
>
> Larry's story is different. He went to a small private college on scholarship and after two years of an "absolutely fantastic time" managed to get himself kicked out of the school. One year of full-time work followed, after which Larry, now married, worked nights to put himself through school during the day. He graduated with honors two years later than he might have if his course had been different. An interview he went to by mistake led him onto the fast track in his current company where he is now president of an innovative subsidiary of the parent corporation.[1]

Although almost all the contributors started corporate life within a year or two of college graduation, almost all of the creators spent time doing other things first before making a full commitment to the corporate world. (The near exceptions were Jon, the slowest of the fast-starters, and Alec, the fastest of the slow-starters.) The creators, in their early adult years, took time out from their eventual occupations to learn both in school and from the world at large. Sometimes this extended learning period was clearly chosen, as in Hal's case, and sometimes, as in the cases of Art and Larry, it was forced upon them. None of them, however, deny that this was an important growth period. Even Art, whose delays were not consciously of his choosing, says, "There was lots of maturation going on here, I developed an appreciation for the liberal arts, and I had to think." The slow-starters did not perceive this as lost time.

IMPACT OF COLLEGE MAJOR

One of the reasons this extended learning period was so useful to the creators was that they did not, by and large, major in "practical" subjects in college and were, therefore, not as vocationally prepared and/or goal-directed as the fast starters. In college, one of the creators had majored in Engineering and another in economics (two of the majors that often lead directly into the business world), but among the others there was a degree in English, one in math, one in psychology, one in industrial arts and an early investment in pre-med as a curriculum with a later degree in Business. One did not complete a college degree. Less than half—three of the eight—completed degrees, however belatedly, in areas directly related to their current occupation. On the other hand, six of the nine contributors completed degrees in subjects that led them directly into their occupations.

College Degrees of Fast-Trackers

Orientation		College Major
Creators:	Rich	Engineering
	Hal	Psychology
	Tom	English
	Art	Electronics + Industrial Arts
	Larry	Pred-Med + Business
	Ken	Mathematics + MS in Mathematical Statistics
	Don	_____
	Alec	Economics + MBA
Contributors:	Andrew	Engineering
	Jon	Economics
	Hank	Engineering + MS in Business
	Jerry	Engineering
	Christine	Psychology
	Brian	Biology + Business
	Sandra	Psychology
	Pete	Business
	Sam	Political Science

There is a tendency for the contributors to have selected a career at an earlier date than the creators and to have prepared for that career in college. On the other hand, the creators demonstrated a wider range of interests than the contributors, and, very likely, a belief that it was all right to experiment with these interests. Explanations for this difference may be found in the family background.

FAMILY BACKGROUND AND PARENTAL AGE

In comparing the fast-trackers' families in size and composition, there are no differences between creators and contributors. On closer examination, however, there is one difference between their families that suggests an explanation of fast and slow starts on the career track. This difference lies in the relative ages of the parents of these two groups of fast-trackers. Taking the birth of the first child as a benchmark, the ages of the mothers and fathers of creators and contributors were as follows:

Age of Fast-Trackers' Parents at Birth of First Child

Style		Average age of:	
		Mother at birth of first child	Father at birth of first child
Creators:	Rich, Hal, Tom, Ken, Don, Art, Larry, Alec	24.0	25.5
Contributors:	Andrew, Jon, Hank Jerry, Chris, Brian, Sandra, Pete, Sam	23.0	29.4

The most striking contrast is in the relative ages of the parents: The creators' parents are very close to each other—on the average a year and one-half apart—whereas in the families of contributors, fathers are an average of six and one-half years older than mothers.

This difference is borne out not only in the average figures but in examining individual data. The ages of the creators' parents are, *in all cases* within four years of each other, and in *all cases but two*, within two years of each other. The ages of the contributors' parents are, *in all cases but one* (the exception is Christine, who will be discussed later in this chapter), more than five years apart and the father is the older. What does it matter how close or how far apart are the ages of parents? Can this explain in any way the differences between contributors and creators?

Research on parental power and influence has found that parents who are about the same age have about the same power and influence in the home in shaping the values, attitudes, and beliefs of their children. Parents of disparate ages have been found to have less equal power and influence, with the upper hand going to the older parent.[2] The similarity in ages of the creators' parents provides a foundation for suggesting that the mothers of these individuals played a greater role in shaping the future orientation of the child than in the homes of contributors in which the father was considerably older, and often well-established prior to marriage.

Other research on developing creativity is pertinent to our argument at this point. One of the factors that has been found to lead to creativity in *male* children is the presence of and interaction with a "strong" mother.[3] The mother, in such cases, is responsible for broadening the child's interests, often beyond the practical, and urging him to think and to achieve. Taking this argument a step further, it seems likely that the mothers of the creators were important in developing a creative orientation in their sons. We may continue this line of thinking by recalling that "creative" individuals take longer to settle on a career path (outside of math and science) than do less creative individuals and that the diversity of interests, indeed, requires a longer processing time before a career is selected.[4] Therefore, it is likely that one factor in the protracted "learning" period of the creators and their slower start in the business world may be found in their backgrounds and in the presence of "strong" mothers.[5]

Other information to support the thesis of greater input from mothers of creators comes from the comments of the fast-trackers themselves. Most of the fast-trackers, creators and contributors alike, mention both their parents positively. However, five of the seven creators with two parents describe their mothers in ways that specifically refer to the mothers' achievement-orientation, and one additional creator describes his older sister in this way as well. Thus six refer to the achievement orientation of either their mothers or, in one case, an older sister. Among the contributors, there are fewer spontaneous comments about mothers and fathers separately, and only one spontaneously refers to the achievement orientation of his mother.

Among the creators, Rich emphasizes his mother's important role in shaping his value system by recounting the incident about the stolen comic book (see Chapter 1). Hal describes his mother as "strong and ambitious for me and she drove me hard in terms of grades, athletics, and everything else." Tom says of his mother, "She had boundless energy, absolutely get it done yesterday, but not lots of feeling." Larry says of his mother: "She takes the initiative; when my parents went into a new business after retiring from their first one, it was Mom who took the initiative and Dad who followed her; she is the brains of the family." Alec does not make mention of his mother but instead mentions his older sister many times over: "She was bright, attractive and able. . . . I most wanted to be better at something than she was. . . . She is perfect, really . . . We got along well."

Among the contributors, Hank and Christine both mention their mothers in a different context than do the others of their orientation. Hank and Christine, however, both have some personal and background characteristics in common with the creators (although the language with which they described their work classifies them as contributors).

> Hank's parents were of vastly different ages (as were those of other contributors) and yet Hank was closest to his mother and learned from her. She is the only mother of a contributor who worked in a business with her husband. Hank speaks of her most strongly (more consistent with the creators than the contributors): "In terms of the business, Mother did the books and supervised the switchboard operations. Mother is the salt of the earth . . ."
>
> Chris's parents are the only ones among the contributors who are similar in age—in this they are like the parents of creators. Her mother is also described as very bright. But because her mother had, at best, a difficult temperament, Chris did not identify with nor model herself after her. Instead, Chris's input from her father proved to be very important (research findings suggest that fathers are as important in stimulating creativity in their daughters as mothers are for their sons). In this, Christine is very much like the creators.

It would seem that both Hank and Christine might have become creators. However, both of these fast-trackers were exposed early to difficult and erratic behavior within their families. Very likely, they came to see that relying on inner feelings and impulses held certain dangers. Christine found being "one-on-one" with her temperamental mother throughout adolescence to be a trying experience. Christine's response to interactions with her mother was, of necessity, to become more controlled in her own behavior, and to be guided by the demands of the task as opposed to the "inner rhythms" followed by the creators. Hank's situation is similar. His much older sister was also very difficult and erratic and gave birth, during Hank's early childhood, to five erratic, difficult children. In having to confront this as a child, Hank says, "I lost my own childhood." He had to be stable, consistent, and keep his eye on the demands of the situation to provide a balance for the temperamental behavior of his sister and her children. Consequently, both Hank and Christine are very successful contributors to the effectiveness of their organization. Given other childhood circumstances, however, they show inclinations to join the creators. They are perhaps, instead of "natural" contributors, "careful" creators who have joined the contributors' ranks.

Among the fast-trackers, therefore, the creators are more likely than the contributors to perceive their mothers as "strong," or as having an investment in achievement. The reverse is true in descriptions of fathers. The creators do praise their fathers but mention their creativity and ethical orientation more often than their achievements. In contrast, the contributors reflect on their fathers' achievements.

Among creators, Rich describes his father as an advisor to all of the family, Hal speaks of his father warmly as being creative and liking change, and Tom says, "Dad is *the* ethical man." Although Larry admires his father's management style and has learned much from it, he refers to his mother as "the brains of the bunch." Alec, too, speaks with admiration of his father, but wanted as a child to model himself after his older sister. The influence of both parents is strong, but the fathers do not have a corner on achievement.

In contrast, the contributors tend to credit their fathers with promoting an achievement orientation. Jon remembers how his dad encouraged him to do the best he could. Brian works to make "Dad proud of me" and is guided by his advice to leave the world better than he found it. Jerry remembers his father's emphasis on education, especially math and science as critical in his formative years. Pete makes frequent reference to his father, whose hard work and achievement he takes as a model for his own behavior. Hank saw less of his father becasue he was so busy, and later became ill, but found a substitute in a friend's father who taught him things, showed him what it meant to work, and who he admired greatly. Christine makes frequent reference to her father and his empathic, caring, helping attitude—and his high level of achievement.

To summarize, the creators started slowly and the contributors started fast on the track to the top. The creators spent more time learning outside the corporate world—in school, in the military, and in preliminary jobs—than did the contributors. In fact, the creators came to a later decision than did the contributors about going to work in business. In contrast, all of the contributors headed toward the business world at an earlier age, and arrived more quickly at the starting gate.

The reasons for this delay can be found in the family backgrounds of the creators. The data suggest that the creators came from homes in which interests were less focused on business than did the contributors. The stronger input from the mother in the homes of the creators is likely to have widened the range of interests and choices that faced many of these fast-trackers, thus extending the search for an appropriate career, or allowing for a delayed entrance into that career. Still, all of the fast-trackers, once a career was chosen, moved ahead *without ambivalence*. Their level of commitment and involvement is in large part responsible for their later success.

The differences in family background between creators and contributors, competitors and cooperators are almost startling in the clarity with which they appear. However, since the sample is small, the inferences from these differences must be treated as hypotheses and not as conclusions. However, the data does suggest that family composition and parental input affect the development of style and that one's orientation to oneself, others, and one's organization may be shaped first and primarily in the family setting. Those in large achievement-oriented families may be more competitive, and those with strong achievement-oriented mothers may be more likely to be creators wanting to "make things different." Style has its origins in the family and affects the timing of major career decisions. In the next chapter, it is clear that style affects the timing of major family decisions as well.

CHAPTER 10

The Timing of Marriage and Children

A Matter of Style

> *Failure at work cannot be fully compensated by*
> *success in love. Failure at work has to be*
> *compensated by success in worklike activities. Only*
> *when work and love coexist in parallel and*
> *appropriate proportions do we achieve happiness*
> *and fulfillment.*
> FERNANDO BARTOLOME AND
> PAUL A. LEE EVANS
> "MUST SUCCESS COST
> SO MUCH?"

Work and marriage are the two traditional commitments that have signified the passage of adolescence and the onset of true adulthood. In the past, and even in the present with its changing values, parents breathe a sigh of relief when sons and daughters have a steady income, a steady relationship sanctified by both church and state, and the prospect of grandchildren in the offing. When all that has happened—and in that order—parents of the young are given to congratulating themselves on a job well done.

Entrance into the worlds of work and family, however, represents the traditional set of expectations for adulthood, which is one measure of maturity. The changing social patterns of the last two decades have overlaid this set of expectations with another: individuals are to find personal meaning and satisfaction in their relationships and thereby may choose the particular life style that best suits them. The achievement of *meaning* or

⎯⎯⎯⎯⟨∞⟩⎯⎯⎯⎯

**Relationship of Amount of Family Time and Career Time
to Career Progress**

STYLE	INFORMATION	RELATED INFORMATION	INTERPRETATION
CREATORS	Married and had children immediately after college; more likely to divorce and remarry	More years spent in families than in careers	More career plateaus
CONTRIBUTORS	Some married early and some late; more likely to postpone childbirth or not have children	More years spent in careers than in families	Rapid and/or consistent career progress

⎯⎯⎯⎯⟨∞⟩⎯⎯⎯⎯

satisfaction in work and family relationships has become a second measure of maturity.

These new expectations affect the work world: more career options are accepted today than yesterday for both men and women. Climbing the corporate ladder is no longer the best thing to do nor a task that can be undertaken only by men. The greater variety of *acceptable* career choices in the current milieu is one result of the new set of social expectations. These expectations, however, affect the personal world more dramatically, supporting a variety of different life-styles: individuals choose to live alone, to live with another outside of marriage, to postpone having children or not have them altogether, or to divorce one spouse and find another, with much more frequency than in the past. New expectations have been shaped by these social changes so that no one is really sure any longer about the signposts that indicate adulthood has arrived.

The personal lives of the fast-trackers reflect many of the changes that have occurred in the culture and, yet, they reflect these changes in different ways according to their style. In the last chapter, the contributors exemplified the traditional work expectations more clearly than the creators: They moved relatively promptly from college into work and began their climb up the corporate ladder. In turning to their personal lives, it becomes apparent that creators and contributors have both responded to some traditional and some of the changing social expectations, but not in the same way. Their personal histories are each unique, but are affected both by their style (which springs from their family of origin), and the cultural values prevalent when they came into adulthood. Both of these shall be examined before turning, at the end of the chapter, to the impact of their personal and family lives on their work history.

PATTERNS OF MARRIAGE AND CHILDBIRTH

All of the fast-trackers are currently married and, in general, have spouses who are very supportive of their careers. All but one of the fast-trackers were married in their twenties, most before they were twenty-five; five of the fast-trackers are in second marriages. Further, thirteen of the seventeen fast-trackers have children and all but two of these have more than one child. Altogether they have twice as many girls as boys. However, the ways in which the fast-trackers are alike are not distinctive enough to suggest a generalized fast-track pattern in terms of either marriage or children.

Once the fast-trackers are separated into groups of creators and contributors, patterns of marriage and childbirth do begin to emerge. Among the creators, there are enough similarities to suggest a typical pattern. Among the contributors, there is more variability, and the variability may, in fact, tell us something more about the contributors in contrast to the creators.

Almost all the fast-trackers initially married women of approximately their same age; in each of the second marriages, the wife was considerably younger than the husband. Among creators, most of the current wives work full-time. All of the children (approximately the same number of boys as girls) are doing well in school or work but only one has headed into the world of big business. Among contributors, fewer wives are working, and children again (over three times more girls than boys) are doing well in school or work, with two of the three eldest headed on career paths that could emulate those of the fast-trackers.

———— •‹✖›•· ————

The Fast-Trackers' Marriages and Children

STYLE	Age at 1st Marriage	# Second Marriages	Age at 2nd Marriage	# Without Children	# of Children
Creators: Rich, Hal, Tom, Art, Larry, Ken, Don, Alec	20-25	4	35-42	1	14 (17)
Contributors: Andrew, Jon, Hank, Jerry, Chris, Brian, Sandra, Pete, Sam	19-34	1	33	3	17

(   ) including stepchildren

———— ·‹✖›•· ————

In short, the creators generally married at a consistently younger age. Six of the eight creators had children and one acquired a stepdaughter, so that seven live, or have lived, with children. Half of the creators remarried at a later age. On the other hand, one of the contributors married at 19, one at 34, and the rest ranged in between. Only six of the nine contributors had children and lived in the same household with children. Only Sandra has married more than once.

The creators show more predictability in their personal lives than do the contributors: they are likely to marry relatively early, often more than once, and they are most likely to have children shortly after marriage. The contributors show more variability in time of marriage than the creators; they are most likely to stay married and more likely than the creators to *not* have children. These tendencies suggest another way to characterize the creators and contributors.

These patterns may, in fact, reflect a greater people-orientation on the part of the creators, and a greater task-orientation on the part of the contributors, suggesting why the creators appear to rush into marriage at the same time as the contributors are rushing into work. Supporting evidence for this point of view comes from a major study of professionals conducted some years ago. In this study, it was found that those whose profession reflected a strong interest in people were more likely to both enter and leave intimate relationships than those whose professional interests were not intensely focused on people-related areas. It was suggested that a strong people interest predisposes one to seek out relationships, to invest oneself highly in these relationships, but also to leave these relationships when they seemed unsatisfactory. On the other hand, a stronger task-orientation led individuals to move more cautiously into relationships and to stay in these relationships, in part, because their expectations of these relationships were not as high. The task-oriented professionals examined and analyzed their relationships less, were consequently less likely to find flaws in them, and more likely to remain in those relationships.[1]

The distinctions between creators and contributors parallel the findings of that study. In many ways, the creators demonstrate a stronger people-orientation and the contributors a task-orientation. The creators, in the interviews, talked more about their relationships and spent a greater amount of time talking about people in their interview sessions. On the other hand, the contributors, who label themselves as matter-of-fact, offered briefer descriptions of relationships and spent more time talking about tasks and projects than about people. The differences in marital histories may be consistent with a people- versus a task-orientation.

If the timing of both work and marriage is a matter of style, the variety of patterns seen in the personal lives of all of the fast-trackers is a reflection of the changes in the culture of the last decades. The fast-trackers were born over a period of twenty-two years and, in part, their lives reflect the cultural conditions prevalent when they came of age.

INFLUENCE OF CULTURAL CHANGES

The last twenty years have seen a time of dramatic cultural change. The figures on divorce, remarriage, and number of children have fluctuated widely. The personal histories of the fast-trackers reflect these changes so that style interacts with culture as an explanation for their marital patterns.

There are five fast-trackers who have married twice, and four fast-trackers who have had no children. This group of nine ranges in age from 34 to 48, excluding both the oldest and the youngest of the fast-trackers, and constitutes a large percentage (75 percent) of the fast-trackers in mid-career. This group of nine—either twice-married or childless—is most representative, therefore, of those fast-trackers in mid-career who are close to 40 in age and born in the 1940s. In contrast, the senior fast-trackers were born in the 1930s and the juniors in the 1950s. Were those born in the 1940s subjected to different cultural influences than those who preceded and followed them? Does the culture, in fact, partially explain the greater number of non-traditional choices in regard to marriage and children of this group?

Social scientists have said that people form many lasting impressions of the world—and form life-time expectations for themselves—during adolescent and early-adulthood years.[2] Thus, the state of the world-at-large during this time of life shapes peoples' expectations of how-things-are and how-they-should-be. Those born in the 1940s came of age in the 1960s, so their perceptions and expectations about the world would have been strongly influenced by the environment of the 1960s. What differences in expectations might this group have from those who came of age in the 1950s (the senior managers) and those who became adults in the 1970s (the junior managers)? A brief review of the circumstances of these three decades may shed some light on differing expectations among these three age groups.

In the 1950s, the United States as a whole was affluent and slightly smug. The world appeared to be stable. Life moved with some regularity and could even be called boring at times. It would be another few years before college students considered burning down administration buildings and protesting the right of the "establishment" to influence the course of the world.

By the time the 1960s were in full swing, however, burning college buildings was taken for granted. Rioting in the downtown areas of major cities claimed media attention. By the late 1960s, the assassinations of political figures were seen as offering a grim prelude to the future. Over all of the late 1960s, too, hung the shadow of the Vietnam War and the challenge this war posed to the authority of the "establishment." This was an age of social protest when the old walls came tumbling down.

As the 1960s gave way to the 1970s, social protest turned into a search for personal fulfillment. The disillusionment of the 1960s—the discovery that youth cannot change the world—funneled energy into changing oneself and one's relationships. Consequently, the values of the culture focused on "doing your own thing," "getting it together," and "having meaningful relationships." At the same time, the growing threat of economic recession cast a shadow across the aspirations of those just coming of age. The economy started to become unstable in the mid- and late-seventies, forecasting the near-depression of the early 1980s. And just as the economy started to waver and the number of entry-level jobs started to diminish, the largest generation ever came into adulthood, crowding the workplace as they had crowded the schools in the years just past. Along with concerns about personal fulfillment, this oversized generation brought with them more concerns about individual economic survival than their older brothers and sisters. Competition among the able and college-educated for "good" jobs was stiff and there were many who did not get their feet on the first rung of a ladder.

The fast-trackers with the most non-traditional choices in their personal lives were those who came of age in the 1960s when change was the byword and stability was suspect; they grew up in disorder and took this as the norm. The way in which they assessed the world was based on principle, not on profitability. Consequently, this generation would be most likely to make choices based on personal principles rather than on public expectations. They would be most likely to "do their own thing" and to ignore the traditional norms. The world that they knew as young adults was one in which old assumptions were questioned, the establishment was suspect, and going to work in a three-piece suit was out, not in. For them, the traditional walls had come tumbling down.

In contrast, the older generation—the senior managers in this sample—knew a stable world in which jobs were plentiful for the bright and ambitious. Whatever impressons of disorder the 1960s brought were superimposed upon their early impressions of stability. Order was something to be created from disorder, not to be thrown out in hopes of creating a utopian world. In contrast, too, the youngest generation—the junior managers in this sample—knew another sort of stability in which norms of personal satisfaction had taken root and competition was stiff. Success required planning and was not expected due to happenstance. Whatever disorder had been part of their very early childhood experience could be tied up and put into the clear emphasis on personal satisfaction of the 1970s.

The oldest and the youngest of this sample follow traditional patterns. They marry in their twenties, they stay married and they have children. Many of the wives do not work. All are supportive of their husbands. The middle age range of this sample, and those close to it, both younger and older, are the ones who demonstrate the greatest variability. In the group that was born in the 1940s and came of age in the 1960s, we find more remarriages, more childless marriages, and more working wives. The upheavals of the 1960s gave more permission to do as one saw best, to seek one's own satisfaction, and to chase after the golden ring. The patterns of marriage and childbirth of this age group, just as the others, are marked by the events occurring in the culture at large. Cultural conditions are clearly an important influence on the family situations of the fast-trackers.

SIGNIFICANCE OF FAMILY SITUATIONS

The next issue, however, is to determine whether or not the family situations of the fast-trackers had any significant impact on their careers. This issue is addressed by asking the following questions. Is there a relationship between the fast-trackers' marriage and family experience and their work life? Does the family situation support or mitigate against a speedy rise up the fast track? The family lives of the creators and contributors tend to differ from each other, and so too do the family lives of those growing up in the 1950s, 1960s, and 1970s. How do the differences in family life affect the careers of the fast-trackers? Is there any way to identify factors in the stories of their marriages and children that might affect their work lives?

One way to assess these distinctions is to compute the amount of time the creators and contributors actually spent living with spouses (*marital years*) and children (*family years*), and to contrast this with the number of years they have been on a career track (*career years*). Contrasting career years with both marital and family years shows the amount of time that the fast-trackers, as individuals or as a group, spent in company with spouses and children—others living in the same space with them—in contrast to the number of years that they spent on their own. The number of career years spent living alone might be related to the amount of energy the fast-tracker has available for work pursuits. Consequently, career years alone and with the family were computed for several groups of fast-trackers. There were no differences between groups divided by age, but there were differences—again—between creators and contributors.

Marital, Family and Career Years of Fast-Trackers

Orientation	Average Age	Average # Marital Yrs.	Average # Family Yrs.	Average # Career Yrs.	Career Yrs. Before Chil.
Creators: Rich, Hal, Tom, Art, Larry, Ken, Don, Alec	43.3	18.5	12.4	17.9	5.5
Contributors: Andrew, Jon, Hank, Jerry, Chris, Brian, Sandra, Pete, Sam	38.1	13.0	6.9	15.3	8.4

In substracting first the marital years, then family years from career years, there are some notable differences between the two groups. The creators, on the average, were married *before* they stepped onto their career track, and spent 5.5 of their career years without children. The contributors, on the other hand, were married 2.3 years *after* they began their careers, and spent 8.4 years living without children. For a greater part of their careers the contributors were not living in a family situation for which they were primarily accountable. Thus, as a group, the contributors had two to three years more as single individuals in which to perform their work and attend to their career. Did this help them or hinder them?

All of the fast-trackers are very successful and it is difficult to distinguish degrees of success among the group. It is also difficult to measure the speed with which they moved to the top in most cases, since increases in responsibility are not necessarily paired with increases in rank and changes in title. Consequently, no definitive answer to this question is possible, given the data at hand. In fact, one could create arguments that answer the question either way. For example, fast-trackers without family responsibilities might move faster because they have fewer demands upon their time and energy; on the other hand, fast-trackers with family obligations might have a greater sense of personal security and more sources of support, so that they are able to move with greater speed along their career paths.

However, if we examine individual stories, the first hypothesis appears more likely. In some cases, those individuals with significant family responsibilities went up the track more slowly than those with minimal family obligations. The stories of Tom and Jon, the first a senior creator and the second a senior contributor, illustrate this point. Tom spent many of his early and middle career years enmeshed in his family, both gladdened and burdened by the activities of his wife and children. Tom went slowly up the track, in terms of visible signs of promotion, during these years. He was on a career plateau for over ten years. Jon, on the other hand, spent much of his time separate from his wife, and until very recently, free of the responsibilities of children. For most of his career, Jon has moved upward at superspeeds. Each of their stories is unique, and not necessarily representative of the group of fast-trackers as a whole. Further, if there is a trade-off between family time and work time, Tom and Jon will both be facing very different situations in the immediate future.

Tom, as the other creators, married early before he had really begun his career. He and his wife had children (three boys) when both were in their twenties. Tom's family demanded more of him than many of the others' did, however, because his eldest son was born with a handicap and required extra care and attention. Caring for this child also put severe pressures on Tom's wife, who grew disconsolate under the strain, and the marriage itself ran into trouble. After Tom's wife had gone back to school, completed an advanced degree, and begun her own career, they decided on a divorce.

After several years, Tom remarried a woman in his company with a child ("The greatest thing that ever happened to me!"), and they later relocated. Tom's first wife, who had joined Tom's company, was then transferred to the same location. By that time the eldest child was completing college (doing superbly despite his handicap) and the second son was well started in another college. The youngest boy, however, still in high school, was angry and rebellious. He came to live with Tom but after a year Tom finally threw him out and told him to grow up. Tom says, "This was a *critical* event." Meantime, he is giving attention to his step-son and spending time now doing things with this child he was either too busy or preoccupied to do earlier. He is concerned with parenting and parenting well. Yet, all of his children are pretty much grown . . . and will most likely not make the demands on his time and energy that they have in the past. A few years from now, he will be entering a new era in his own life when for the first time, parental responsibilities will decrease. ("Hurray!" he says.)

Jon's situation also is unique. Although classified as a "traditional" marriage in the previous analysis because he has been married, has stayed married, and has had children, Jon's family life has varied from the norm along a number of dimensions. His life, too, has been affected by the cultural changes of the 1960s and 1970s and he and his wife have made decisions that suited their own needs, but that differed from most of his peers.

Jon was married just after his middle twenties to a woman of the same age who had already begun a professional career. Four years into his marrige, he received an offer of a double promotion that involved relocating to a new area of the country. His wife refused to move because she had just established a business with several partners; she wanted to stay put. The result was that although they bought a house near Jon's job, she returned every week to their former location, rejoining Jon on the weekends. They did this for eleven years, during which time her business became increasingly prosperous and was finally bought out by a major firm. At that point, five years ago, she joined Jon in his work location.

The decision to maintain a commuting marriage had required that they postpone having children. Once in the same location, although already in their forties, they decided to begin their family. Now with a three-year-old girl and an infant boy, Jon and his wife are spending sleepless nights with little children. On the day of his interview, Jon described—grinning happily—how tired he was and how many times he had been awakened by a very small girl who was adjusting to the freedom of a new bed and kept popping into her parents' bedroom during the night, exclaiming, "Here's Sarah!" These young children may, in fact, have more impact on Jon's career than just an occasional day of fatigue. They are already figuring largely in new career decisions.

Almost all of Tom's career years have been spent with children and in struggling (or temporarily fleeing) the difficulties involved in relationships with others. Yet, his world is also enlivened by these people and they form the central point of his story. The learning that has resulted from his interaction with his children may very well have provided a foundation for his success in "empowering" others in the workplace and may help him in future endeavors of even greater scope. He, himself, is "empowered" by his relationships with others.

On the other hand, Jon spent most of his career years with minimal responsibilities for his wife and with no responsibilities to children. Although he rose *very* quickly in his organization, he is now focused strongly on family events. His delight in his wife and his children is evident. One could ask, has he won or lost by delaying involvement with his family?

There is no answer to that question. Or, perhaps, the answer is that each of the fast-trackers has followed his or her own course, not always because of individual choice, and has confronted the givens in life as well as choosing the way in which to respond to these givens. It is clear, however, that the fast-trackers' joy in work is paralleled by a joy in relationships; despite difficulties along the way, energy is devoted to both spheres of life, forming part of the complex tapestry of interests and activities that are characteristic of all the fast-trackers.

In summary, the fast-trackers invest a lot of energy—if not time—in their relationships with spouses and children, and these relationships form a central part of their lives. In both work and love, the fast-trackers' patterns are affected both by their individual styles and by changes in the culture as a whole. Style originates in and strongly affects our relationships, both at home and at work. Style, however, is one of the two components of leadership. As we turn to an analysis of the career path of the fast-trackers—with its superspeeds and potential for abrupt derailment—the focus shifts to substance, the other component of leadership.

CHAPTER 11

Equation for Success

Style + Substance = Leadership

> *I define destiny as the pattern of limits and talents*
> *that constitutes the "givens" in life . . . it is in the*
> *confronting of these limits that our creativity*
> *emerges. Our destiny cannot be cancelled out; we*
> *cannot erase it or substitute anything else for it. But*
> *we can choose how we shall respond, how we shall*
> *live out our talents which confront us.*
>
> ROLLO MAY
> *FREEDOM AND DESTINY*

The 1980s have been a time of greater economic instability than Americans have known since the years just prior to World War II. Many of the assumptions sustaining American economic institutions in the past have proven faulty in the tumult of the past few years. Contrary to what Americans have believed for many years, often without even thinking about it, bigger is not necessarily better: change for the sake of change is not always positive; quantity does not win out over quality; there is not always enough to simply throw out the mistakes and start again tomorrow. Stiff competition from countries not previously in the marketplace and the reality of diminished resources have forced members of the American corporate community to reexamine their basic premises, to reevaluate their objectives, and to start anew; thus, they are currently seeking a more solid foundation in quality of product, economy of use, and commitment of *all* their people to common goals.

Many businesses have closed their doors; others, once considered unassailable in the marketplace, are restructuring their hierarchies and

---

The Development of Leadership

I. INDIVIDUAL FACTORS:

	Predispositions:
CHILDHOOD	Heredity & Culture
&	
ADOLESCENCE	+

Early Experiences Primarily in the Family

1. Parental Expectations
2. Parental Support
3. Parental Evaluation

+

Early Adult Experiences in and after College

ADULTHOOD

+

Career Experiences

1. Junior Stardom
2. The Executive Transition
3. Senior Statesmanship

+

II. ENVIRONMENTAL FACTORS:

Organizational Circumstances

1. Degree of Change
2. Degree of Opportunity

S T Y L E + S U B S T A N C E =

= LEADERSHIP

---

revising their management practices in order to remain competitive by making the most of their people and their resources. Companies resistant to such changes are disappearing from the economic landscape with alarming speed, along with other relics of the past. Companies willing to confront the new realities, to fight for honors in a new competition ruled by quality and economy, are creating structures that may sustain them into the future.

Yet, for those who blaze new trails the destination is never guaranteed; for those who are first to tread in new directions, a safe arrival is never a sure thing. Therefore, the undertaking of American business to survive in what has become a new economic world is an uncertain one, which calls for the best that our people can bring forth.

The economic realities of our time call for leadership, and the lives of the fast-trackers exemplify one way in which that call is being answered. Their stories, taken collectively, illustrate both what leaders do and how leadership is developed. From their histories can be extracted guidelines for the development of leadership at all levels of organizations—both in and out of the corporate community. Old questions are demanding new answers; many of these answers are emerging from this group of corporate stars, some of whom will move to the very top of America's big corporation in the immediate and not-so-immediate future.

It is, in some sense, reassuring to explore the lives of these fast-trackers. Among them are some of America's future leaders, and this fact provides a source of hope. Yet many more, at all levels of organizations, must join them if the American economy is to have a chance of maintaining its supremacy in the years just to come. If the fast-trackers represent a much larger number of leaders, then American is fortunate. If not, then steps must be taken to develop the leadership that is latent throughout the population as a whole in order to ensure that the call to leadership finds sufficient answers among those throughout our corporate and non-corporate organizations.

From the lives of the fast-trackers can be extracted guidelines for the development of leadership for people of all ages and all levels of responsibility. The similarities among individuals in this group of fast-trackers demonstrate what leaders do, and what qualities characterize leadership. The differences among them illustrate that leaders are not cloned or manufactured from a given model, and that leadership is founded on recognition and development of individual strengths. Hence, in some way, each leader is unique.

In this chapter, we summarize and clarify the components that shaped each of the individuals in this book. We ask both about the limitations and the opportunities that individuals face in developing their own leadership talents. Each of the individuals in this book, and leaders in every setting, have confronted their own particular "destiny" and their inherent limitations in shaping the substance and style of their particular brand of leadership. What are these limitations? Or, in other words, what are the givens? At what point may individuals choose to respond to these limitations, often turning them into opportunities for further growth and learning? These are the questions we ask here. In the next part of the book we shall turn to the guidelines for the development of leadership. The demand for leadership is today a challenge to each one of us; it is within the scope of our own personal situations, both given and chosen, that we may respond.

What gives the fast-trackers the ability to perform these essential functions of leadership? What are the personal characteristics, the developmental and environmental factors that have led them to create a positive difference in their organizations? There are many similarities among the family backgrounds and career paths of the fast-trackers, which indicates that the origins of leadership lie in early family situations and that beginning abilities are refined throughout the career. Moreover, the current unstable economic environment has given the fast-trackers opportunities that were rare in the more stable economic setting of previous decades. The ability to act originates in themselves and in their family backgrounds, has been refined through the course of their careers, and is then highlighted by the nature of current organizational needs.

DEVELOPING A LEADERSHIP STYLE: INDIVIDUALS AND THE FAMILY

The early family setting is the first training ground for leadership. Much of our early family is not chosen, but instead has been given. As people interact with those close to them, responding in many ways to the givens of their lives, they develop the rudiments of style. They develop varying degrees of confidence, communication skills, and commitment to goals. They learn to examine the world to see how they will make it different (the creators) or how they will make it better (the contributors). In the early environment, children begin to develop their way of being in the world. This is the beginning of *style*.

As *individuals*, the fast-trackers are uniform in demonstrating unusual amounts of energy, mostly because they manage their energy wisely. They set priorities and focus on what matters and stay away from things that do not. They work very hard at what they do, and go ahead with all the stops out. They do not ask privileges for themselves—and rest is a privilege—but secure these privileges for others. They give all that they have to the accomplishment of the task. Yet the task does not take precedence over people: All of them—to different degrees—place a priority on caring for and about others. Energy, priorities, work, commitment, and caring characterize all of the fast-trackers.

Among the senior fast-trackers, there is an additional emphasis upon thought and the creation of a philosophy. The behavior of those at the highest levels is not based on past practices, nor on random nor impulsive activity, but rather on a coherent philosophy of what matters. Each of these individuals may phrase this a little differently. Andrew talks about teams and plans; Jon about directions and communications; Hal about change; Rich about strategies; Tom about destiny. In whatever words, however, each of these men shapes his own particular approach and verbalizes it to those who work for and with him.

The question of where these fast-trackers get these characteristics is one that often preoccupies the parents of these corporate stars, a handful of whom also have children who fell by the wayside and did not, or are not, leading functional and productive adult lives. Clearly, we are born with a certain set of characteristics or at least the raw material for these characteristics. Psychologists are finding that, very early, children seem to be timid or assertive, that many other characteristics cluster around these two traits, and that the degree of timidity or assertion may be inborn.[1] Thus, people are partly who they are because of the roll of the genetic dice. They come into the world with at least a predisposition toward certain ways of being.

These predispositions are then shaped by childhood experience. All the predispositions, plus early experience, form the "givens" of life as people move into late adolescence and early adulthood. What people do from this point forward, however, is very much in their own hands. What they do with the "givens" that they have been handed is a measure of their individual choices. Accepting and responding to a unique set of "givens" is at the heart of style and the beginning of being able to be oneself in interaction with others.

These givens and early responses achieve further distinctiveness in the early *family* setting. Three factors appear to be present in the childhood family experience of most of the fast-trackers that account for their early orientation toward success. First, there are the expectations set by the parents for the child. Most of these expectations are not verbalized, but are demonstrated in the parents' own behavior. The salient question is, How high are the expectations? As a rule, successful people have been held to high expectations by those who are important to them. Second, there is the degree of support that the parents give the child in meeting these expectations. Most of this support is on the emotional side of the ledger. Successful people, in general, have come from homes in which the parents believed that this child could meet these expectations, and encouraged and rewarded his or her efforts; the parents stood behind the child. Third, there is the assessment of the child's value by the parents, and how that assessment is communicated. Was he or she judged as very good? Good? Not quite what was expected? Falling just below the standard? Were evaluative remarks phrased in such a way as to point to new and better directions that the child might take, or were they more sweeping condemnations of behavior? Parents show how they judge a child by saying things like, "That was great!" or, on the other hand, "What in heaven's name did you do that for?" Successful people have, by and large, measured up to their parents' expectations and have been evaluated positively by those parents.

All of the above positive conditions were found in the backgrounds of these fast-trackers. For each of them there was a good fit between their native abilities and/or dispositions and the high expectations that surrounded them in their home environment. They were expected to work hard, to perform, and to excel. They were expected to measure up to caring and upright parental standards. They were given parental support and encouragement and sometimes felt they were pushed by their parents. And, by and large, they measured up to parental expectations: they were "good," "successful," and "better than most." From early in their childhoods, they were all considered winners.

The fast-trackers were born with a good fit for a particular brand of success and then met with an environment that nurtured their particular talents. They learned in their home environments to use their talents to contribute to the world at large. As adults, however, the continued use of their talents is their choice, and not the choice of another. Entering the adult world between 16 and 24, individuals have a large set of givens: not only the characteristics inherited at birth, but the expectations, support, and evaluations of their parents, siblings, and other important figures. As they move through the late adolescent years into adulthood they have an increasing choice in how to respond to the givens. They have the opportunity at some time during this period to decide how they will respond to the givens in their lives. Everyone receives a mixture of pros and cons in the givens that they are handed by others. The question for adults is what they are now going to do with what has been handed to them.

Individual choice, the willingness to follow through, comes from within. Early abilities may be laid to rest by the difficulties of mid-life; early successes may wear off by mid-career. An individual's inflexibility may lead to total derailment from the fast track, or to life on the sidelines or in distant pastures far from the center of action. Whatever talents individuals may have, whatever pluses they may have received from their parents, the choice in adulthood to persist and go forward is theirs.

Psychologists have noted for some time that, although the characteristics of backgrounds that lead to success in modern life are generally well defined, there are cases in which the most remarkable people emerge from completely unexpected settings. Longitudinal studies are being conducted to study the "superkids" who come from homes in which expectations are minimal, support is non-existent, and evaluations of the child are negative, if he or she is evaluated at all.[2] Yet, somewhere, sometime, these young people make the decision to head for the top of the ladder in terms of human growth and development (though not necessarily in terms of worldly success). Their life courses are proof that it is possible for individuals to have the ultimate say about their own lives, and to determine the final balance of victory or defeat. In the end, choice resides with the individual.

Art's life history is one example of this phenomenon. Raised on the city streets, the child of a semi-literate welfare mother and a non-existent father, Art became a typical "bad kid"—smart on the street and dumb in school. Somewhere at the entrance to adulthood, however, when Art was a senior in high school, he made a decision to take hold of his life and to follow an upward path. He is the only one in his family or of his childhood friends to make this determination. His transition from the dumb kid to the smart kid (in terms of usual academic expectations) took time. He went to community college. He went to night school. He took extra units at a not-so-good college. Finally, he achieved his degree and began a career that may well take him to the top of one of the world's biggest companies.

He sees pluses and minuses in his background. The minuses emphasize the loss of 20 years of possible education and development. The pluses are the up-side of this loss: He does not have any pre-learned patterns about how things are supposed to be in the executive world; he arrives at new solutions to old problems and sees things that are normally overlooked, because he never learned "how things should be." He is building his world anew, and his ability to question, to think things through, to see patterns not perceived before, are an asset to his company as a whole. Somewhere, somehow, this success was built on Art's choice. With what he was given, he did a great deal.

The individual characteristics of leadership, all of which are lived out in the personal histories of the fast-trackers, are the combined products of genetic heritage, early environment, and individual choice. The way in which people develop their own unique characteristics in response to situations within their families and other childhood environments is the beginning of style. Continued learning about oneself and others throughout life provides the context for later refinement of style. Style is the expression of an orientation, or an approach to the world. Style is recognizing and accepting who one is, and then being that person in interaction with others. Style is being oneself.

DEVELOPING THE SUBSTANCE OF LEADERSHIP: LEARNING THROUGH THE CAREER PATH

Individual development throughout the career lifetime reflects both continuity and change. There is continuity in the fact that human beings, in growing to new heights, become even more of who they already are, refining and developing the unique heritage that each brings from early childhood into adulthood. There is change, however, in that all individuals who continue to grow—developing further and refining what they are already—strengthen and deepen their self-awareness and self-understanding. With increased awareness, priorities shift, and less visible aspects of the individual are highlighted while others are played down. Lifetime learning creates different contexts in which to act. Therefore, those who are 50 are different from those who are 30; they cannot be the same, because much of a career lifetime lies in between.

Growth in self-understanding is one part of the substance of leadership, which occurs only when individuals are open to a lifetime of continued learning about themselves and others. Growth in understanding of others, of the organization, of one's business in life is another part of the substance of leadership. The process of learning throughout the career path results in the wisdom of those who finally arrive at leadership positions: guiding others to the accomplishment of goals based on a common understanding. The process of learning at each career stage is reflected in the stories of the fast-trackers as they face the challenges of each new rung up the ladder.

In the early years of the career—the pre-adolescent phase—the fast-trackers as a whole are individualistic and achievement-oriented, focusing on what they themselves can accomplish through their own efforts. Much of this must be forgotten in the mid-years of the careers—the adolescent phase—when the transition from individual to group achievement, from solo flights to partnership, and from competition to cooperation must be learned. Then in the senior years—the career adulthood—these learnings are focused on creating an environment in which *many others* can achieve, and where the measure of one's own work is, in fact, the measure of the work of others.

In each new phase of the career, moreover, increased responsibilities for others provide entirely new dimensions, which require reevaluations of priorities and objectives. Thinking for oneself alone, or for those whom one sees every day, is very different from thinking for many people with whom one has only occasional contact. It is different to have one's mistakes count only against one's own measure, than to have errors, forgetfulness, or negligence count against the welfare of hundreds or thousands. The increased responsibility of each career phase thus leads to another step in learning about oneself, others, and the organization. Priorities are aligned anew, on an increasingly larger screen.

The speed of movement and the acquisition of tangible rewards and promotions is more improtant on the small screen than on the big one. The leader of many is creating a common unit out of a great diversity of people. Among the many, there will be some fast and some slow, some sharper and some duller. Goals are accomplished, however, by utilizing the best of each, by tolerating diversity, accepting imperfection, and still moving, unflinchingly, toward the overall objective. Working at this level, the speed of movement along a career track through different levels is scarcely relevant. Tangible rewards assume second place next to watching others grow and learn, using the talents that they have to make a difference in their worlds.

The movement through the three phases of the career, with the consequent increase in responsibility and decrease in importance of independent achievement, is a tremendous learning experience. At any level of any organization, those who continue to grow and learn emerge as leaders in their community. The hallmark of any kind of leadership is, simply, to continue to learn from experience: to accumulate, sift, and shape the substance of experience and, at the same time, to clarify one's individual style, and to become the unique person that each one is.

The result of such learning is that, like the senior fast-trackers, leaders are *very* clear about who they are and what they do. In other words, the result of a lifetime of learning is wisdom. The junior fast-trackers are clearly *bright*; the senior fast-trackers are *wise*. There is no short-cut to the development of wisdom. It is the reward for a lifetime of remaining open to the lessons of experience.

THE DEMAND FOR LEADERSHIP: ORGANIZATIONAL CHANGE

The turbulence of the economy in the 1980s has not only created new uncertainty but has also created a new demand for leadership. In fact, it is only in environments that are unstable and changing that leadership is required.[3] If everything is to be as it was yesterday, there is no call for individuals to set new directions, to stave off danger, and to guide people to a better world. It is when nothing is as it was yesterday that such a call is issued. The 1980s is indeed one such time and the uncertainty and instability of this age is demanding a response for those able to take on the mantle of leadership.

The fast-trackers have responded to this call for leadership. They are setting new directions in a time of change. Reviewing the characteristics and personal histories of these fast-trackers, each, whether creator or contributor, is in some ways less traditional and less conservative than those who have sat at the top of major corporations over the last decades.[4] They are responding to the current situation, acting within an unprecedented context, and they recognize that new directions must be found in all functional areas, that individuals at all levels of organizations must assume more responsibilities. Thus, the call to leadership in the 1980s emanates from a different contextual environment—and is eliciting a different set of answers and solutions—than in the past.

The fast-trackers are leaders not only because of their own developmental background but because their talents have matched the demands of the situation in their organization. All of the fast-trackers have found a context in which their talents could be used most effectively. All of them have found a setting in which their particular strengths matched the particular needs of an organization. It is unlikely that any of them would have been on the fast track to the top if the organizational context in which they work did not call for their particular talents. Leadership is the result not only of personality and development, but of the right fit with what is needed by the context in which people live and work. Leadership reaches the "nth power" only when individual talent meets organizational need.

Whether or not the fast-trackers consciously chose their current environments is a subject for some debate. Did they fall—by chance—into their current positions, or did they walk—by choice—into the contexts in which they work? The fast-trackers' clarity about who they are and what their organization does, suggests strongly that in some way, the fast-trackers chose to be where they are and that one of their talents is recognizing where their strengths may be most needed and then putting themselves in that place. The fast-trackers are leaders—and each a different sort of leader—because their personality strengths, their developmental history, *and* the needs of their organization come together in their work. All of these factors are critical in defining the nature of leadership and in developing leadership philosophies.

LEADERSHIP PHILOSOPHIES

The fast-trackers themselves speak spontaneously about leadership in general and their own style of leadership in particular. In summarizing their views of leadership they provide guidelines for others who are moving along similar paths.

Larry gives advice to new managers and to those aspiring to the fast-track as follows: He says that the "principles of good managements are: (1) team-work, (2) high standards, (3) no bullshit, and (4) listening." Another version of this, described at a different time, is "Treat others fairly and work your tail off." Finally he says that basically it comes down to "guts and risk-taking." Several of the components of leadership are included in Larry's one comment about "no bullshit." To follow this advice one must be self-aware, communicate clearly, and act wholeheartedly.

There are the same emphases on communication and action, along with an equally strong emphasis on thought (philosophy) and planning (or strategy), in the words of the senior statesmen of this group.

Tom emphasizes commitment and action when he says: "The cultural change took clarity and discipline and *attention to making it happen*. There was an unfailing commitment on the part of the senior management team which was absolutely essential." Jon emphasizes direction and communication and insists that it is important to tell people where they are going: "Most people have a lot of common sense. Explain things and tell them how it is . . . Point the ship in the right direction and make sure everyone coming in the wake understands where we're going." Finally, Rich emphasizes the importance of planning: "What I mean by a strategic business plan is really using long-range goals as an incentive for personal growth and development. This is a process that produces amazing results. . . . It is a critical success factor."

What these fast-trackers have to tell the world is critically important. Yet their actions more than their words are cause for hope, for in their actions they demonstrate the answer that we all must give to the call for leadership. We must be ourselves, talk with others, and act on what we believe. But we must also think, plan, and evaluate what we do. These components come together in the essentials of leadership, the subject of the concluding chapters of this book.

PART IV

The Essentials of Leadership

Six Steps to Success

> *Leadership, unlike naked power wielding, is thus*
> *inseparable from followers' needs and goals. . . .*
> *the fundamental [leadership] process is an elusive*
> *one; it is, in large part, to make conscious what lies*
> *unconscious among followers.*
> JAMES MACGREGOR BURNS
> *LEADERSHIP*

What leaders do may be defined very simply. Leaders *clarify what matters, demonstrate that it is possible to achieve those things that matter*, and *act so as to create a difference in their worlds*.[1] These three functions of leadership are each accomplished by completing two of the six steps that lead to success in any venture. Clarifying what matters results from increasing awareness and making sense of our knowledge. Making it possible to do what matters requires communication and planning. Finally, creating a difference rests on the two steps of action and evaluation. All of the fast-trackers do each of these things.

Essentials of Leadership

LEADERSHIP FUNCTION	STEPS TO SUCCESS
I. CLARIFYING WHAT MATTERS:	1. Awareness or Not Pretending Knowing Oneself (Substance) Being Oneself (Style)
	2. Sense-Making Finding Patterns (Substance)
II. MAKING IT POSSIBLE:	3. Communication or Talking and Listening Knowing What to Say (Substance) Saying it with Clarity (Style)
	4. Planning or Charting a Course Drawing Time-Lines and Assigning Tasks (Substance) Involving Others (Style)
III. CREATING A DIFFERENCE:	5. Acting or "Going for the Gold" Knowing What To Do (Substance) Motivating Others (Style)
	6. Evaluating or Summing It Up Assessing the Result (Substance) Spreading the Word (Style)

CLARIFYING WHAT MATTERS

The fast-trackers know what matters. Knowing what matters requires first an awareness of what is going on in one's world, and second, the willingness to utilize this awareness to draw out the patterns that are there.

For Rich, what matters is making a new idea into a reality: "I am taking the concept of this company from a grand experiment to the real world." For Tom, it is empowering the people: having them make decisions, take responsibility, and in the process, increase market share. For Hal, who sees himself as an architect of change, the vision of a participant company is clear and is drawn from an awareness of changes in competition and values in the world outside the company. Larry summarizes crisply—for himself—the importance of working on things that matter: "Lots of people spend time on things they can't control, can't fix. I don't."

Awareness or Not Pretending

The fast-trackers do not pretend that something is what it isn't. They are open to the information that comes from within and without. Alec is the most forthright about the direction of his own abilities and emphasizes that he only establishes new projects and does not maintain old ones. Andrew always does "what's there" and "takes on the next thing." Just as they are clear on what they do, so they pay attention to their world. Sam makes the clearest statements about his early childhood, when he was "like a fly on the wall absorbing everything." Rich says with a smile, "Well, sometimes you just have to listen," implying that this is so even when the words are not particularly welcome. All of them learn from others, from the managers older than they who were part of their work lives, and from all the people who are currently part of their teams. They are open to new information about themselves, about people, and about their organizations.

Sense-Making

After acquiring new information, the fast-trackers then think about what they learn until all the pieces fit together into a sense-making pattern. Ken, in his earlier job of training new managers, came to the conclusion "that the most important thing is to be able to take all the different bits of information and fit them together into a whole." He repeats this twice for emphasis and then says, with some slight astonishment, "but some people just can't do that and those are the ones we let go." Rich talks about his early bosses and how, within a scientific framework, they took pieces of data and moved them around until they fit into a pattern. Art is always creating a new matrix, fitting information into new patterns, and creating a new framework where none existed for him before.

> For example, even in small matters such as what knife to use at a formal dinner, Art says that he has no preconceptions. He has to watch everybody and learn from what they are doing and, in the process, may learn more than other people who already know about silverware and thus have to pay less attention. In creating his matrices, he puts in place the rules that he sees in operation around him—but, taking nothing for granted, he often creates new rules that better fit the current situation than the ones other people have learned.

It is these matrices, frameworks, and patterns that then become the foundation for the essential philosophies that distinguish the senior managers in this sample from the others, and that give them the vision and direction to lead large numbers of people in the world's biggest organizations.

MAKING IT POSSIBLE

In order to demonstrate that what is important can in fact be achieved, individuals must communicate with others, sharing their own knowledge and listening to what others know, and then formulate a plan to achieve objectives held in common.

> Jon "communicates with the people again . . . and again . . . and again," sharing with them the directions he envisions for the company. Tom is constantly talking, listening, and responding to others in person, on the telephone, or in the mail. Rich listens to his people—sometimes more than he talks—and encourages others to spread his message. From the widespread communication throughout the company, he shapes the outlines of a "common understanding" and works with others to develop a strategic plan. Hal believes that communication and planning are the keys to "moving the mountain without it knowing that it is being moved."

Communication or Talking and Listening

All of the fast-trackers emphasize communication, and some are specialists: Christine sees herself as the interface between the engineers and the manufacturing wing of the organization; Hal, early in his career, was the only person who could talk to both the personnel folks and to the engineers and became a focal point for these two groups. Others have built their philosophies on a foundation of good communication. Tom goes to many meetings around the nation to personally see all of his people and to talk to them about changes in the company; he is now making videotapes to reinforce the message of his personal visits. Art says, "You have to talk to them, you have to talk to everybody . . . as if they all counted. . . ."

Planning or Charting a Course

Planning is central to Rich's philosophy and his view of leadership in organizations. Rich sees the process of creating a plan as enriching its overall value far beyond the plan itself, because such a process involves many, many people, whose commitment to the outcome is increased by their involvement. Additionally, having a plan becomes a channel for communication with peers and superiors in one's own as well as in other functional areas. Tom, on the other hand, pokes a little bit of fun at the idea of a plan by saying that his task is to raise seven elephants off the stage at once, without wires. When asked, "How?" he chuckles and goes on to other matters. However, on his desk sits a very cohesive and workable plan for making this come about (figuratively raising seven elephants, etc.), a plan that has been distributed to central figures in his organization.

CREATING A DIFFERENCE

All of the fast-trackers have had an impact on their environment by making things different or making things better. They act—and then they evaluate the results of that action.

As a very junior person in his first company, Alec went ahead and made decisions on the marketing of this company's major product. These decisions were revised in somewhat heated discussions with the president of the company (on the day when the decisions arrived on the president's desk all of the intervening layers of management were absent and Alec had to meet with him alone). Alec won some and lost some but the fact that he acted, for the most part in the right direction, made him a star in this company.

In his junior years, Rich created a new plant built on a team concept. He did not just think about it, he did it, and it became a model for change within the company. In the same stage of his career, Hal created a new computerized system that was instituted not only in his division but in corporate headquarters and began his journey to the top. In the junior years, the actions of these men have direct effects. At senior levels, effects are indirect: these men all *do* things but their goal and purpose is to empower others to do things. They are less visible as actors; rather their people act and create sweeping effects. The influence of the senior statesmen can best be observed in the actions of their people.

Action, or "Going for the Gold"

Since they were children, all of the fast-trackers have been at home with action. They do not procrastinate. They do not put off until tomorrow what can be done today. With the knowledge they have at hand, they make a decision and they act on that decision. They know that they will learn from whatever they do. They know that they can cut their losses if they take a wrong turn, and they know that they can get back on the path with a different tactic, a different approach. They act and then assume the consequences for their actions. Each of them has had years of practice in doing this, since they were six, ten, or fourteen. Jon describes the ability to make a decision and act as one of the prime requirements for high levels of leadership, and finds that others have been derailed along the way because they refused to limit their options, always wanting to keep many possibilities open until another day had passed. "No," he says. "You set a direction and then you go in that direction. That's all there is to it."

Evaluation, or Summing It Up

The fast-trackers follow action with evaluation. They examine what has been done and what can be done to make it better. "I learned from this experience . . ." is a phrase that is often used by the fast-trackers to preface a story about a work experience. By thinking about what happened after the fact, they know how to do it better the next time.

The three functions of leadership—clarifying what matters, making it possible and creating a difference—are what the fast-trackers do. The six steps—awareness, sense-making, communication, planning, action, and evaluation—spell out how they carry out each of these functions. Doing each of these things had led them to their position at the helms of their own ships. Because they do these things, any one of them may someday steer an even bigger ship on the seas of change—either charting a new course and creating a new map, or adapting the marks on an old map to take account of changes in the seascape. Both those who create the new and those who adapt the old are essential to the process of navigation on a changing sea.

In the next chapters each of these six steps is examined in more detail. Any who undertake to carry out *all* these behaviors in any sphere, of any size, will have joined the ranks of the fast-trackers and assumed the mantle of leadership in his or her chosen sphere.

CHAPTER 12

On Not Pretending

Beyond the yellow brick road of naivete and the muggers' lane of cynicism, there is a narrow path, poorly lit, hard to find and even harder to stay on once found. People who have the skill and the perseverance to take that path serve us in countless ways. We need more of these people.
JOHN KOTTER
POWER AND INFLUENCE

There are many routes to the fast track. The seventeen individuals in this sample received an early exposure to the business world and leapt onto the fast track between the ages of 21 and 30. Other individuals with different life histories may move onto the fast track later in life, pursue other intellectual or artistic interests, or create, from the ground up, their own operations in business, professional, or artistic fields. Regardless of the point of departure, or the direction in which one is heading, most people want to find the same joy in their work as the fast-trackers in this book; want to be challenged and have their limits tested; want to experience the satisfaction of achieving their own objectives. Most people want to shape their own lives, and not be at the mercy of others. In this context, the lives of those on the fast track provide a model for those on other tracks, for those in and out of the business world, and for those who pursue independent interests outside the realm of big business.

If there is but one lesson from the fast-trackers, it is to manage one's time, talent, and energy well. In fact, the lesson is to manage time, talent, and energy *superbly*. The fast-trackers make every moment count—in their work, in their relationships, and in their leisure activities. As we examine their lives, we see that there are a number of steps leading to this level of productivity and satisfaction. *Anyone*, in any position in life, may

To Not Pretend

1. Own up to our strengths and weaknesses.
2. Accept that we are not, and will not become, equally strong in all areas.
3. Learn to say "I don't know."
4. Acknowledge the gray areas in ourselves and our worlds.
5. Accept that we do not always operate at our highest levels.
6. Recognize in others the same degrees of strength that we see in ourselves.
7. Accept that we are where we are because of choices we have made in the past.
8. Accept that we do not fully control our destinies.
9. Live in the present and not in the past.

take these steps and find the result to be greater effectiveness at work, greater satisfaction in relationships, and greater excitement and enthusiasm for the process of living. None of these steps is easy, however, for each basically requires that we be ourselves, do what matters, and take the risks of sharing with others and acting on our beliefs. The fast-trackers do each of these things consistently.

The first phase in the development of leadership, the first step toward the fast track, is to *stop pretending*, especially to ourselves, that we are something we are not. We all pretend some of the time, but none of us does this very well. Watching other people closely we can detect the signs of pretense: they stop looking at us directly, twist in their chair, fiddle with papers, pencils, or their clothing, chew their lip, or hesitate in their speech. They are signaling us, in fact, that they are putting a significant amount of energy into *not telling us* exactly what they think, but instead telling us what they think we want to hear, or what they have learned would be a good thing to say. They are spending time and energy avoiding being themselves. Moreover, their pretense is generally noticeable to an astute observer, who is then left to guess what was really intended as opposed to what was said. What's more, "those people" are often us.

Pretending is, in many ways then, a waste of energy. The fast trackers *do not* do this. Their time, their talents, and their energy are all directed toward some productive goal. They do not wear themselves out hiding their real selves from others but instead use this energy to accomplish what they believe to be important. If we choose to follow their example and stop pretending, we must do several things:

First, *we need to own up to our strengths and weaknesses*. We all have things we do well and things we do less well. Unless we are honest about these things, we will spend lots of energy trying to demonstrate that what we do poorly, we in fact do well. Reluctant to be evaluated in our areas of weakness, we may find reasons to delay doing things in these areas at all. We may procrastinate, fail to ask the right questions for fear of appearing incompetent, say it's not possible (not because of our skills but because of some objective reason in the world, i.e., "it's *their* fault") and, in general, dilly-dally along until the time for action is past. As others learn that we are not to be relied upon in certain areas, they come to doubt that we can be relied upon even in our areas of strength. Not being clear about our weaknesses casts suspicion on our strengths.

Second, *we must accept that we are not, and will not become, equally strong in all areas*. There is a sense of internal tension that often accompanies such an awareness. We would all like to be competent in every area and able to do all things; however, none of us has been given the talent to be all-encompassing in our abilities. Consequently, we are good in some things and not so good in others. Yet, perhaps we learned that we *should not* be like this, perhaps we heard somewhere, from parents or teachers or friends, that good people *are* always good at math, or good with details, or good in writing. So we fear that by admitting to not being good in one of these areas, we are, in fact, not being a good person generally or a person of value. This confusion exists in all of us; it is only when we accept ourselves as people of value (*all* of us have value) that we can then admit to areas in which we do not measure up.

Third, *we must learn to say "I don't know,"* and to say it with a reasonable degree of comfort. In whatever position, at whatever level, there are things beyond our ken and we must let others know, when relevant, that we do not have the answers. This will enable a working team then to explore what is not known and, perhaps, discover new approaches, new possibilities, and new answers. To pretend to know what is not known puts a cap on creativity and experimentation.

Fourth, *we must acknowledge the gray areas in ourselves and our worlds* and give up the idea that something is either this or that. This means that we must discriminate degrees of knowledge, degrees of competence, and degrees of strength in different areas. In so doing, we give up the comfort of believing it is either so or not so. Those individuals who can recognize *degrees* have the ability to fine-tune their judgment and to understand when it is important to act in one way or another. Those who live in a categorical world where something (a trait, a characteristic, an ability) is either this or that lack the basic prerequisites for making good judgments in complex situations.

Fifth, *we must accept the fact that we do not always operate at our highest levels*. There are peaks and valleys in everyone's performance in all areas of life. If we acknowledge where we are, however, we must also acknowledge that at least part of the time, we fall short of our potential. And we must accept the tension that results from this recognition. (This is a tension that performers, competitors in athletic events, and many others know well: the ability to create, to perform at any given moment is not entirely under our conscious control and yet we must go forward, knowing that whatever we do may be less than our best.) To retreat from this tension, we must either ignore the reality of ourselves, pretending that we are something we are not, or we must ignore the possibilities, believing that we can be no more than we are. To acknowledge both the reality and the vision, the limits and the possibilities, requires that we walk a narrow road along which we can continually see both our limitations on the one hand and our possibilities on the other.

Sixth, *we must recognize in others the same degrees of strength and capability that we see in ourselves*. We can watch and listen to others and pay attention to their behavior, withholding initial judgments about who they are and what they do. Extending our understanding to others, we will recognize areas of strength and weakness, we will recognize gradations of skill, we will acknowledge areas of conflict and tension. We will discriminate pretense from genuine awareness in others as well as ourselves. In doing this, we will have the basis for making better judgments in the workplace, for putting the best people in the best jobs and for offering them opportunities even there to grow beyond their limitations.

Seventh, *we can accept that we are where we are because of choices we have made in the past*. In doing this we stop saying "It's your fault," but instead, by accepting that *we* did it, we take charge of our own lives. We have, in fact, steered our own ships and created our own courses. Many of us would prefer to deny the existence of choice in our lives, because we do not want to take responsibility for the consequences. We do not want to own up to the fact that we are where we are because of what *we* did rather than what *they* did. Not pretending, however, leads directly to acceptance of self, acceptance of others, recognition of the choices that have led us to this place, and responsibility for those choices. This is sometimes a heavy burden to bear.

Eighth, *we must accept that we do not fully control our destinies* even though we are in charge of our lives. We entered the world with many givens and in the course of our childhoods acquired many more. Moreover, as adults in a complex world we may decide what we will do and what response to a given situation we can make, but we cannot determine the behavior of others nor the nature of the situation itself. Thus, we must admit that life is not predictable; it is uncertain and often unfair. Yet we have what we've been given, and what we do with it is in our hands.

Finally, not pretending means that *we live in the present and not in the past*. When we pretend, we are taking something that we learned from our past—such-and-such is the way to be—and are superimposing it on the present. Bringing such material along from the past blocks clear awareness of the present. (For example, when we view others as they were some years in the past—this is easy to do with grown-up children who have gone away to live their own lives—and are certain that we know what matters to them, we are most likely to block out any contradictory information and miss entirely the opportunity to know them in the present.) With each pretense we block out an area where we might otherwise be open to new awareness. Consequently when we pretend, we are responding to the past and not to the present. Our judgment, our response to current information, is diminished. To live in the present, to take in fully what is here and now, is the consequence of being true to who we are.

Each one of these nine points is part of not pretending. Acceptance of ourselves and life as it is—and recognition of how we might make it better—is the foundation for productive use of time, talent and energy. Clarity about oneself and one's world is the basis on which each of the fast-trackers has made his or her way toward the top.

Alec does not pretend about what he does well and what he does not. He knows he is exceptionally good at directing new ventures and not so good at maintaining old ones. He admits, too, that he has trouble delegating tasks to others and that sometimes he lacks important interpersonal skills. Because he admits this, however, he is able to compensate for his areas of weakness. He has hired a second-in-command with excellent people skills who works well with a diverse group of important associates. In a way, because he does not pretend to have skills he does not possess, he is able to provide a "buffer zone" in the guise of his immediate subordinate. This enables his team, at least for the time being, to operate well with people; also, with an eye to the future, he has given himself room to develop in this area. His clarity about himself has provided for effectiveness in the present, and opened up possiblities for later growth. This is the most that we can ask of ourselves.

Ken is dynamic and enthusiastic and reaches out easily to others. However he thinks and acts very quickly, and is often impatient with those working for him, who are most often slower to respond than he. Ken admits to a lack of tact and diplomacy when his speed is countered with another's slowness, when what he wants to happen yesterday gets put off until some future tomorrow. However he admits to this impatience in himself and is striving to find a greater tolerance for other people's ways of operating. At the time that I met him he had just left a meeting in which he would have become "abrupt and critical" if he had stayed. It was better, he said, that he left. This recognition of his own tendency to criticize others who do not move at his lightning pace allows him to compensate by leaving others to work things out at their own speed. If he were unable to admit to his own lack of diplomacy with others, he might barrage them with criticism and negative commentary, thus interfering with the effectiveness of his operation. Clarity about himself, as in Alec's case, has allowed Ken to make appropriate compensation for his own less-well-developed characteristics.

How different each of these fast-trackers turn out to be from society's prevalent stereotypes of businessmen bluffing their way through encounters in which they have too little information and knowledge, making unfounded and exaggerated claims to back up untenable positions. Instead, these fast-trackers tell it like it is, make fine-tuned judgments about what will work and what won't, what is appropriate and what is not. They may make grand claims for some of their ideas but they *believe* in those ideas. When they talk on a grand scale they are thinking and feeling on a grand scale, using a big picture to cover a small experience.

The mark of high levels of leadership in any organization, in any system in fact, is good judgment. We are never going to have clear signposts pointing to the right answer. However, living in a complex world in which the gray areas override the black and white ones, we increase our odds of making good judgments when we have the greatest amount of information—information about ourselves, others, and our organizations. Those who do not pretend, who admit who they are, who accept responsibility for their lives and live in the present, even as they plan for the future, are those who are likely to have the best shot at making the right decisions for themselves and their organizations. These are the leaders of tomorrow.

In short, we may be able to develop many of the characteristics of the fast-trackers and to enjoy their high level of work satisfaction by: admitting our strengths and weaknesses; accepting the tensions that accompany clarity; admitting that we don't know many things, and that there are degrees of almost everything; accepting our limits and accepting others as they are. In doing this we take charge of our own lives, even as we accept the unpredictability of events in general. We live appropriately in the present, responding to *what is* even as we work to shape *what will be*. Our time will be better used, our judgments more finely tuned, and we will be ready to move speedily ahead toward the top of whatever mountain represents our chosen destination. These are the consequences of not pretending.

CHAPTER 13

On Making Sense

*Only with many changes in the works can the
manager discover new combinations of opportunities
. . . The process is not highly abstract; rather the
manager searches for a means of drawing into a
pattern the thousands of incidents which make up the
day-to-day life of a growing company.*
H. EDWARD WRAPP
"GOOD MANAGERS DON'T
MAKE POLICY DECISIONS"

*Upon this gifted age, in its dark hour,
Rains from the sky a meteoric shower*
*Of facts . . . They lie unquestioned, uncombined,
Wisdom enough to leech us of our ill
Is daily spun, but there exists no loom
To weave it into fabric. . . .*
EDNA ST. VINCENT MILLAY
"HUNTSMAN, WHAT QUARRY?"

Clarity about ourselves may take us onto the fast track, but clarity
alone will not speed us on the upward journey. Being oneself is the
beginning, but to take the next step we must think about what we know,
select the important components and significant bits and pieces of our
knowledge, and identify the *patterns* that emerge from relating the separate
components to each other. We must not merely accept what we know, we
must make sense of it. This is the second step in the process of developing
leadership and moving onto the fast track.

The *senior* fast-trackers have mastered this ability on a large scale. For
them their work directions and decisions fit into a larger pattern that has

To Make Sense (of Our Career Path)

1. Accept that there is something each of us does well.
2. Remember how our parents spent their time during our childhood.
3. Explore how supportive our parents were.
4. Recall how well what we did measured up to our parents' standards.
5. Recognize our own uniqueness within our families.
6. Remember in childhood and adolescence how we chose to spend our time and what activities were most satisfying.
7. Identify in adult lives the ways we spend our time and the activities in which we are successful.
8. Begin the process of matching our skills with opportunities in organizations
9. Identify what training, education or job experience we need to be prepared for jobs which make best use of our strengths.

emerged from and now guides their lives. Tom talks of destiny and empowering the people, and views everything in this context. He is always asking himself how events relate to his destiny, and help or hinder him in empowering the people. Rich centers his thinking about work around what he calls "strategic planning," and around his feelings for helping people. He looks at his current situation and asks: "Where do we hope to go? Where are we now? What is missing in the present that will take us to the desired future?" Situations in the workplace are all examined to reveal the presence or absence of necessary steps leading toward the envisioned future goal. Hal speaks of being an "architect of change" and of having a vision of what a well-managed company can be. Jon knows that he is directing a ship—closing off some channels and guiding his people through the clear passages, explaining to them all the while the purpose of their voyage. Andrew, more briefly than the others, describes his thinking as built on a team concept. Through a particular interpretation of the facts, each of these senior statesmen has made sense of his world.

The *mid-level* fast-trackers are aware of the importance of sense-making. Ken says clearly that the ability to make sense of isolated pieces of information is the key ingredient of success along the fast track. Art emphasizes again and again his belief in the importance of creating matrices that make sense of his activities. Jerry talks about his philosophy as providing principles for action for his management team. Don refers often to the philosophies of his early bosses, and the lessons he took away from them which he now shares with others. Yet none of the men or women at this level presents the all-encompassing philosophical viewpoints typical of the senior men. In their work, in their immediate setting, they make sense of what is before them and identify patterns, identify what matters. But still in the adolescence of their careers, much of their sense-making is either borrowed from others they respect, or is still specific to a given situation. In announcing their viewpoints about work, the company, and their role in the company, they exhibit the beginnings of a philosophy. However, their frequent use of former mentors as reference points demonstrates that what they believe is not yet fully their own. Integration occurs at the end of career adolescence, as corporate stars who survive the Executive Transition enter the adulthood of their careers.

The focal point of the *junior* stars' thought is still their career path and movement along the fast track. Most of them are in the process of making sense of their heady success. They look back over their earlier lives and ask, "What brought me here?" They look at their work and ask, "Where next and how fast?" In examining their own career paths they are making sense of much information about themselves, their histories, and their impact on others. They do not, and are not in a position to, present views of organizations as a whole or philosophies that outline large directions. They are still in the process of placing themselves in the larger world, and making sense of that place in the world.

Among all the junior fast-trackers, Alec is perhaps clearest in his perception of where he is, and why he has arrived at this point. He knows that he "does new things" and that this makes him somewhat unusual among his peers in the corporate world and, because he is unusual, he has perhaps been required to explain himself (at least to himself) more than once. He has had to examine both his personal and corporate experience, in order to find the best match for his abilities in the larger world. He has done this well. Later, one expects that he and the other junior stars will apply their sense-making capabilities to the entire organization. The first steps in this direction are seen in those one step more senior, those at mid-career who are in the Executive Transition.

All the fast-trackers seek to find the patterns in their worlds. However, the focus of their sense-making capabilities differs at each developmental level. The junior people make sense of their own career tracks. The mid-level people are beginning to integrate the teachings of their mentors, and to reach out tentatively in the direction of a philosophy about the corporation. This philosophy, however, is not yet theirs; the ability to make sense of things comes to fruition in the senior men. Each of the seniors has developed a sense-making philosophy that encompasses the workings of large organizations, and the directions of individuals within these organizations. They interpret their own actions within the framework's large-scale view.

All of us make sense of information and find patterns in what we do. Some of us do this more consciously than others. We may learn from the fast-trackers collectively, and from the junior fast-trackers in particular, how to think about ourselves and our careers; such thinking will start us up the track that we have already stepped onto by not pretending. The place to begin in sense-making is to examine what we do well and look for a good match in terms of the organizational world. This begins with thinking about our personal histories, and those things that are *givens* in our lives.

First, *we must accept that there is something each of us does well,* and that we have probably been doing it for a long time. The fast-trackers began at six, 10, and 14 to prepare themselves for their later careers. They realized what they were doing by 25 or 28 or 30. Others may not become aware of what their lives have taught them, and what their specific preparations have been, until they are even older. Yet, what we do well (and success on the fast track occurs because we work from our strengths) we have been doing and learning to do for a long time. Part of what we do well has been shaped by our childhood experiences; in seeking the patterns of behavior that represent our strengths, it is helpful to examine our personal histories and those things over which we had little control.

Second, to explore what was given, *we need to remember how our parents (or other significant adult figures) spent their time during our childhoods.* As small children watching bigger, more important people doing something consistently, we probably reckoned that what they were doing was important, valuable, and meaningful. The fast-trackers watched their parents work hard, often at small businesses where serving the customer mattered. They learned as children the importance of hard work and serving others. Some of their brothers and sisters rebelled against these values, but the fast-trackers accepted them as their own. Regardless of our decisions to rebel or accept them, the values exemplified by the lives of our parents or significant adult others are very important in understanding our own values.

Third, *we need to explore how supportive our parents were* in helping us to do the things that they valued; how encouraging or discouraging; how generous with opportunities to work along with them. Did we watch them at work? Did we only *wonder* what it was they did all day when they were not with us? To what degree were we given opportunities and encouragement to learn the ways of our parents? In those instances where there were few opportunities to learn from our parents, what other resources did we have? Were there relatives, teachers, older friends we admired, and did they support us and encourage us in learning how to do what they did? From the histories of the fast-trackers we learn that most of them found support within their families but some found support in teachers, in friends' parents, and in relatives outside the immediate circle. What they learned from these supportive others still sustains them today, and is one of the reasons for their success. Somewhere we have all decided that doing certain things matters more than doing something else, and we have received support and encouragement for this set of beliefs.

Fourth, *we need to recall how well what we did measured up to our parents' standards*, or those of significant others, based on their values and what they thought was important. In general, the fast-trackers' parents thought they did splendidly, yet many had other sons or daughters who failed to measure up to these expectations and seemingly, therefore, chose other directions in life. Yet even in these alternate choices they seemed to be trying to improve upon or disprove altogether their parents' values and actions. The degree to which we measured up to some standard in our parents' eyes, or in the eyes of significant adult others, affects our degree of self-confidence, our sense of unique personal value, and our willingness to be ourselves and to examine our own lives. The activities that were valued in our homes, the support we received for doing these things, and how well we were perceived as doing them are all part of the givens that we bring into adult life.

Fifth, *each of us must recognize our own uniqueness within our families*. Each of us came into the world with a unique genetic heritage, and therefore we are more than the product of our early backgrounds. We bring with us into the world certain sets of predispositions, and the combinations of these predispositions is unique to us. We might ask then, what qualities in ourselves distinguish us from our parents, what strengths and weaknesses do we have that they might not have. These things, too, are givens forming part of our personal destinies.

Sixth, *we may remember in childhood and adolescence how we chose to spend our time and what activities provided the greatest sense of satisfaction*. What did we do most often? What did we enjoy doing? When did we feel most successful? How did these activities relate to our parents' values? Did these activities show that we were moving in directions valued by our parents, directions slightly different, or in other ways altogether?

Seventh, *we may then identify in our adult lives the ways in which we choose to spend our time and the activities in which we feel particularly successful*. The way we spend much of our time, in the past and in the present, has constituted a training ground for the development of specific strengths that may be translated into characteristics useful in the world of work. The settings in which we have succeeded suggest the nature of the environments in which we best use our strengths. From the combination of these recollections, we may identify more clearly our areas of strength and the settings in which these strengths are most likely to be utilized. What we come up with may not, in fact, resemble a job description or a specialized skill in a particular trade or discipline. Describing our strengths may, in fact, be more general than either of these: yet in getting this far we have made sense of our experience, allowing that experience to form a pattern that identifies a particular set of skills, based on innate talents, early training, and continuing experience. To thus define our skills requires a high level of thought—the same kind of thinking, in fact, that the fast-trackers use in the workplace.

Eighth, *we can then begin the process of matching our skills with opportunities available in organizations.* Are there already-existing positions that make use of our skills? Or can a position be created to match our particular strengths? Do our skills fit best in the business world, or in another sphere altogether? Do our skills involve building something new like the creators, or making things work better like the contributors? Whether in business or in other spheres, there are different needs for different kinds of talent. When we have achieved a fair degree of matching, we know that we may pursue a career where we enjoy doing our work; and loving one's work is clearly one of the characteristics of the fast-trackers and of leaders in every sphere.

Ninth, *we may then identify what further training, education, or job experience we need in order to be prepared for the jobs that make the best use of our particular strengths.* The process of learning is an on-going one. The very good matches that fast-trackers' strengths have made with specific organizational needs do not occur magically, or without clear awareness about oneself and an organization. By making sense of who we are, we begin the process of seeking out the work best suited to us, greatly increasing the odds that we will be able to say, along with the fast-trackers, that our work is "great fun!"

Attending to each of the above issues is an exercise in making sense of our experiences and our knowledge of self and others. Applying the same pattern-making thought to larger and larger spheres results, during the years of senior management, in the clear philosophies of the oldest men in this sample. Entry onto the fast track is assured by giving up pretense for clarity about ourselves and our skills. However, movement along the track occurs—except for a few preliminary starts and stops—because we can outline a direction and recognize significant landmarks along the way.

Perceiving a direction takes thought. It is the result of being able to make sense of our world, to bring the important things into focus, omitting the distracting details. Knowing our direction means, in fact, that we have made sense of our world.

Once we have a direction and a set of priorities, we do not waste energy on matters irrelevant to our central purpose. We can match our skills with the needs of an organization (or some other entity) and work from our strengths. Then we may clarify those things that matter, we may establish a clear set of priorities, and in directing ourselves toward their accomplishment take charge of our own lives. At the same time we can respond constructively to events beyond our control. To do so requires not just knowing, but thinking. The next phase in developing leadership emphasizes talking and listening.

CHAPTER 14

On Talking and Listening

The influence a leader exerts in altering moods, evoking images and expectations, and in establishing specific desires and objectives determines the direction a business takes. The net result of this influence is to change the way people think about what is desirable, possible, and necessary.
ABRAHAM ZALEZNIK
"MANAGEMENT AND
LEADERSHIP: IS THERE A
DIFFERENCE?"

All of the fast-trackers communicate clearly with others, and most of them emphasize the importance of communication with associates on a steady and consistent basis. They know, too, that communication is not just talking but listening. Many times they comment on what they learned from others by watching *and* listening; particularly in recalling their junior years, they frequently volunteer information about how much they learned by watching and listening to those with more experience than they. Now, as they talk to others, the fast-trackers generally recognize intuitively the effect that their communication has on the beliefs and behavior of others. Communication *is* influence, and things get done in organizations only because people influence other people. Communication is, in effect, the reason that things happen at all.

Jon enthuses about the communication groups he has established in every organization he has run in the last six to ten years. He recognizes that these groups are central to his success with people. Tom has made new efforts, in large regional gatherings and through videotape, to communicate to *all* his people across the country and, as nearly as possible, to establish a one-to-

—◦◦◦◦◦◦◦◦◦◦◦—

To Talk and Listen

1. Accept that what we say influences others.
2. Listen attentively to others knowing what they say matters.
3. Watch as well as listen to perceive the full complexity of communication.
4. Know what matters to others so that we may weave their hopes and dreams into common group goals.
5. Stop pretending in our conversations with others.
6. Avoid withholding information to prop up our own sense of control.
7. Speak out more often, make more mistakes and learn from these mistakes.
8. Increase our comfort by remembering that no one else will pay as much attention to us as we do ourselves.
9. Spend time talking and listening about things that matter.

—◦◦◦◦◦◦◦◦◦◦◦—

one relationship with many of them. Art says you have to talk to the people all the time to let them know that they matter, while Larry states that there is to be "no bullshit" in communication—you have to tell it like it is. Jerry solidified his own position several years ago by creating new channels of communication in his organization, and modeling clear communication for his people. Hank is still seen as a counselor and a good sounding board for many in the organization, and Pete will talk to anybody almost any time—*if* they are willing to run along with him as he goes from one end of the building to another. Good and clear communication is central to the success of each one of the fast-trackers.

The journey along the fast track is one that is always shared with other people. The fast-trackers are adamant about their interdependence with others, and the help they have received along the way. Thus while clarity about oneself may bring one onto the fast track and thinking about priorities may establish the primary direction, it is sharing with others that makes the journey up the track possible at all. Nobody ventures forth alone. Only by developing a cadre of mentors, associates and supporters can one withstand the rigors of the fast track: the rapid pace, the uncertainties and the loneliness of a journey to the top. Good communication is the only means of developing such support.

Furthermore, the farther one travels along the fast track the more dependent one is, in some ways, on other people. Initially, one's merit is evaluated in terms of one's own efforts. Later, one's merit is evaluated in terms of the efforts of others. At the late middle and senior levels, one's own leadership qualities are assessed by what other people do and how well they do it. Leaders—and the fast-trackers are leaders—work through others. Only by influencing others to move in chosen directions can goals be accomplished. Communication therefore is a primary tool at all levels, but increasingly important as one goes farther along the track.

Communication rests on clarity and thought. Therefore, not pretending, and making sense of what is known, are prerequisites to good communication. In order to communicate well, one must first have information that is important, and then must know out of all the information available what is most important. With good communication, leaders tell others what is happening at the moment and what may happen in the future; they tell people what is important about what they are doing now and clarify the road to achievement of those objectives. In talking and listening to others, leaders help others to clarify their own thinking about what is desirable, just as they do their own. In the process, they help others to make sense of their world.

There are several steps to increasing skill in communication and they rest upon a clear understanding of oneself and others, and the ability to make sense of what is known. We all can profit from improving our communication.

First, *we must accept that what we say influences others* and take time, before speaking, to be honest with ourselves about what we know and don't know. We can pay attention to what we say. Many of the remarks we make that are misinterpreted, or perceived as detrimental to somebody else, are often those we toss off without thinking when we think it doesn't matter. What we say *does* matter and it is important that we give it our full attention. If we can't pay attention to what we say, then it is better to be quiet and to talk at a later time.

Second, *we can learn to listen attentively to others knowing that what they say matters*. When we decide to listen we owe the other person our full attention. Whether or not we listen fully and how we respond influences the behavior of others. If we cannot listen fully at one time or another, we need to make a commitment to listen later, and keep that commitment.

Third, *we must watch as well as listen to perceive the full complexity of communication*. When others speak because they are *clear* about their message, most of what they have to say will be communicated in words. When they speak out of *pretense*, however, most of what they say will be communicated non-verbally in small gestures or movements indicating nervousness, discomfort, or boredom. We pick up these signals by watching others. We learn from the clarity but also from the pretense of others.

When others are clear, the signals come across without static. When others are pretending, on the other hand, there is static in the air. The static occurs, in most cases, because of a strong emotional response. Underlying pretense is fear or anger or sadness. By acknowledging pretense and recognizing the emotions that prompt individuals to pretend, we, in fact, learn even more about and from others. Our judgments about people will be more finely tuned because of this knowledge.

Fourth, *we must know what matters to others so that we may weave their hopes and dreams into the common goals of the group,* knowing that people will be motivated, will work at top levels, when they see that their own hopes may be realized. The visions of any group or organization can encompass the dreams of its members if we have taken the time to clarify what matters to them and to us, have made sense of what matters, and have woven all of the threads into the larger tapestry that describes the vision of the group.

Fifth, *we ourselves may stop pretending in our conversations with others.* We can say "I know" and "I don't know" with equal comfort when each is appropriate. We can admit areas of vulnerability and lack of knowledge. We can "talk without bullshit," as Larry says, and, like Tom, earn respect for our honesty. The winning strategy is to tell it like it is, or not to tell it at all.

Sixth, *we can avoid withholding information to prop up our own sense of control.* Although sometimes we may not tell others what we think because it is not clear in our own minds, it is not appropriate for the situation, or the information is not relevant to their concerns, we err when we withhold important information in order to strengthen our own sense of control. By choosing to maintain a spurious sense of control, we in fact diminish our influence with others in the organization. The real sense of control we seek is to be found only in not pretending, in making sense of the world, and in sharing with others.

Seventh, *we can speak out more often, perhaps making more mistakes, but learning from these mistakes.* We can accept that good communication, like everything else worthwhile, is only acquired through practice; thus we must talk and listen, sometimes misspeaking in order to learn how to communicate better, more clearly, and more appropriately. We must stumble and fall down before we can walk; we cannot learn by never trying.

Eighth, *we can increase our own comfort by remembering that no one else will pay as much attention to us as we do ourselves* and no one else is likely to be as critical of us as we are. In communicating with others, and in our behavior altogether, our mistakes may actually count for less with others than they do in our own imaginations. Consequently, we can try and try again. Not just once, but many times.

Ninth, *we can spend time talking and listening about things that matter* and avoid spending this time on things that do not. The fast-trackers talk and listen well—when the topic is important. They do not have much patience for rambling, irrelevancy, and self-indulgent speech. They know when someone is about to waste their time, just as they know when they might be about to waste their own. Consequently, good communication for the fast-trackers, and for leaders as a whole, is direct and to the point. Such communication must be clear both about what is and about what matters.

Again, it is important to stress that good communication is at the heart of organizational effectiveness, and is essential for success on the fast track. The reason all of those widgets went out the door in the past is because somebody talked to somebody else, designed a system, made it bigger and better, told other people how to use it, and attended to whatever problems arose. Circumstances changed, the market changed and competition got tougher; people talked about this with each other, and foresaw the end of the widget age and the beginning of the new techno-widget age. This transition itself occurred because somewhere, somebody talked to a whole lot of people, and a new idea was implemented and became reality. Those on the fast track tend to be the ones who talk and listen first, who know what changes have occurred, who forecast the ones yet to come, and who, by talking and listening, lead people into new industrial landscapes.

Communication is influence. By talking and listening to others, the fast-trackers each bring about significant changes in their immediate units or in the larger organization. Through good communication they motivate others, neutralize opposition, and persuade sufficient numbers of people to approve new projects and see them through to completion. As Larry points out, persuasion and influence are the key to organizational results. "If somebody thinks he has to *command* somebody else in order to get work done, that guy is not a leader," he says emphatically.

Leaders—and these fast-trackers—are excellent communicators. In their communications they clarify the nature of the game to be won. In other words, they identify the goals that matter and how they can be attained, and elicit commitment to playing this game and achieving the end results. They do not command; they talk and listen, persuade and influence.

All communication influences others: good communication increases understanding and enlarges the knowledge base on which decisions are made; poor communication creates distortions in others' perceptual worlds and decreases the chance that decisions will have a sufficient knowledge base. In well-functioning organizations, communication channels are open and information flows freely through the organization. The reverse is true in ineffective organizations.

The importance of communication cannot be overstated. All leaders of people are masters of the art of communication. They know how to get their point across. They know how to draw on the wells of untapped motivation that lie within people. Leaders communicate their vision of what is possible, demonstrate what is attainable, and motivate others to work toward those goals in which they believe. Communication determines whether or not a leader will succeed or fail in moving an organization toward effectiveness. The fast-trackers, above all, know how to talk and listen well.

CHAPTER 15

On Charting a Course

In my work environment the best way to gain acceptance of a new idea or a different way of doing things is to communicate the suggested change to the people who will be affected by it. I give them as many details as I can because it is their work and they are the real experts. . . . I bring the entire group together and then I bring a flip chart to write down their concerns so that I can give them feedback at a later date.

GENERAL SUPERVISOR
GENERAL MOTORS
CORPORATION

Leaders not only clarify what matters for those who work with them, but demonstrate to their followers that doing what matters is indeed possible. In order to clarify what matters they must be open to information about themselves, and others, and they must think about that information until a pattern of priorities emerges. In order to demonstrate that doing what matters is possible, leaders talk with and listen to others and they develop a plan.

Frustration at work is usually the result of two irreconcilable sets of beliefs: (1) things are not the way they should be; and (2) there is nothing I can do about it. Managers and their employees have both said again and again that if only *somebody else* would run things right, the world would be a better place. When asked why in fact they themselves don't act so as to "make things right" (whatever that means to them), each replies, "I can't." The transition from "I can't" to "I can" is achieved through the planning process.

To Chart a Course

1. Make realistic assessment of the current situation.
2. Discover what others want to see happen.
3. Build a common understanding in discussion with others.
4. Assess our people and determine who is likely to favor a plan and who is likely to oppose it.
5. Devise the actual plan itself.
6. Elicit commitment of all involved in implementation.
7. Begin to implement the plan.
8. Persist over time revising tactics when necessary.
9. Recognize that difficulties are opportunities for new learning.

All of the fast-trackers are leaders, though of different scope and scale depending on their relative position and seniority. All people who acknowledge themselves and others as they are have stepped onto the fast track; by thinking about who they are, what they do well, and what is needed in the world-at-large, they select a direction on the fast track and identify the early landmarks along the way. In talking with others they develop a cadre of supporters who move along the track in concert with them, helping and being helped in turn. Yet only by identifying both the characteristics of the current situation and the more distant objectives, and by outlining the specific steps necessary to move from the present into the future do they increase the odds that they will continue to move along the track. Only by developing a plan is it possible to demonstrate not only to one's immediate supporters, but to all those coming along behind, that it is indeed worth the effort to go the next step, because the objective has been sighted and is within reach.

Sitting at Hal's desk I leafed through a stack of papers, recognizing some materials designed for projection to an audience as an accompaniment to a speech. One message was printed in large type on each page. Taken together, the pages spelled out a series of objectives leading to the changes Hal plans to bring about in his company. When I asked what was next, Hal responded that only now were they figuring out just how to implement these objectives. In other words they were still at the beginning and did not have a plan. The next week, sitting near Tom's desk I saw a similar stack of papers and turned them over one by one. In a different company, in a different part of the country, objectives were again listed in large type, one per page. Yet halfway through the stack a difference became apparent, because following the objectives the specific action to be taken was listed. "By August 16, in XYZ location, such-and-such will be in place . . ." "Are you on schedule?" I asked. "You bet," Tom replied. "It's happening!" Thus Hal was in the process of creating a plan for action, and only when he had accomplished this task could he demonstrate to the other senior managers that his dream was possible. Tom had already taken the next step, had shown that what he wanted to achieve was possible, and was in the middle of implementing his dream. A plan is essential for action. While one may still wonder if Hal will be able to create the changes that he believes in, one knows that Tom will do this. The difference is in the plan.

Almost anything we wish to do can be done if we commit the time and energy to making it happen. Once we make time and energy available, however, we still have to find the way to move from A to B. How do we arrange all the pieces so that starting at A, we arrive at B? How do we work our way through the mazes of support and opposition, resources and roadblocks, that open up in the wake of any new venture in any organization? How do we go from start to finish without giving up our dreams?

The fast-trackers know how this is done: first by being clear about the desired goal, and second by finding a way to make that goal a reality through strategy and planning. They do this by analyzing the component parts of the goal, and by measuring each one's similarity and dissimilarity to current organizational realities. Can part X of the overall goal be attained because it is similar to other activities of group A in the organization? Can part Y be attained by enlarging a project already undertaken by group B? Can part Z be shaped so that it attains some of the goals already acknowledged by either group A, B, or even C? What parts of the project beyond X, Y, and Z must be sold to others in the company? What are the varied timelines for achieving each component part? Within the total picture, what goals of how many different groups will be met by the accomplishment of this project?

The planning and analysis process is never accomplished in solitude or alone; new and continuing knowledge of others and the organization is needed so that current and up-to-date information is part of the process. All of this knowledge must be reshuffled and reorganized until the pieces begin to form a path from the present into the desired future. By talking and listening, new information must be sought, and commitment elicited, from others. These processes work together to demonstrate that it is possible to bring a new idea into the everyday reality of the organization.

Rich is emphatic about the importance of this process, and his philosophy of management hinges on the key factors associated with strategic planning. He elaborates on the benefits of planning that reach beyond the obvious. Having a plan makes clear, to all members of the company, the direction in which the company is moving. The process of creating this plan involves many people in the organization, and opens up new channels of communication and new topics of discussion, building teams where none existed before. Just having a plan, however tentative, is cause for meetings and discussion with other senior managers, resulting in the keeping open of important channels of communication. The planning process also focuses attention on current operations in new ways and highlights "holes" in the present setup, providing new insight on how to strengthen *what is* as well as to create *what will be*. Planning is central to the work of the fast-tracker and all who anticipate creating changes in organizations.

The plan itself requires:

- definition of goals and objectives
- assessment of one's people and material resources
- development of strategies to bypass possible roadblocks, and
- a means to elicit the necessary commitment of all involved.

Thus, those developing plans require both a broad organizational picture *and* the ability to break the large picture down into measurable steps. They require both conceptual and analytic skills. In order to elicit commitment, those involved in the planning process must also ask the following questions: "Can we make our plan relevant to the needs and desires of those in the company? Can we get approval for the plan? Can we motivate the people to accomplish the goals?"

A plan that demonstrates the possibility of achieving desired ends will elicit the commitment of at least some in the organization. Achieving small successes in implementing the plan will win over yet another group. It is not necessary for leaders to have a full commitment at the outset; significant ends are often achieved in a piecemeal fashion. It takes time to chip away at years of "it can't happen" and "it can't be." As a leader creates a plan, however, and communicates with others, the leader demonstrates that what is important can and will be done.

There are nine steps to follow in the planning process; although they are not always discrete from each other, each of the nine steps occurs along with, or in sequence with, the others:

First, *we must begin with a realistic assessment of the current situation*. We cannot pretend that it is other than it is. The only basis for initiating change is the reality of the present. Part of our knowledge is knowledge of the business, of the competition, of the marketplace. We must ask what is needed and what is being done. From this, we can begin to formulate an idea about what is necessary; it will then become our task to make the necessary possible.

Second, *we must discover what others want to see happen*, for only by meeting others' dreams will we elicit their full involvement. We find out what others want by watching and listening. We even help others to clarify what they want by listening and talking, listening and talking. Out of this interaction with others, as a result of the integration of business knowledge with human desires and dreams, we can shape the beginning of a direction.

Third, *we must build a common understanding of the situation in discussion with others* that will be the foundation for new teams able to work on the idea when it is ready for implementation. By talking with others, by building on their hopes as well as our own, we create a common perception or understanding among groups of people. Groups of people with common perceptions about things that matter *are*, in fact, teams.

Fourth, *we must assess our people and determine who is likely to favor this plan, and who is likely to oppose it,* as well as large numbers who will not be actively for or against at this point. A good proposal never pleases everybody; a proposal that pleases everybody is one that does not rock the boat nor make changes in the lives of many people. All of us are resistant to change, particularly change initiated by someone else. So any proposal promising to create significant change is likely to be opposed, at some point in the process, by those whose lives will be affected by the implementation of this plan. We must know our people. The attitudes and beliefs of the people involved in any idea probably have more impact on the final result than the idea itself. A bad idea can be reworked and revised by the involvement of committed people; a good idea will only die in the hands of those who are not committed to its achievement. We must be ready to devise tactical maneuvers to make the most of those who are committed to the idea and to diminish the impact of those who are opposed.

Fifth, *we must devise the actual plan itself* utilizing all our knowledge of the business and the people, our recognition of what is necessary and what is possible. Timelines must be blocked out, responsibilities assigned, and contingency plans developed to go around anticipated roadblocks. The actual planning requires that the goal be analyzed in terms of its component parts, and then that the process of achieving the goal be broken down into steps—all within the context of the total organization. The resulting plan will be logical and realistic *and* have the full commitment of many in the organization.

Sixth, *we must elicit the commitment of all of those who will now be involved in the implementation of the plan*. People become committed to goals and objectives because these ends meet perceived needs of their own.

These needs may be personal (the plan provides benefits for them) or more general (it serves an idea or a cause that they believe in). Those who sell their plans to others must show them how the implementation of this idea will make *their* dreams a reality, thus engaging their commitment.

Seventh, *we must take beginning steps to implement the plan.* We who lead such an effort have a primary task: to keep both the importance and the possibility of attaining specific objectives clearly visible to the people involved in the project. This is the essence of motivation. People work hard for those who can demonstrate that their work and their efforts matter. This is leadership.

Eighth, *we must persist over time, revising our tactics when obstacles are encountered.* Leaders in general, and fast-trackers in particular, do not lose sight of their vision when they run into inevitable roadblocks, but maintain the overall goal even while carrying out strategic retreats. Persistence more than any other characteristic is the one trait likely to lead to successful implementation of a new idea.

Ninth, *we must recognize that each difficulty encountered along the way is an opportunity for new learning.* While we learn relatively little from success, we learn much from perceived failure when events show us that our expectations have been out of line with reality. Recognizing difficulties as learning opportunities means that the next plan will be even better than the current one, and that even greater visions may be implemented in the future than in the present. Continual learning speeds the journey along the fast track.

High levels of self-awareness, ability to work with others to create an effective team, and persistence in seeing a project through to the end are the components that create an aura of success for all those working on bringing a new idea into reality. Each of the fast-trackers has fallen heir to an image of success, even though each has undoubtedly met with a fair share of failure along the way. The fast-trackers have done what they set out to do. They can be relied upon by others. Their words, their directions, carry weight. By giving allegiance to these fast-trackers, their followers increase the chances that their personal goals will be realized (they too will learn from being part of a successful team). Each of the fast-trackers is thus what Hal calls "a natural leader." "How," I asked, "can you identify a natural leader?" Hal replied simply: "Others follow him."

CHAPTER 16

On "Going for the Gold"

*I ask how I can make something work and then I do
it. If I can't make it work, I dump it.*
LARRY
MID-LEVEL FAST-TRACKER

*I followed my dream. There was setback after
setback. Now we are beginning to break even.*
TOM
SENIOR FAST-TRACKER

When the fast-trackers tell stories about their personal history, all the
way back to their early years, they talk about what *they have done*—and
they have done a lot. In childhood they delivered papers, shoveled walks,
raked leaves, and helped paint houses. In adolescence they dug holes for
big construction projects, turned hamburgers at fast-food chains, sold a
variety of retail products, and served food in restaurants. In their adult
lives, they created new concepts, established new management precedents,
reorganized plants and other facilities, and dramatically increased the
productivity of their units. They are where they are because of what they
have done. They think, talk, listen, plan, and then act. And when they
move into action, all systems are go, nothing is held in reserve. They go for
the gold.

The process leading to action involves gathering knowledge, thinking, talking with others, and planning. When action follows upon the heels
of this process it is most likely to bring about the desired outcome. If it does
not bring expected results, the process itself will point to alternative steps
that might achieve the overall goal. When we follow through, from the
initial steps of gathering information to the final stages of implementation,
we spend our energy well. We may attain the original objective slowly or

To "Go for the Gold"

1. Prepare for what we are about to do.
2. Proceed on course without reservation.
3. Not complain about limitations and restrictions.
4. Revise tactics and timetables to account for new information.
5. Acknowledge that goals may need revisions.
6. Adapt course of journey to accommodate significant dreams of others.
7. Accept contributions of and share credit with others.
8. Assume responsibility for what we have done and for what we have not done.
9. Know that achieving our destination only marks the beginning of the next journey.

quickly, directly or indirectly, or not at all. But we have given it our best shot and, if we have learned along the way, we will have greater success in our next ventures. Success in attaining an objective is always a matter of playing the percentages. By preparing well for action, we increase the odds that we will succeed. We up the percentages, and cannot hope for more.

When we act without preparation, or prepare for action and do not act, we lower our chances of success. We are investing energy in and placing our bets on processes that are themselves incomplete. There are sufficient factors outside of our control that may mitigate against our success, so that we do not need to add more by neglecting to prepare fully. Even when we go through the entire process—gathering knowledge, thinking, discussing, planning and acting—we have no guarantee of a successful outcome. First, we may have insufficient knowledge, or insufficient practice in necessary skills, to achieve our desired ends. Second, there are many factors beyond our control in any process involving a considerable amount of time or people. We can choose how we might respond to these factors, but we cannot command them.

Action is a learning process. If we discover in the process that our knowledge or our skills fall short, we know what we must learn before we try again and we have, in acting, already increased our level of expertise by adding to the amount of time we have practiced certain skills. We need only to be willing to admit our shortcomings in order to profit from this experience. When external forces introduce new variables into the situation, changing the intended outcome, we can learn to make more room for the play of chance in our planning processes, to allow for the unpredictable and to take into account the complexity and diversity of life. When we fail to act we miss opportunities for learning and development. When we act and fall short of our expectations, we have created new opportunities to learn.

The fast-trackers have earned the respect of their colleagues because of what they have done. From the fast-trackers we can learn how to act well. We can learn how to prepare for action and then to act, without reservation. When we act with needless reservations, denying with one hand what we do with the other, we are hedging our bets; we are holding back in the face of uncertainty—and life is always uncertain—to avoid taking responsibility for our actions.

The chief characteristic of leadership *is* responsibility, and to act is to be responsible. However, we often fail to see that not to act is also to be responsible—for what we *might* have done. We may say it doesn't matter, and so do nothing. Yet doing nothing is also significant and just like doing something, doing nothing counts in the final equation of what makes a difference in the world. We can try to avoid responsibility for the way things are; once we choose to act, however, we have to consciously accept that responsibility.

Further, the result of successful action is more responsibility. Leaders (those who have acted successfully) accept the fact that what they do is tallied up as significant in the world's balance. In addition, one of their chief functions is to instill this belief in their followers, helping them to recognize the significance of their actions. Leaders clarify the goals that are to be sought, and define each worker's contribution to the larger picture. In this way, they create meaning for themselves, and for others. They see and communicate the importance of each individual action in terms of the larger goal. What they do matters, and they show other people that what *they* do matters as well. They highlight the significance of everyone's contribution to the task.

Having stepped onto the high-speed course, chosen our direction, joined with others, and set our objectives, we are now ready to move forward with the accelerator on and the brake off. After all, it is action that speeds us along the fast track. We are aware that the outcome is not guaranteed; that whatever we do in the present cannot insure the future; that we are in charge of ourselves but cannot control the situation as a whole; that even without full control, we nonetheless accept responsibility for the outcomes of our action. We know, moreover, that we will make a difference in the world. We can recapitulate this process in a series of steps:

First, *we prepare for what we are about to do*. We accept life as it is, sort out what matters, work closely with others, and take the time to develop a plan. Then we are ready to go.

Second, *we proceed on our course without reservation.* Once on the road we do not press the accelerator and the brake at the same time. We do not delude ourselves that half-effort on our part means being only half accountable. We accept the uncertainties of life, and go all out for what we have decided to do.

Third, *we do not complain about the limitations and restrictions we encounter.* Such limitations only require that we focus our energy more clearly along certain paths, that we manage our time more carefully, and that we think more inventively about our course. Limitations highlight our priorities and focus our energies. We do not let them stop us completely or keep us from our goal.

Fourth, *we revise our tactics and our timetables to account for new information* without losing sight of the goal. We recognize the difference between tactical maneuvers and long-term objectives and do not confuse the two. Thus, we may regroup along the way but not lose sight of our goal.

Fifth, *we acknowledge that even our goals may be transformed along the way* and that considerable new information may cause a larger reevaluation of our aims and purposes. However, the goal was initially defined as one way to approach a more global aim, a larger vision. We may, once in a while, have to cast this vision into a new form and give different outlines to our goals. The ultimate outcomes that we seek may be achieved in a variety of different guises.

Sixth, *we are willing to adapt the course of our journey to accommodate the significant dreams of others* who take the journey with us. Individual dreams and priorities are the foundation of the larger vision and such dreams demand our time, attention, and recognition when such does not conflict with ultimate achievement of the larger aims.

Seventh, *we accept contributions of and share credit with others* along the way, recognizing that it is more important to get where we want to go than to be acclaimed for our efforts. Success lies in achieving the objective, not in wearing the crown of victory.

Eighth, *we assume responsibility for what we have done and what we have not done,* recognizing the impact of our actions on others, knowing that both what we do and what we don't do is counted in the balance. Although often perceived as a burden, we shoulder the responsibility that accompanies action—the responsibility that is the mantle of leadership.

Ninth, *we know that achieving our destination only marks the beginning of a new journey,* and that what we have learned is not a final accounting but only a foundation for future growth. We know that the responsibility we have just shouldered will grow considerably in the future and that any success is merely the groundwork for a new and bigger challenge. Yet we are equal to the task.

The journey along the fast track is not an easy one. It is lined with uncertainties and weighed down by responsibility. Yet in their encounters with self and others, in the interplay of limitations and possibilities, and in their achievement of goals along the way, the fast-trackers find joy in their work and in their relationships. All of us may not choose to move along this track, but all of us can.

When and if we choose to move along the fast track we will find ourselves, like the fast-trackers, shifting gears frequently. Life on the fast track is not all work and no play; the fast-trackers lead complex lives and are involved in a variety of activities, and strongly invested in primary relationships. The complexity of their lives, in fact, is essential for movement along the fast track. Thus, one of the lessons we must learn is that to stay on the fast track, we cannot lose our momentum. We cannot let down all the way after each eight-hour day. We cannot move from an active mode to a passive mode with any regularity and not burn up unnecessary energy. Instead, we must shift gears as we shift to different spheres of activity, maintaining a moderate to high level of energy. We need to always maintain a state of readiness for what might happen, an openness to opportunities, which would not be possible if we indulged with any frequency in a passive mode. The fast-trackers stay revved up most of the time. They find their rest and relaxation, their sense of refreshment, in shifting from one activity to another, in moving between worlds.

None of us sustains a continuous focus on only one activity, nor constant attention in a particular direction, remaining unflaggingly alert to all the possibilities that exist. On the road, for some unbroken stretch of time, we all suffer from highway hypnosis. In continuous contact with others at work or at home, we take things about other people for granted and fail to be sensitive to new possibilities that may be emerging. Remaining attached to an idea over time, without letting go and stepping back, we lose our excitement, perceiving only the mundane and trivial or the grandiose and overwhelming; in each case, we lose the energizing force of contrast. In never leaving, we cannot return. Remaining in the same place, we cannot perceive anew. Consequently, we must break our stride, change our pace, and shift gears into another place and time in order to make the most of what matters.

The fast-trackers shift gears frequently. One raises horses, another gardens, a third collects folk art, and many are involved in recreational sports. In addition, and of primary importance, the fast-trackers are invested in their relationships, in their wives and husbands and the activities of their children. In many different arenas, the fast-trackers *act*: they do things and take responsibility for what they do. Having sorted out what matters, they make what matters possible. In acting on their beliefs, they make a difference in the world. The fast-trackers are all comfortable with the phrase "I can." They do not say "I can't." As they mature through higher developmental levels and progress through the three phases of their careers, their "I can" applies to bigger and bigger worlds. Everyone who is willing to stop pretending, make sense of their knowledge, communicate with others, plan and then *act* will experience the sense of capability and of power that is common to all of those on the fast track. Those who say "I can" make a difference in the world.

CHAPTER 17

On Summing It Up

> *. . . the role of leader, then, is one of orchestrator and labeler taking what can be gotten in the way of action and shaping it—generally after the fact—into lasting commitment to a new strategic direction. In short, he makes meanings.*
>
> THOMAS PETERS AND
> ALAN WATERMAN
> *IN SEARCH OF EXCELLENCE*

The last step of the leadership process is the key to continued growth and learning, and only by continuing to grow can fast-trackers avoid derailment or sidelining. Having progressed through the early phases to the action phase, leaders are now ready to evaluate what has happened: to sum up the pluses and minuses of their accomplishments; to draw from a particular experience the generalizations and principles that will allow them to meet even greater challenges in the future. In summing up, leaders evaluate the past to prepare the ground for the future. In this process, they stand accountable for the difference they have created in the world.

The evaluation process together with the actions preceding it consti-tute the essentials of the third task of managerial leaders: to create a difference in their environments. If all of the phases of the leadership process have been completed, the leaders will have first clarified what matters and will then have made it possible. They will have given up pretense; identified sense-making patterns from their knowledge of them-selves and others; talked with and listened to their co-workers; involved them in the planning process. Then by acting and evaluating their actions, they will have created a difference in their organizations, changing *what is*

To Sum Up

1. Recognize that evaluation is necessary for further growth.
2. Assess what we have done: what worked and what did not.
3. Determine what individuals and what individual skills were critical in achieving specific outcomes.
4. Assess the specific situation that contributed to the outcome.
5. Go deeper and understand general principles of human behavior which led to specific outcomes.
6. Imagine transferring our learning to other situations.
7. Recognize that this process of evaluation yields a philosophy.
8. Anticipate that each new position will make greater demands upon us.
9. Accept that we must constantly look beneath the surface, draw out the guiding principles and apply them again and again to new and more important situations.

into *what can be*. This process in its totality then becomes the foundation for new acts of leadership on an even grander scale.

The fast-trackers talk freely about the pluses and minuses of their past actions. They are willing to admit how much they learned from experiences they viewed negatively at the time of occurrence. Alec remembers his skirmish with co-workers at 18, in which he came out on the short end of the stick and had to quit his job. He has thought about this since, and is still thinking about it. By evaluating that situation many years ago he learned about the downside of organizational politics, and has been able to avoid similar situations in his career along the fast track. Hank has thought about and evaluated his more recent encounter with a difficult political situation, which resulted in the many months he spent "in limbo." By making sense of what happened at that time, he has drawn up some guidelines for his behavior in the present and the future. More alert to the sensitivities of others and more aware of the possible implications, he now acts to defuse potentially explosive patterns before they gel. Both of these experiences, originally perceived as negative by the two fast-trackers, resulted in increased sensitivity, understanding, and self-awareness, and led to behavioral changes that have increased the odds in favor of their ultimate success. In light of such circumstances it is hard to consider any experience that promotes learning and growth as truly negative. Perceived failure is often the greatest incentive for new growth and development.

We also learn from circumstances that are not negative at the time of occurrence. Stories from two of the senior managers show how their philosophies of management developed from the evaluation of certain experiences.

> Observing one of his mentors along the way, Jon first saw the benefits of being absolutely clear about expressing the company's course, and now believes in setting a clear direction and in communicating this directly and explicitly to all employees. He describes implementing his belief about clarity of direction in his first job as president of a subsidiary company: "I tried it and it worked!" He says of his next position as president of a larger company, "I did it again and this time I added communication groups throughout the company—they loved it!" In evaluating each of his experiences, Jon isolated the important elements of his behavior as a leader, transferred them to his next position, and added to them. In his next position, he will build upon all of his previous experience, refining his philosophy and modifying his behavior to both clarify the direction of, and broaden the base of communication through, an even larger and more diverse group of employees.
>
> A philosophy of management that can be applied to many situations has evolved for Rich as well, because he has thought about and evaluated his experiences. His first introduction to strategic planning occurred in a small division in which he had considerable personal contact with the employees. Strategic planning was central to his supervision of the merger of this division with another. However, he says, he did not see the full importance of strategic planning until he moved to a much larger division, in which his opportunities for personal contact with field managers and workers diminished greatly. He refined his ideas about strategy and planning while setting a direction with senior management, and established channels for communicating the message down through lower tiers of management for the workers themselves. Currently, in another new situation as president of an experimental enterprise, Rich is thinking about strategy again, and sifting out the central strands from his earlier experiences that are applicable to the new situation. In this new company the expectations of managers and workers are vastly different because they anticipate doing "new" things and are resistant to anything "old," whereas workers in his other company opted for the tried and true and resisted innovation. As he helps workers in his current company find a balance, his approach is causing him to rethink, reevaluate, and expand his understanding of strategy and planning. Although his principles are sound, their application to a new setting requires an adaptation of both belief and behavior, and provides another opportunity for essential growth and learning.

None of the fast-trackers has avoided the evaluation of his or her own behavior. Each is willing to look at past endeavors and to accept that in so doing one will find areas of weakness, areas of vulnerability. Yet each one knows, intuitively if not consciously, that this will always be the case. The fast-trackers' expectations are high and their behavior is unlikely to match these expectations on a day-to-day basis. Yet they must acknowledge their deficits, and still go ahead on the basis of their strengths, aware that they will come to the next accounting still falling somewhat short of their dreams.

Many of us resist the evaluation process because we do not want to look closely at our behavior, at what we might have done, might have been. All of us expect too much of ourselves. Anything we do is necessarily imperfect. We live in an imperfect world and are, ourselves, fallible human beings. We cannot *do* perfectly. Yet we are able to imagine perfection. We can see how something might be, if all things went well, and everything worked at peak levels. It is against our own imagined ideals of perfection that we measure ourselves. So in acting and in being imperfect we are already in touch, at some level, with a sense of falling short, of not being what we could be. To add to this a conscious process of evaluation often seems unfair. The process of evaluation, after all, will only reveal what we hope is not true, yet know to be so.

However, by acting and then evaluating our actions, we set the stage for new learning. In action and through evaluation we create a difference in the world; in the action we accept responsibility, through evaluation we become accountable. Yet in our evaluation of what we do, we may find ourselves wanting, and this makes us uncomfortable. By not acting we may hope to avoid this discomfort; by acting and not evaluating our actions we avoid the confrontation between actual accomplishment and imagined ideals. When we allow this discomfort to hold us back from the phases of either action or evaluation, the world becomes poorer.

In fact, if enough imperfect people work together they can closely approximate our idea of perfection; and the effort that such imperfect beings make could mean the difference between survival and extinction, between victory and defeat. Actually, we have an obligation to owning up to who we are (imperfect human beings) and what the world is, and to justly assess our strengths, and to use these strengths to make the world better—no matter how uncomfortable we may be in the process.

Thus it becomes possible for all of us to make a positive contribution to the world at large. At the same time, however, it is necessary to recognize things that we cannot do, the situations we cannot change. Possibilities and limitations exist together in all people. If we are honest with ourselves and clear-eyed about the world, we can discriminate those aspects of things that are changeable from those aspects that are unchanging, and direct our strengths toward those areas in which they will have the greatest impact. Because such discrimination requires acknowledging shades of gray, and requires fine-tuned judgment, many choose to simply ignore the possibilities. They assume their limitations are all-encompassing and say "it can't be done." In contrast, leaders on the fast track are willing to live with these complexities, ambiguities, and shades of gray. Leaders look at the world, assess both possibilities and limitations, and say, "I can."

Evaluation of our accomplishments marks each leg of the journey up the fast track. The process begins with self-knowledge and assessment of others; proceeds through establishing priorities, having discussions, planning, and action; and culminates with summing up what has been. The summing up is simultaneously an ending and a beginning. All individuals on the fast track recognize the steps that form the process of summing up:

First, *we recognize that evaluation is essential for further growth,* and that only those who continue growing stay on the fast track. Staying on the fast track requires that we assess where we have been in order to formulate better guidelines for where we are going. We may choose the measuring sticks that apply to us. For example, by entering a certain sphere of work we *choose,* in effect, to be assessed according to the standards of that workplace. Yet, regardless of the standards to be applied, we must accept that in our chosen spheres our abilities will be measured, and we must know that only by accepting the realities of measurement may we further our own growth.

Second, *we assess what we have done: what worked and what did not.* We take the time to look clearly at ourselves and at the results of our actions, weighing the positive results—those that enhance human life—against the negative—those that diminish the human enterprise in some way. We ask whether the good outweighs the bad, and reevaluate our actions in light of answers to this question.

Third, *we determine what individuals and what individual skills were critical in achieving specific outcomes.* If we can identify the characteristics, experiences, or skills essential for a successful outcome, are we able to train or develop these skills in others? Can we become more insightful in selecting individuals with the critical skills and giving them a major part in future actions? Through selection or training, can we increase the numbers of people able to move in this direction?

Fourth, *we assess the specific situation that contributed to the outcome of our actions.* Was the outcome, either success or failure, related in part to the place in which we were working, the nature of the organization, or the specific timing of our actions? Was the outcome, in other words, dependent on the timing or the setting of our actions? If so, can the important features of time and place be replicated in the future?

Fifth, *we may then go deeper and understand the general principles of human behavior that led to a specific outcome,* and in doing so, move beyond the specifics of individuals, place, and time to a deeper layer of understanding. By going to this depth, we may find ourselves elucidating general principles about human behavior that are widely applicable in many situations. We then leave behind the factors relevant only to specific individuals and organizations, growing in our awareness of human beings and their organizations.

Sixth, *we may then imagine transferring our learning to other situations* and imagine expected outcomes in these situations. As we do this we prepare ourselves to adapt or add to the lessons already learned. In our imaginations we test out what we will later enact in the real world, and thus prepare ourselves for what is yet to come.

Seventh, *we recognize that this process of evaluation, in fact, yields a philosophy* of management, a philosophic stance toward human beings as a whole, that is the mark of the senior managers in this study. We have through this process prepared ourselves for further leadership actions. We have learned invaluable lessons from the process of evaluation. Without evaluation, there is no philosophy.

Eighth, *we may anticipate that each position we accept will make new and greater demands upon us,* and that having a flexible, growth-oriented philosophy is essential to survival on the fast track. On the fast track we continually face new challenges, take on more responsibilities, and are accountable for the outcome of more and more influential actions. Only by making sense of what has happened in the past can we survive, let alone prosper, on this fast-paced course.

Ninth, *we must accept that we must constantly look beneath the surface, draw out the guiding principles, and apply them again and again to new and more important situations* for as long as we continue on the fast track. Whatever we learn will be the foundation of our future success. Continued growth and learning is the primary key to survival and success on whatever fast track we have chosen for our own life journey.

Leaders are measured by their actions, and by the impact they have upon their worlds. In assessing such impact, the responsibility of action is paired with the accountability of evaluation. If we are to follow the precepts of many of the fast-trackers, we are charged with leaving the world a better place than we found it. As we work toward this goal, we assess at each leg of the journey what we have done, why events transpired as they did, and what characteristics were essential in achieving the desired ends. As we do this, we identify basic principles of human behavior and cast them in a shape that becomes our own philosophy of leadership.

If, on the other hand, we choose to operate without following all the steps of leadership development, we may in fact create good in the world quite by chance; however, since we do not know what happened for sure or why it happened, we are as likely to undo this good as to build upon it in our next series of endeavors. Only those actions subjected to examination are likely to become the foundations of a continuing and enduring contribution to the world. What we did once (consciously) we very likely may do again, utilizing our strengths to contribute to the ultimate welfare of others.

Once we know what, who, where, and why we have created a philosophy. The philosophy places our actions in a large context and gives meaning to our own work and that of all the others who may follow us. The senior fast-trackers have developed an encompassing organizational philosophy over time, and are inspiring and empowering their people as they lead them to seek new meanings in work. The mid-level managers have parts of a philosophy in place and are filling in the empty spots as they work through the ambiguities of the Executive Transition. The junior managers are at a beginning point, still more concerned with themselves than with the larger organization. If they continue on the fast track, they will, however, eventually tease out from their experience the principles and generalizations that allow them to move into the ranks of senior management.

Each of these fast-trackers, and each of us who develops our capacity for leadership, will have some day developed a philosophy of leadership that gives new meaning to the world, awakens latent hopes, and inspires a higher level of productivity among the many who work alongside of us. With the full development of a philosophy—derived from being and thinking about who we are, talking, listening, planning, and acting—we will have arrived at the point where each of us may make a positive difference in our organizations and in the world at large.

EPILOGUE

The Fast-Trackers Today

*Indeed, the first rule of survival is clear: Nothing is
more dangerous than yesterday's success.*
ALVIN TOFFLER
THE ADAPTIVE CORPORATION

In writing this book, the stories of the seventeen fast-trackers were the
basis for creating a framework for understanding careers along the fast
track. The fast-trackers were portrayed as creators and contributors,
skyrocketing through the stage of junior stardom, rockily bumping along
through the Executive Transition, and emerging onto the stage of senior
statesmanship, anchored by a comprehensive philosophy, to lead large
groups of people. Creators have been described as more focused on people,
and consequently leading more turbulent personal lives because of the
attention focused on this dimension of their lives. The contributors were
viewed as more focused on task—and, once established, maintaining a
more stable set of relationships in their personal lives. Both groups,
moreover, were viewed on the road to leadership as they developed and
integrated substance and style in their approach to their careers. Does this
framework for understanding the stories of the fast-trackers help us to make
sense of their current experiences as well as their past experiences? Does
this description of the lives of fast-trackers have any predictive value?

In order to answer these questions, all of the fast-trackers were
contacted by telephone approximately one year after the first interview and
asked to describe (1) significant events of the last year, (2) any consequent
revisions in their career aspirations, and (3) their key learnings from their
experience. The fast-trackers responded with their usual clarity about the
events of the last year and their reflections upon these events. The events
themselves were varied and perceived as either major or minor, positive or

negative, in terms of their progress along the career track. These descriptions provide us with some new information about the fast-trackers and with a way to test the expectations about their future progress that are implicit in the message of this book. From the fast-trackers' second interview we learn, in fact, more about survival on the fast track.

EXPECTATIONS ABOUT THE FAST-TRACKERS

The message of this book is the basis for generating a set of expectations about how the fast-trackers will fare in the future. Clearly, these expectations cannot be used to *predict* either survival or derailment on the fast track for specific individuals. Rather, they establish certain courses as likely possibilities for the fast-trackers in general, for creators and contributors, and for those at different stages of the career path. These expectations might be described as follows.

First, we might expect that no specific event, perceived positively or negatively, would foretell the fast-trackers' future success. The fast-trackers' careers have clearly not proceeded in a linear fashion but they have zigzagged up their corporate pyramids, sometimes with long stops along the way. Even temporary derailment, as in Hank's case, did not prohibit future upward movement. The end results of the fast-trackers' journeys are not foretold by any single event or even any set of associated events within a given time period. The fast-trackers are *en route* and have not arrived: moving up, down, and sideways at any point in time always remain as possibilities.

Second, although the key factor in the success of the fast-trackers cannot be encapsulated in a single event, it is clearly associated with an openness to learning from experience along the way. We might expect, therefore, that the fast-trackers will continue to succeed in one manner or another as long as they are willing and eager to continue learning, as long as they do not pull a switch and stop making sense of their experience. This means that they cannot rely on the guidelines offered by yesterday's success but must take a new sounding of their current experience and shape their action to meet ever-changing situations.

Third, survival on the fast track is related to continual learning about both substance and style, about knowledge of the business and knowledge of themselves, others, and patterns of interaction. In terms of the career stages, we might anticipate that the greatest emphasis would be placed on style for fast-trackers who are either approaching or transiting the difficult middle career stage.

Fourth, we might expect that creators would continue to build something new at work. At home (particularly in mid-life), they would be more likely to institute changes in their family settings via divorce and/or remarriage. At the same time, the contributors would continue to make things more effective at work and would maintain stability at home as they have done in the past.

Fifth, we would expect differences in the perceptions of success of those in different stages of their careers: the junior stars, focused on the substance side of the leadership equation, might be expected to feel very good about themselves and their careers; those in the middle years, coming to terms with the importance of style as a leadership component, might be expected to take a grimmer view of their prospects; finally, the senior statesmen, having achieved an integration of substance and style, might be expected to emphasize substance and style equally as they view the corporate scene from the top of their particular company.

The fast-trackers, then, might be expected to reveal a variety of outcomes one year later. Although the individual uniqueness of the fast-trackers would still be paramount, certain patterns might be expected to emerge in various subgroups: We would expect more changes in personal lives for creators, and more of a downbeat about career progress from those in the middle, as opposed to the junior and senior career stages. Are these expectations borne out in the second interviews with the fast-trackers? What, in fact, is it that they have to tell us?

THE FAST-TRACKERS ONE YEAR LATER

In general, the experience of the fast trackers in the present confirms the expectations we have drawn from their past. By and large they are surviving on the fast track and they are excited about what they are learning—both about the business and themselves. The one divorce and impending remarriage is that of a mid-career creator, and his remarriage will mean that five of the eight creators and three of the four mid-career creators will be living in a second marriage. The bleakest views of career prospects also come from the mid-career group, from one creator and two contributors, who are "sniffing out possibilities" in other companies. In fact, not only the mid-career group but the seniors and the juniors are easily grouped by the similarities in their reflections on the past year. The senior statesmen present the most holistic viewpoint of corporate events and thus present a good starting point for summarizing the current perceptions of the fast-trackers.

The Senior Statesmen

The five senior statesmen responded to the questions in a like manner, each of their responses reflecting the *integration* of their thinking about their work and personal lives and about the people- and task-oriented factors in their work experience. In addition, they did not separate their own personal career path from the welfare of the organization as a whole; in this sense, their thinking was organizationally rather than individually centered. Overall, their responses reflected concerns of both *substance* and *style*, yet not viewed as separate components but rather intertwined.

All of them perceived their organizations as doing well—two of the senior men in the face of what were perceived as severe external difficulties for the organization. They were excited and enthusiastic about the possibilities for their companies to either forge ahead to new heights or to confront and deal with the blows struck by a turbulent economy. Each of these fast-trackers identified strongly with his organization. The organization and not the person was the subject of almost all responses.

Rich talks about the siege he and his organization have been through in the last year and the learnings that have come from this. "This year," he says, "I had to dig down deep inside myself, decide what really mattered, then put my head down and keep going. What is exciting, is that it works!" He goes on to say that he and his company are now a lot stronger because they went through this experience together. "We learned a lot about what we are trying to do. We have come out on a new level, on a new plateau, and have a better foundation than ever. I don't think it ever gets easy," he continues, "each step raises new issues and new hurdles to overcome."

In a similar vein but in less troubled circumstances, Hal says he has developed a different perspective on his company. The change he has worked to bring about is finally occurring. "I can *see* the change now— more importantly, I can *feel* the change." But this learning has not come without hardship, and he comments later that he has also become aware of how *really* difficult it is to change attitudes and behavior and he is still searching for the best process with which to produce "an awakening among all the people."

Tom is enthusiastic about the ability of his division to meet the challenges of a highly competitive environment: "I see evidence of major, major change in my organization in terms of people factors. People are much more attuned to our common vision. This is moving faster than I thought it would. I feel like we're ahead of schedule. These changes are heartening and are the essence of the year for me."

Andrew and Jon are again, as they were in the original interviews, relatively brief in their responses—focusing slightly more than Rich, Hal, and Tom on the task factors in their business environments. Yet both of them, in different ways, are excited and enthusiastic about the changes that are occurring in their respective companies. Andrew, close to the top of a corporation embroiled in current difficulties, is excited about the recognition of these difficulties throughout the huge corporation and the commitment and speed with which both staff and operational units are responding to the challenge posed by the environment. In contrast, Jon's company is doing well and he expands enthusiastically on the possibilities for long-term growth and profitability. He concludes by saying, "I'm still excited about my job; that's the bottom line."

These statesmen were nearly as quick, however, to mention events in their personal as in their organizational lives, and to see these events as having both stressful and uplifting consequences. Illness in Rich's family, devastating in itself, is drawing the family together in new ways. Personal business losses, outside the corporation, led Hal to reaffirm the importance of supervision and to recognize the dangers of over-delegation, and he is using all his business knowledge to help his wife develop her own business—an exciting experience, he says. Hal is also involved in rebuilding his house and is enthused about the process. Jon is thrilled to have a new baby but dismayed that this has severely limited his wife's travel time with him, and he is consequently finding his job-related travel more burdensome. Tom describes strengthened relationships with wife and son and believes that he is bringing a new measure of integrity into his life. In each case, the personal experiences of these men have generated new growth and learning that affect their work as well as their personal lives.

Rich, Andrew, and Jon identify their own aspirations totally in terms of prospects for their corporation and do not mention their own aspirations separately from a prognosis for the corporation as a whole. Hal and Tom do mention their individual aspirations specifically. Hal, however, discounts these aspirations by affirming that he feels more rewarded by making a difference in the company than by any thought of future promotions. Yet, the excitement he is finding in his work he now plans firmly to recreate— either in his own company or in a second career. Tom allows that he is more open to new possibilities within the company than before and that he might, in fact, be willing to create a new vision at another level of the corporation. "I'm more open," he says, "to staying around and working for the company I love."

In short, the balance and integration reflected in the responses of the senior fast-trackers exemplify once again the balance of *substance* and *style* in their thinking and behavior. Their responses reflect an awareness that good and bad experiences are both grist for the mill of learning, that the good and the bad are often paired in life, that tasks are accomplished because of people, not things, and that there is a strong relationship between one's life at work and at home.

The Mid-Career Managers

The managers moving through the difficult Executive Transition *differentiated* the components of their responses to each question more clearly, perceiving their own individual career track as separate from the business as a whole, and distinguishing business knowledge from personal considerations. Most of them remarked separately on issues related to *substance* and *style*—unlike the senior statesmen.

Moreover, in discussing changes in the business, five of the eight (in contrast to only two of the five seniors) perceived their companies as in trouble or their own job situations as not meeting their expectations. Although they balanced their negative reviews of their companies with positive ones, the negative and the positive were not seen as opposite sides of the same coin, but rather as separate and distinct threads in the tapestry shaping their work lives. Moreover, their responses centered on their business experience, and only three mentioned events in their personal lives. Yet for one of the three, Ken, personal life changes were paramount.

When asked about their expectations, most of the senior fast-trackers had responded first in terms of the prognosis for their company. The mid-career fast-trackers, however, responded first in terms of the possibilities for their own career paths. Further, within this group of eight there were three small groupings: two who saw themselves as still on an upward path, three who were committed to maintaining their current positon for at least two years making no predictions about career movement after that time, and three who saw themselves as stalled in their current position and who were looking for jobs elsewhere. This was the only age and career group, moreover, that perceived, at least momentarily, their own careers on a potential downhill slide.

In describing their learnings from this year, the mid-career managers (with the exception of Ken) mentioned specific learnings about the business—they gained both breadth and depth of business knowledge—yet more frequently mentioned learnings about people and about themselves specifically.

The first group is composed of Hank and Larry, who were both enthusiastic about their career possibilities. Each is president of his own division: Larry has continued in his post as head of an innovative division and has established this division on a solid footing this year; Hank has been promoted to president of a major division and foresees further movement if he succeeds in his new job. In describing their learnings from this past year, both show some of the integration reflected in their seniors' responses: Larry expounds upon the difficulties in a start-up effort—how hard it is to create change in *any* organization—and concludes with a list of the personal characteristics (patience, discipline, and self-control) he has acquired in the process; Hank, from a different point of view, talks about the changes required in his own management style as he has quintupled the numbers of his employees and must now develop new strategies of communication in order to reach all of his people. Each of these men is beginning to develop the identification and integration characteristic of the senior statesmen.

The second group includes the three managers who did not anticipate immediate promotions but were still content with their careers. Two of them are working in companies that have experienced considerable up-heaval in the last year, and both are in divisions that have continued to show a steady growth and profit. One whose experience has been particularly uncertain this year due to the business environment has found that circumstances in his work have been particularly rewarding in reaffirming his own beliefs. He is delighted that "perseverance and the right cause are winning the day." Another one, in a less-troubled setting, has expanded the influence of his division into new areas, and has spent more time coaching others ("I do a lot of missionary work," he says). Only slightly disap-pointed at missing an anticipated promotion, he concludes, "I love what I do."

Ken, the third member of this group, is the most enthusiastic about the state of the business. He describes what is important to him about the business now: "We're just learning how to be successful, we're flying up the learning curve." However, he is not anticipating any immediate moves as a result of these changes, assumes such a move is somewhere in the future, and says, "I wouldn't be shattered if I were passed over—but I don't expect that to happen." This is, for all three, a time of growing in the job without any expectations of imminent promotions. Ken, is the only one of the mid-level managers who are either moving up or consolidating their current positions to discuss his personal life at all, and for Ken, his personal life is central this year. He is making the same decision that four of the other creators made when they were in the mid-career years: divorce and remarriage. These personal changes are forcing a reevaluation of his life and he exudes a new exuberance:

The biggest change has been taking control of my life and my expectations. I realized I had very high aspirations on the career side and very low aspirations on the personal side. I had it backwards, in fact, so I began making some changes. There were difficult decisions to be made and it was hard to implement these decisions. But it's been tremendously exciting — a wonderful experience and I am beginning to enrich my personal experience in other ways as well. And I've done this without losing sight of things at work. I didn't know that was possible.

Finally, the third small subgroup of mid-career managers is composed of the three fast-trackers who were striking a particularly downbeat note about their organizations and their careers. Each described the narrowing of "windows of opportunity" in their respective companies. Two of them had watched as an expected promotion went to another manager rather than themselves. All three are in the job market, seeking a position that might better meet their needs. With the exception of Ken, the only other mentions of personal events came from this group as they reflected on the effect that a major job change might have on their families.

All three of these individuals were clearly learning from the disappointments they had confronted this year. One spoke of the strong reminder he was receiving about the role of circumstance in human lives and the need for sustained self-confidence in the midst of disheartening circumstances. Another emphasized the importance of learning patience in confronting issues and people in a troubled division of a big corporation, and the need for continual reevaluation and testing of perceived truths. Finally, Brian comments on a learning common to many of the young mid-level and older junior people when he states that: "I never realized that peoples' perceptions and communications have as much to do with business outcomes as the work itself." Patience and reevaluation are keywords for this career stage, now forcefully placed in the forefront for these mid-career managers just as they were in Hank's and Larry's lives in parallel circumstances only a few years ago.

The learnings of this last group illustrate the increased emphasis on style, in contrast to substance, that is the focus of those in mid-career. Perceptions, communication, patience are as important as the work itself. The fact, however, that new emphasis must be placed on the style side of the leadership equation does not, in any way, predict the future. These troubled mid-career individuals may learn from their experience and soar on to new heights as did Hank and Larry, or they may choose otherwise and move onto other tracks in other worlds. The choice is largely their own.

The Junior Stars

Those still on the early rungs of their career ladders were the most positive and least negative of any of the groups. None of them comment at any length on severe business difficulties, even though these young stars represent the same companies whose ills were catalogued by the mid-career and senior fast-trackers. All of them perceive themselves still on an upward slope. In describing the recent events in their lives, moreover, three of the four make easy reference to their personal as well as business experiences. In their responses, these junior people reflect an awareness of the importance of both work and personal concerns, task- and people-oriented issues, yet, at this stage each of these dimensions remains in its own distinct category.

None of the junior people perceives his or her career as endangered. Alec, in the most senior position of the four junior stars, perceives his job as a steady learning process. Sandra and Sam have both been moved to jobs with more responsibility within the last year, and Sam has made such moves twice. Each of them anticipates promotions within the next year. Pete, on the other hand, has decided to consolidate his current position and work steadily with others in his network. He plans, he says, "to stay in the back seat for about two years" before heading further up the ladder.

Whereas most of the mid-level people talk about new business learnings, only Sam among the juniors places much emphasis upon the knowledge gained in the business. The others talk about learnings in the people sphere and in terms of themselves. The growing awareness among much of this group that people skills will play a large role in future advancement is shown in Alec's somewhat caustic remark that, "I am spending more time in the care and feeding of my counterparts than I used to; a year ago I would have said that this was a waste of time." The preparation for the coming Executive Transition is underway and the older junior people are preparing themselves for the shift in focus that will come with this time.

The junior people, as frequently as the seniors, talk about personal concerns and describe a search for balance between their personal and family lives. Pete, for example, says he wants to see his wife more and is looking forward to a time when he will spend more time at home. To make sure this is not interpreted as his wanting to slack off, Pete says, "this means I will work closer to 50 hours a week instead of 70."

Still, it is clear that the junior people by and large have the luxury of focusing chiefly on substance—on learning the business. Only a beginning awareness is evident that getting the organization's work done does not just mean "doing work," but spending time building alliances, creating networks, and helping others climb with them to the top of the mountain.

LEARNING ON THE FAST TRACK

The framework for understanding the fast-trackers—creators and contributors in three career stages—works as well with the current activities of the fast-trackers as it did with their past. First, it is clear that the key to success, regardless of individual diversity and corporate upheavals, is tied into openness to continued experience, evaluation of this experience, and the consequent learning from experience. The continued enthusiasm about learning on the part of the fast-trackers fits with our sense-making framework. Second, the only major personal life change occurs in the experience of one mid-career creator, which is also in accord with expectations. It is the creators, not the contributors, who most often in mid-life have made dramatic changes in their personal relationships. Third, the only fast-trackers expressing outright dissatisfaction with their work and who are, therefore, exploring other job possibilities, are those who are in the risky mid-career stage. The challenges of this stage have been described as differing considerably in degree and nature from those of the junior and senior stages. Fourth, the senior fast-trackers continue to demonstrate the highest level of integration in their thinking, bringing together substance and style, their personal and work experience, and viewing problems and opportunities as opposite sides of the same coin. This accords again with the framework developed for understanding the lives of those on the fast track to the top.

Yet, the message here and elsewhere is that this is a life and a path without guarantees, and the final outcomes are not determined. Surviving on the fast track is not an easy course and requires a continual willingness to evaluate new information, reevaluate the past, and make new decisions. Yesterday's success is no predictor of tomorrow's achievement; and, on the other hand, today's disappointments are not predictive of tomorrow's defeat. As long as we are open to new learning and to using this learning for the betterment of others we will continually be faced with new challenges that test our strength. As Rich reminded us, each new step opens up new issues and reveals new hurdles that must be surmounted. Thus, the journey on the fast track is a process and there is no final and absolute destination.

If we remember the importance of both substance and style, and are not afraid to grow and learn, along with the fast-trackers we may create new worlds, make new things happen, and do something better than it was done before. All of these are functions of leadership—and we need many more leaders. Each time we increase our awareness, make sense of our knowledge, talk and listen with others, plan, and then *do something* we are adding incrementally to the sum total of leadership in the world and are increasing the odds that collectively we may all be on the fast track to personal satisfaction and career success. What's more, we neglect to do these things only at our peril, for the collective future lies in the hands of each one of us, not just in the hands of those who are on the fast track in major corporations. From them we may learn, but ultimately the responsibility is our own.

Appendices

DESCRIPTIONS OF THE FAST-TRACKERS

Each of the fast-trackers is described below in more detail than elsewhere in the book. Each description gives the fast-tracker's age, physical appearance, job description, and a brief career and personal history. Statistics on each of the fast-trackers are then given in the chart that follows.

Senior Statesmen

Rich is 52 this year; tall, slim, greying, and quiet in manner. He is currently the president of the most innovative division of a major corporation. He has arrived at this position after heading up small operations, then small divisions, and finally major ones within the company. He was the first child of three boys born to working-class parents who, in times of hardship, pooled forces in a family business. He was married soon after college, took his first job with his current company, left to spend four years in the service, and returned to the same job. He has five children: the eldest is working and now returning to college in the evenings; the other four are either pursuing professions or completing college degrees. His wife has supported him throughout his career, while pursuing her own artistic interests on the side.

Andrew is 51, a slight man of average height with grey hair and modest demeanor. He was promoted recently to a group vice-president of a very big corporation and is overseeing the interests of one part of the business from corporate headquarters. Andrew's career within the company has been one of slow but steady progress building upon his engineering background. He was an only child who grew up with his mother, grandmother, and his grandfather, who had his own small business. His grandfather became ill, was bedridden for several years, and then died during his adolescence. Andrew has four children, three of whom have gone to college and entered professional, generally scientific, careers. His fourth child is in elementary school.

Hal is 48, an exuberant, solidly built man of average height with a shock of greying reddish-blond hair. Currently, he is a senior vice-president of his company, working closely with the president to set the company's future directions. He has worked with this company since he interrupted a graduate school career in clinical psychology and has moved through various divisions quickly, often because of innovations that he initiated and implemented. He has an older brother and a younger sister. His father is a professional who in his seventies has just completed another advanced degree. His mother pushed him to do his best throughout his school years. Hal married for the second time in his thirties and and is the stepfather of a daughter who has just entered college. His wife is active in many volunteer organizations.

Tom is also 48, an almost flamboyant, enthusiastic man of average height and slim build with white, curly hair. He is vice-president of a division of a major company and has been instrumental in helping to set his division on its future course. The eldest of twin brothers born of parents who worked together in their prosperous small business, Tom went to college and spent four years in the service. He then joined this company— almost on a whim—and has stayed there ever since, promoted quickly at first, followed by a long plateau, and then rapid moves upward again. He was married soon after college and had three boys, the eldest of whom has survived physical handicaps to succeed in his college career, the middle one has just graduated from college, and the youngest is still in high school. Tom remarried in his early forties, a woman with one child who is also on the "ladder to the top" within the company.

Jon at 46, is a very tall, slim, grey-haired man, quiet in manner but exuberant about his currently growing family. He is vice-chairman of a major company, in charge of large areas of its operation, both at home and abroad. His career with the company has been a rapid climb—after a slow start—and he has moved directly toward the top of the corporation. Jon is the eldest of two sons of a father who was also a business manager. He has been married since the beginning of his career to a businesswoman who maintained her prosperous professional operation in another state for eleven years, commuting by plane on weekends. Now that he and his wife reside in the same place, they have begun a family and have two children, a toddler and an infant.

Mid-Career Managers

Art at 43 is a smallish, wiry man with close-cropped, iron-grey hair, who exudes a sense of energy and urgency both held in tight control. He is vice-president and general manager of a major division of a very large corporation. He joined this company in his late thirties, having moved rapidly through the ranks of another company on the basis of his outstanding sales ability. He is the second of two children of a mother who spent her life on welfare in an urban environment, and he is the only one of his immediate family or childhood associates who is actually earning his own living. Married after high school, his first wife supported him through a college degree, and guided him into the sales job that really began his career. Their two children, both boys, live with their mother. He has remarried a woman within his company and they are contemplating beginning a family of their own.

Larry, now 41, is a boyish, trim man of average height with light-brown hair and a wide grin. He is president of an innovative division within his company charged with bringing a new entity into being. He joined this company, almost by mistake, following a delayed college graduation, moving up rapidly then laterally for a time before his current assignment. He is the second son of six children born to a farm family who all worked together in the family business. Kicked out of his first college, Larry went to work, married, and then began college again while working full-time. He and his wife have one son who is soon to begin college.

Hank at 39 is a large, prematurely gray man who looks older than his years. He is vice-president of a major division of his company. Beginning his career in another company, he reevaluated his goals when promised promotions were relatively slow and joined his current company. His rapid progress upward in this company was set back for a year just before his current assignment. He is the second of two children of parents operating a small business in a farm community. Following college and graduate school, he devoted himself to work for several years before marrying. His wife supports his career and pursues her own interests in the art field. They have no children.

Jerry, also 39, tall, solid, energetic, and red-haired, is the division manager of one operation in a large corporation. He began his career with this company immediately following college and has moved steadily forward since that time, although promotions have slowed in the immediate past. He is the eldest of four boys of a working-class family. He himself is the father of six children, the eldest about to enter college, and the husband of a wife who is just recently working part-time.

Ken, at 38, a tall, thin whirlwind of activity with light-red hair, is director of a large concern within his corporation. After completing college and an initial graduate degree, he ran his own business for three years while contemplating further graduate work. He chose not to return to school, and succeeded instead in a number of different positions that taught him his current business skills. He then joined a major company, moving only in the last five years to his current employer. He is the eldest of two sons of a plant manager and working mother. He is now married to a working wife and is engaged in a business with his brother-in-law. He and his wife have no children.

Don, also 38, is a boyish-looking, quiet, firm man with brown hair cut straight across his forehead. Beginning in a non-managerial slot, he rose through his company with record speed, becoming the youngest division manager in the firm. He is only slightly disconcerted that he has not moved upward since this last promotion. The second son of four children of working-class parents, his college career was interrupted by his father's death, and he has not yet returned to school to complete his education. He married soon after high school and has two girls now living with their mother in another state. He has remarried, a professional woman with a small child, who also has executive prospects and ambitions.

Christine at 37 is a pixie-like, small, blond woman with a direct gaze and a quiet manner. She has concentrated her energies on her career since joining her current company shortly after completing college. She is the second of two daughters of a professional father and non-working mother. She married her husband at the same time as she began her career and he supports her work strongly. They have no children.

Brian, 36 this year, is a small, active, red-haired man who is rarely still. He has moved into his current position as divisional manager only recently, on the strength of his innovative efforts that brought him company-wide visibility. He is the second son of four children of a military family—his father is at the top of the enlisted ranks. Following college, he succeeded in entering another company, excelled in all that he did, was dismayed by the promotion prospects, and finally succeeded in entering his current company where his talents have brought him early recognition. He is married and has no children.

Junior Stars

Sandra at 34 is a striking, tall, dark-haired woman who appears slightly older than she is. She was the youngest district manager in her system and was careful not to reveal her age, believing that her youth might be held against her. Still a district manager, she is now lobbying for an overdue promotion. The oldest of four children born to professional parents—both her mother and father had managerial positions—she was married following college and is the mother of a young daughter. Both she and her daughter now live with her second husband, a professional in her company.

Alec at 33, tall, dark, lanky with hair reaching down to his collar, is reserved and slow to smile. As a district manager in his firm, he is very young for his position, and widely regarded as much older than he is. His promotions have been rapid—now in three different companies—based on his success in creating and promoting innovative products. The second child and only boy of three children of a successful businessman father and non-working mother, he excelled in college and in graduate school, and walked into his first job almost immediately following completion of his second degree. He is married to a working wife with similar academic credentials. They have one daughter.

Pete, just 31, is a tall, slim, exuberant black man, who rarely stops either running or talking. The youngest in his operation to become a district manager, he is constantly moving, constantly talking, and constantly challenging and encouraging his people. He began his career with this company immediately following high school, got married, worked full-time, went to school full-time and finished his degree in four and one-half years. The second son of ten children, he worked in his father's business after school during the week and worked a second job on the weekends. His wife works full-time and is also the primary caretaker of their two young daughters.

Sam, at 30, is a short, friendly but intense man with wavy dark hair, who has moved rapidly through the ranks of three companies and is now being groomed for the next level position. He began his career after college

---

Statistical Description of the Fast-Trackers: Early Families

Name	Age In 1986	Parents In Household	Parents' Occupational Status	Age Difference Of Parents	No. Of Older Brothers	No. Of Older Sisters	No. Of Younger Brothers	No. Of Younger Sisters
Rich	52	2	Blue Collar	2	0	0	2	0
Andrew	51	1	Small Business	—	0	0	0	0
Hal	48	2	Professional	1	1	0	0	1
Tom	48	2	Small Business	2	0	0	1	0
Jon	46	2	Managerial	8	0	0	1	0
Art	43	1	Unemployed	—	0	1	0	0
Larry	41	2	Farming	1	1	0	2	2
Hank	39	2	Small Business	6	0	1	0	0
Jerry	39	2	Blue Collar	5	0	0	4	0
Ken	38	2	Managerial	1	0	0	1	0
Don	38	2	Blue Collar	3	1	0	1	1
Chris	37	2	Professional	1	0	1	0	0
Brian	36	2	Military	7	1	0	1	1
Sandra	34	2	White Collar/ Professional	5	0	0	3	0
Alec	33	2	Managerial	4	0	1	0	1
Pete	31	2	Blue Collar/ Small Business	6	1	2	0	6
Sam	30	2	White Collar	14	0	0	1	3

with much soul-searching about giving up his lucrative sports position. He is the eldest son of four children of a white-collar family. His retired father has now begun his own business and "will never stop working." He is married to a non-working wife (which is the exception among people he knows) and is the father of two small children.

———··◁∞▷··———

Statistical Description of the Fast-Trackers: Current Families

Name	Job Title	Age Entered Career Path	Age at 1st Marriage	No. Of Marriages	No. Of Children	No. Of Stepchildren
Rich	Divisional President	28	24	1	4	
Andrew	Corporate Vice-President	23	21	1	4	
Hal	Corporate Vice-President	24	25	2		1
Tom	Divisional Vice-President	27	24	2	3	1
Jon	Corporate Vice-Chairman	26	29	1	1	
Art	Divisional Vice-President	25	21	2	2	
Larry	Divisional President	24	22	1	1	
Hank	Divisional Vice-President	23	29	1	0	
Jerry	Divisional Manager	22	21	1	6	
Ken	Divisional Director	30	21	1	0	
Don	Divisional Manager	24	21	2	2	1
Chris	Divisional Manager	22	22	1	0	
Brian	Divisional Manager	22	34	1	0	
Sandra	District Manager	23	24	2	1	
Alec	Division Director	24	22	1	1	
Pete	District Manager	23	19	1	2	
Sam	District Manager	23	24	1	2	

———··◁∞▷··———

APPENDIX B
DESCRIPTION OF INTERVIEWS AND INTERPRETATIONS OF MATERIAL

It is important to identify the source of the material for this book very clearly and then to distinguish the different levels of interpretation that appear throughout the book. In response to a uniform questionnaire (see Appendix C), all of the fast-trackers were asked to outline their family, educational, and career histories and to talk about significant people along the way. They did so in interviews averaging three hours (the shortest was one and one-half and the longest six hours). Information was not transcribed nor was it written down by the fast-trackers. Notes were taken on the basic content, and specific and potentially important statements were set off in quotes within the notes. These were later transcribed.

Thirteen of the fast-trackers I met for the first time in the interview session. Four of the fast-trackers were individuals with whom I had had prior contact. Following the interview session I have been in contact with fourteen of the fast-trackers and have met on an occasional basis with about half of these individuals. Consequently, *most* but not all of the information in this book comes from the interview sessions. Some was gathered in consequent meetings or telephone calls initiated by the fast-trackers.

The information from the fast-trackers is of two kinds:

(1) *Quantitative or measurable data,* such as the numbers and ages of brothers and sisters, parental occupations and ages, date of career promotions, and so forth. No attempt was made to corroborate this information because of the assumption that it was relatively accurate as it stood. Describing fast-trackers collectively, most of this information appears in tables throughout the book.

(2) *Perceptions and recollections* of the fast-trackers are at least an equally important part of the information elicited in the interview sessions and include: what *they think* about themselves, their parents, brothers and sisters, their co-workers and their current families; and what *they remember* about their early home and school experiences as well as past events along the career track.[1]

This information appears in the text and is generally set off with indentations on both margins. When possible, this information is presented in the fast-tracker's own words. Often, however, since no recordings were made of the interview sessions, I have retold their stories and the indented material is written in the third person. I have also taken the liberty of filling in the gaps in this information, have shared the written material with the fast-trackers, and received their approval. The stories of the fast-trackers, therefore, whether in their words or mine, are set off from the rest of the text. In addition, some short statements from members of this sample appear in the regular text itself, as illustrative or supportive material and are set off with quotation marks.

It is extremely important that readers of the book understand that all of this material is drawn from the *perceptions and recollections* of the fast-trackers and represents what they think and what they remember. In talking about their families, for example, they make many descriptive and some evaluative remarks about their families. These remarks are illuminating in terms of *understanding the fast-trackers themselves* and may or may not reflect the actual reality of the situation or person being described. For example, the fast-trackers as a whole speak well of their parents; yet someone said to me recently, "maybe their parents weren't so wonderful as all that." Maybe not; the degree of goodness of parents is not the issue. What is important is that by and large the fast-trackers, looking back, remember them as wonderful. This recollection shapes the fast-trackers' attitudes and behaviors—it says nothing, in fact, about how parents of these individuals actually behaved.

Finally, from the quantitative information and perceptions of the fast-trackers I have drawn intepretations based on my own experience: graduate school training in human development, four years of part-time clinical training and counseling, seven years of consulting in major organizations, and six years of university administrative experience. When the interpretations rest on knowledge gleaned from particular research endeavors, this is documented. When the interpretation is one that might rest on a common pool of psychological understanding, I have not documented the sources of this interpretation. The interpretations drawn from the fast-trackers' *perceived* experience are generally identified as interpretations within the overall text.

Consequently, in this book, there are three levels of information: (1) quantitative data about families, college experiences, and careers as told by the fast-trackers; (2) the fast-trackers' current perceptions and past recollections of their lifetime experience; and (3) interpretations that I have made of both the quantitative data and the perceptual information. Each level rests to some degree on the other, and conclusions become more tentative as one moves from data, to perceptions, to interpretations. It is expected that readers will discriminate the degree of objectivity and subjectivity at each level and respond to the information accordingly.

APPENDIX C
SAMPLE INTERVIEW FORMAT

Exceptional Managers Corporate Questionnaire

1. PERSONAL INFORMATION

Name_____ Birth Date_____

Sex: M   F   (circle one)   Race: _____

Job Title: _____

Company: _____

Location (City, State): _____

Job Description: _____

_____

_____

Number of Employees Supervised Directly: _____

Indirectly: _____

Other information about the company that would be useful in terms of understanding the scope of your responsibilities:

_____

_____

_____

_____

Exceptional Managers Corporate Questionnaire

2. EDUCATIONAL HISTORY

High School Attended: _____

Location (City, State): _____

What did you do in high school in addition to attending classes:

_____

_____

_____

What were your grades like in high school?_____

Year of Graduation: _____

Undergraduate College Attended: _____

Location (City, State): _____

Major Area of Study: _____

What did you do in college in addition to attending classes?

_____

_____

_____

What were your grades like in college?_____

Year of Graduation: _____

Graduate School(s) Attended: _____

Location (City, State): _____

Major Area of Study: _____

What did you do in addition to attending classes?

_____

_____

_____

What was your cumulative grade point average? _____

Degree and Year: _____

SIGNIFICANT TEACHERS AND/OR INSTRUCTORS

Identify one or more significant teachers or instructors in your educational career who had some impact in determining your career path.

1. Name _____ School _____

   Desribe his/her significance to you and give an example if possible:

   _____

   _____

   _____

2. Name _____ School _____

   Describe his/her significance to you and give an example if possible:

   _____

   _____

   _____

3. Name _____ School _____

   Describe his/her significance to you and give an example if possible:

   _____

   _____

   _____

Exceptional Managers Corporate Questionnaire

3. WORK HISTORY

For each job or position that you have held since you first began working, list the job title, dates held, company, and location of the job. Give a brief job description. List part-time or temporary (e.g., summer) jobs which you held while you were in school in the section provided and full-time jobs later. Consider each promotion or transfer within a company as a new job. Use more paper if necessary.

PART-TIME OR TEMPORARY POSITIONS

1. Job Title: _____

   Company: _____

   Location (City, State): _____

Years in job (give dates): _____

Job Description: _____

_____

_____

Part-Time _____   Full-Time _____

2. Job Title: _____

Company: _____

Location (City, State): _____

Years in job (give dates): _____

Job Description: _____

_____

_____

Part-Time _____   Full-Time _____

3. Job Title: _____

Company: _____

Location (City, State): _____

Years in job (give dates): _____

Job Description: _____

_____

_____

Part-Time _____   Full-Time _____

FULL-TIME POSITIONS

1. Job Title: _____

Company: _____

Location (City, State): _____

Years in job (give dates): _____

Job Description: _____

_____

_____

Number of Employees Supervised Directly: _____

Indirectly: _____

2. Job Title: _____

Company: _____

Location (City, State): _____

Years in job (give dates): _____

Job Description: _____

_____

_____

Number of Employees Supervised Directly: _____

Indirectly: _____

3. Job Title: _____

Company: _____

Location (City, State): _____

Years in job (give dates): _____

Job Description: _____

_____

_____

Number of Employees Supervised Directly: _____

Indirectly: _____

4. Job Title: _____

Company: _____

Location (City, State): _____

Years in job (give dates): _____

Job Description: _____

_____

_____

Number of Employees Supervised Directly: _____

Indirectly: _____

5. Job Title: _____

Company: _____

Location (City, State): _____

Years in job (give dates): _____

Job Description: _____

_____

_____

Number of Employees Supervised Directly: _____

Indirectly: _____

6. Job Title: _____

Company: _____

Location (City, State): _____

Years in job (give dates): _____

Job Description: _____

_____

_____

Number of Employees Supervised Directly: _____

Indirectly: _____

7. Job Title: _____

Company: _____

Location (City, State): _____

Years in job (give dates): _____

Job Description: _____

_____

_____

Number of Employees Supervised Directly: _____

Indirectly: _____

8. Job Title: _____

Company: _____

Location (City, State): _____
Years in job (give dates): _____
Job Description: _____
_____
_____

Number of Employees Supervised Directly: _____
Indirectly: _____

9. Job Title: _____
Company: _____
Location (City, State): _____
Years in job (give dates): _____
Job Description: _____
_____
_____

Number of Employees Supervised Directly: _____
Indirectly: _____

ANTICIPATED POSITIONS

List the positions that you expect to hold in the future—if "things go well for you."

1. Job Title: _____
Company: _____
Location (City, State): _____
When anticipated (give dates): _____
Job Description: _____
_____
_____

Number of Employees to Supervise Directly: _____
Indirectly: _____

2. Job Title: _____
Company: _____
Location (City, State): _____
When anticipated (give dates): _____
Job Description: _____
_____
_____

Number of Employees to Supervise Directly: _____
Indirectly: _____

3. Job Title: _____
Company: _____
Location (City, State): _____
When anticipated (give dates): _____
Job Description: _____
_____
_____

Number of Employees to Supervise Directly: _____

Indirectly: _____

SIGNIFICANT MENTORS, SPONSORS, AND/OR GODFATHERS

Identify one or more significant mentors, sponsors, and/or godfathers in the course of your career who have had a significant impact on your career path.

1. Name: _____
   Title: _____
   Company: _____
   Work Relationship With You: _____
   Years Most Affected by Relationship: _____
   Describe his/her significance to you and give an example if possible:

   _____

   _____

   _____

2. Name: _____
   Title: _____
   Company: _____
   Work Relationship With You: _____
   Years Most Affected by Relationship: _____
   Describe his/her significance to you and give an example if possible:

   _____

   _____

   _____

3. Name: _____
   Title: _____
   Company: _____
   Work Relationship With You: _____
   Years Most Affected by Relationship: _____
   Describe his/her significance to you and give an example if possible:

   _____

   _____

   _____

Exceptional Managers Corporate Questionnaire

4. FAMILY HISTORY

Name of Father _____ Birthdate _____
Name of Mother _____ Birthdate _____
Father's Occupation: _____
Mother's Occupation: _____
Your Brothers and Sisters:

Name	Sex	Birthdate	Occupation
_____	___	_____	_____
_____	___	_____	_____

_____   __   _____   _____
_____   __   _____   _____
_____   __   _____   _____
_____   __   _____   _____

Your Spouse's Name: _____ Birthdate _____
(First Marriage)
Spouse's Occupation: _____
Date of Marriage: _____
Children:

Name	Sex	Birthdate	Living with You (Y/N)
_____	__	_____	_____
_____	__	_____	_____
_____	__	_____	_____

Your Spouse's Name: _____ Birthdate _____
(Second Marriage if applicable)
Spouse's Occupation: _____
Date of Marriage: _____
Children:

Name	Sex	Birthdate	Living with You (Y/N)
_____	__	_____	_____
_____	__	_____	_____
_____	__	_____	_____

Spouse's Children (if applicable):

Name	Sex	Birthdate	Living with You (Y/N)
_____	__	_____	_____
_____	__	_____	_____
_____	__	_____	_____
_____	__	_____	_____

SIGNIFICANT FAMILY MEMBERS IN REGARD TO
CAREER DECISIONS

Identify one or more family members (they need not be listed above) who have had a significant impact on choices you have made in your career:

1. Name: _____
   Relationship With You: _____
   Years Most Affected by Relationship: _____
   Describe his/her significance to you and give an example if possible:

   _____
   _____
   _____

2. Name:_____
   Relationship With You:_____
   Years Most Affected by Relationship:_____
   Describe his/her significance to you and give an example if possible:

   _____

   _____

   _____

3. Name:_____
   Relationship With You:_____
   Years Most Affected by Relationship:_____
   Describe his/her significance to you and give an example if possible:

   _____

   _____

   _____

Exceptional Managers Corporate Questionnaire

5.COMMUNITY AND PROFESSIONAL ACTIVITIES

Describe any other activities outside of the family and the workplace in which you have been or are now involved which have been or are now significant in thinking about your career:

_____

_____

_____

_____

_____

_____

_____

_____

OTHER SIGNIFICANT PEOPLE IN REGARD TO CAREER DECISIONS

Describe any other individuals who have had a significant impact on your thinking in regard to your career. Describe their relationship to you, the years in which they had the greatest influence, and illustrate with an example if possible.

_____

_____

_____

_____

_____

_____

_____

_____

Notes

Introduction

Frontispiece: Cox, A., *The Cox Report on the American Corporation,* New York: Delacorte Press, 1982, p. 182; and Zaleznik, A., "Management of Disappointment," In E. Collins (ed.), *Executive Success: Making It in Management,* New York: John Wiley & Sons, Inc., 1983, p. 239.

1. Kovach, B. "The Derailment of Fast-Track Managers." *Organizational Dynamics, 15,* Autumn 1986, pp. 41–48.

2. Welch, Jack, "Managing Change." Keynote address, Dedication Convocation, the Fuqua School of Business, Duke University, Durham, NC, April, 1983.

3. Of those that nominated individuals, three held high-level positions (either divisional vice-president or corporate director) in human resources departments in three of the corporations; two were line managers, one at the division level and one at the district level, in the two other corporations. Nominations were made on an informal basis after conferring with peers and sometimes superiors. Of those making nominations, three were white males, one was a black male, and one was female. Despite this diversity, all of the initial twelve nominees were white and male. The sample was extended to include two women and one black male and two other individuals who were nominated later in the process.

Part I

Frontispiece: Kotter, J., *Power and Influence,* New York: Free Press, 1985, p. 39.

1. Elaboration on and theoretical support for the model of leadership as substance and style exists in Kovach, B., *The Essentials of Leadership* (unpublished book manuscript, 1985). The model was initially worked out by the author with Randy Kovach in the five years of developing 18 days of management training programs, "You and Your Organization," for Rochester Products Division of General Motors Corporation—Grand Rapids, Michigan, and Rochester, New York—from 1982 through 1987.

Chapter 1

Frontispiece: Boettinger, H., "Is Management Really an Art?" *Harvard Business Review,* January–February 1975. In Harvard Business Review, *Paths Toward Personal Progress: Leaders are Made, Not Born.* Cambridge: Harvard College, 1982, p. 40.

Chapter 2

Frontispiece: Selznick, P., cited in *Chronicle of Higher Education,* May 28, 1986, p. 20.

1. Simon, H.A., "What We Know About the Creative Process," in R. Kuhn (ed.), *Frontiers in Creative and Innovative Management,* Cambridge, MA: Ballinger Publishing Company, 1985, p. 12.

Chapter 3

Frontispiece: Zaleznik, A., "Management of Disappointment," in E. Collins (ed.), *Executive Success: Making It in Management,* New York: John Wiley & Sons, Inc., 1983, p. 230; and Peters, T.J. and Waterman, R.H., *In Search of Excellence: Lessons From America's Best Run Companies,* New York: Harper & Row, Publishers, 1982, p. 287.

1. See Galbraith, J., *The New Industrial State,* New York: Mentor, 1978, p. 317. Consider also other similar distinctions such as a very early one made by C.P. Snow in which he distinguished between conceptualizers and problem-solvers, and commented on the more difficult and less directed early adult years of the conceptualizers (*The Search,* NY: Scribner, 1959). Recent research studies also distinguish adaptors and innovators, see for example: Kirton, M.J., "Adaptors and Innovators: A Description and Measure," *Journal of Applied Psychology,* 1976, *61,* 622–629, and Kirton, M.J., "Adaptors and Innovators in Organizations," *Human Relations,* 1980, *33,* 213–224. Similar distinctions around processors, integrators, and producers have been made in our own research using the *Personal Expectations Inventory (PXI)* as reported in *Organizational Sync* (Englewood Cliffs, NJ: Prentice-Hall, 1984), as well as in unpublished validation studies on the PXI (1983, 1984, 1985). Corroborating evidence for such categorization of the fast-trackers is seen in their scores on the PXI: almost all of the creators are processors and almost all of the contributors are integrators; there are only three exceptions, one creator and two contributors who are producers.

2. Further descriptions from senior fast-trackers classified as cooperative creators are as follows:

   Rich describes his current job with an emphasis on implementing a vision, building partnerships and having fun: "I am taking the concept of this company from a grand experiment to the real world. We are asking old questions and getting new answers. If the answers were always the same, it wouldn't be any fun . . . We're supposed to initiate change . . . We do not need to do everything ourselves. We are *not an island* . . . We need to think of ourselves in partnership with others."

   He speaks of his past history in much the same vein: "We created a plant culture by building teams with the belief that if you treat people right you'll be productive. Creating that plant was an emotional experience, very powerful."

He concludes with a summation of his feelings about his current task: "There's a lot of excitement here. What motivates me is the feeling I have for the people."

Tom views his entire career history in terms of living out his destiny, implementing visions and building partnerships. He was first aware of a sense of destiny—something he must do—about the age of ten. "It was not something I thought about," he says, "doing something with people. It was something that I felt I was going to do." He spoke of his early career years as a partnership with his boss: "We had a dream. We anticipated big technology breakthroughs . . ." And in foreseeing what was to come they created a system that was ahead of its time. Describing his work six or seven years later, he says, "we created a whole new way to market; nobody had ever done this before. We had a ball. It was a tremendous experience." And, in describing his next job, he notes the same pattern on a bigger scale; "We created the most successful marketing organization in the company . . ." And in his next job, "I followed my dream . . . there was setback after setback . . . now we are beginning to break even . . ." and now, a few years later, "What I'm doing now is why I came to the company in the first place—to realize my dream . . ."

Tom's dream is to do something great for people, to share ownership with them and to empower them—and in the process increase their individual productivity. He says at one point, "The power I have comes from the people . . . power comes from putting power on the street." And later, "I am here to bring a new sense of ownership to all the people." And, again, Tom accentuates the importance of working in partnership with others: "All my life I've been creating partnerships with people . . ."

3. A second mid-level fast-tracker, Don, comments as follows:

"Unless your people work for and with you, nothing is happening." He attributes his rapid early rise up the corporate ladder to the fact that he is creative and finds new ways to do things. Early, this ability led to the development of several new systems now used company-wide. Says Don simply, "I am where I am because I'm creative." Yet he is also known for his ability to develop and motivate his people.

4. Larry, another mid-level competitive creator, shares much in common with the other creators when he talks about what he does and what he wants to do. He is willing to take risks, to go out on a limb in order to create a dream. He says, "I ask how I can make something work and then do it—if I can't make it work, I dump it," then, "Making this work is a question of mind-set and attitude, it takes guts and risk-taking," and finally "I want to create a company, I want to have a lasting impact on this world."

Other statements, however, clearly place him in the competitive camp. He says that early in his career, "I learned that the important thing was to get your market share up . . . I had a lot of discipline . . . I like competing . . . my area was always top." And later, in describing himself, he says again, "I'm a very competitive person, I don't lose very often."

5. Suzanne Langer, in *Philosophy in a New Key* (Cambridge, MA: Harvard University Press, 1957), emphasizes the critical importance of an *orientation*. She writes, ". . . the driving force in human minds is fear, which begets an imperious demand for security in the world's confusion: a demand for a world-picture that fills all experience and gives each individual a definite *orientation* amid the terrifying forces of nature and society."

6. Jon, another senior cooperative contributor, also has always done what came next since he "settled down and got to work" in his mid-twenties. At that point, after a stint in the military, he came to a new appreciation of the value of life and, with the help of his new wife, put many of his insecurities aside. From that point on, he says, "I just decided to do the best I could as fast as I could do it." And he has done exactly that.

His concern for the people who work with him, however, is evident, and his management style rests on both decisiveness *and* strong communication. He makes sure that all the people are coming along, not in partnership with but in the wake of, decisions made by upper management.

Part II

Frontispiece: Margaret Thatcher in interview appearing in *Parade Magazine,* in "Newark Star Ledger," July 13, 1986; and Drucker, P., *Managing for Results; Economic Tasks and Risk-Taking Decisions,* New York: Harper & Row, Publishers, 1964, p. 6.

1. The interrelationship of power and love (similar to that of substance and style), as well as their different emphases, are traced throughout all the life stages in Forisha-Kovach, B., *Power and Love* (Englewood Cliffs, NJ: Prentice-Hall, 1982).

Chapter 4

Frontispiece: Livingston, J.S., "Myth of the Well-Educated Manager," in *Paths Toward Personal Progress: Leaders are Made, Not Born,* Boston: Harvard Business Review, 1982, pg. 66.

Chapter 5

Frontispiece: Simon, H.A., "What We Know About the Creative Process," in Kuhn, R. (ed.), *Frontiers in Creative and Innovative Management,* Cambridge, MA: Ballinger Publishing Company, 1985, p. 19.

Chapter 6

Frontispiece: personal communication, August, 1986.

Chapter 7

Frontispiece: Katz, R., "Skills of an Effective Administrator," in *Paths Toward Personal Progress: Leaders are Made, Not Born,* Boston: Harvard Business Review, 1982, p. 31.

  1. See Peters, T.J. and Waterman, R.H., *In Search of Excellence: Lessons from America's Best Run Companies,* New York: Harper & Row Publishers, 1982.

Part III

Frontispiece: Livingston, J.S., "Myth of the Well-Educated Manager," in *Paths Toward Personal Progress: Leaders are Made, Not Born,* Boston: Harvard Business Review, 1982, p. 68; and Prentice, W.C.H., "Understanding Leadership," in *Paths Toward Personal Progress: Leaders are Made, Not Born,* Boston: Harvard Business Review, 1982, p. 6.

Chapter 8

Frontispiece: Zaleznik, A., "Management of Disappointment," in E. Collins (ed.), *Executive Success: Making It in Management,* New York: John Wiley & Sons, Inc., 1983, p. 232; and Douvan, E., "The Marriage Role: 1957–1976," presentation at the American Psychological Association Annual Meeting, Toronto, Ontario, Canada, August, 1978, p. 14.

  1. Four fast-trackers had parents who, among them, had a laundry, a farm, a telephone business, and a vehicle rehabilitation business. In addition, another's father started his own business before selling out to a large company and becoming a manager for them, yet another's father and mother owned a store during the depression years, and still another lived with his grandfather who had his own small business. In all, seven grew up, at times, in a small business environment where the choices were determined by the parents themselves and not by others, and where the hours of work were long and demanding. Two other fast-trackers had fathers who managed manufacturing concerns from the top and two had fathers who practiced a profession. Thus, eleven of the fast-trackers were exposed to family situations in which the working parent or parents did not report to an immediate boss and where the demands of the vocation took them long beyond an eight-hour day.

  2. A similar story is told by the fast-tracker who did not want to be like his father. For him, it was the high school basketball coach "who got me out of the streets and into more activities. He generally improved my behavior. This was a rare human being that dedicated his whole life to helping turn kids' heads around."

Chapter 9

Frontispiece: Rousseau, Jean Jacques, *Emile* (critical edition): Stuttgart, p. 479; and Mead, M., "Adolescence," in H.V. Kraemer (ed.), *Youth and Culture,* Monterey, CA: Brooks/Cole Publishing Co., 1974, p. 55.

1. Another early adult experience of a mid-level creator is the story told by Ken. He spent some time in graduate school creating a graduate program in statistics unlike any others in his university. He used this as a base to set up a consulting center within the university and to incorporate the new computer technology into the curriculum. Following completion of a master's degree, he was offered scholarships to go on for his doctorate three years in a row. He turned them down each time, "just for this year," to devote time to managing a restaurant, a sole proprietorship. He loved the pace of activity, the constant bouncing from item to item. "Bouncing is my life," he says. He left the restaurant business, finally, because his wife thought it was too demanding, and took two jobs over three years with different companies in which he converted his technical and statistical skills into a marketing expertise. With these years behind him, he was able to use his marketing skills to leap onto the fast track in first one company, and now another, and has moved rapidly upward since his late start. He is somewhat regretful, however, of the time he spent elsewhere: "I feel like I'm five years behind."

2. Art's story reflects one more experience from a mid-level creator. Art did poorly in high school: "I never thought much about schooling and felt peer pressure *not* to do well. I was very insecure, had poor self-esteem, and acted in accord with that. I scored well in mathematics. At least in math, I could study for three hours and get an A. There was a specific answer. In social studies, you can study for three hours and still get an F. That didn't interest me. Senior year, however, I began to come out of this. I met some new people and got involved in sports. I graduated with a C average (much better in math) and decided to go on to junior college. There I made the Dean's list." With an Associate's degree, Art got a technical job in a big company and hated it. He kept at it for four years while he took more courses at night so that he could get into a four-year college. When he was ready, he went to a local college and in three years earned a bachelor's degree. At that point, with the help of his wife, he located a job in the same company that had career potential for him. Outstanding achievements led to rapid promotions and, later, a change of company. With a slow start, Art is now very close to the top.

3. Information on conjugal power relationships are discussed by Gillespie, D. "Who Has the Power? The Marital Struggle," in *Journal of Marriage and the Family, 33,* 1971: 445–58. Although she does not specifically mention age, she discusses the relationship of personal and real resources in determining the marriage balance and the increasing upper hand of the primary breadwinner as the marriage progresses (especially as children are born). Other sources on parental power and the influence of the primary money-earner are: Brossard, J.H.S. and Boll, E.S., "Marital Unhappiness in the Life Cycle," *Marriage and Family Living,* 1955, *17,* 10–14; McDonald, G.W., "Parental Identification by the Adolescent: A Social Power Approach," *Journal of Marriage and the Family,* 1977, *39,* 705–719; Safilios-Rothschild, C., *Toward a Sociology of Women,* Greenwich, Conn.: Xerox College Publishing, 1972. This research fits

with common images of marriage partners: imagine the media's portrayal of two young people, newly married, who have gone to school together and are bringing to the marriage roughly equal amounts of knowledge and experience and contrast this with another image, frequently portrayed in novels and films, of the established man, with his career well-in-hand, choosing a much younger bride whom he intends to educate and bring into adulthood as he sees fit. In the first case, the couple will argue about what will happen and how it will happen until common patterns are established between them. In the second case it is more likely that the wife will adapt to patterns already established.

4. Domino, G., "Maternal Correlates of Sons' Creativity," *Journal of Consulting and Clinical Psychology,* 1969, *33,* 180–183; Schaefer, C.E. & Anastasi, A., "A Biographical Inventory for Identifying Creativity in Adolescent Boys," *Journal of Applied Psychology,* 1968, *52,* 42–48.

5. Barron, F.X., *Creativity and Psychological Health,* Princeton: Van Nostrand, 1963; Erikson, E.H., *Young Man Luther, A Study in Psychoanalysis and History,* New York: W.W. Norton & Co., Inc., 1958; Hudson, L., *Human Beings: The Psychology of Human Experience*, Garden City, NY: Anchor Press, 1975.

6. Contributors comment on their mothers as follows: Jon says that his mother likes plants and flowers, and visits frequently. Pete says his mother was immensely supportive, emphasized integrity, and taught them to be open; however he also says that in his family, women were not supposed to work, and the men were supposed to take care of them. Two of the contributors, Brian and Sam, mention their parents without specifically indicating either mothers or fathers—they are as likely to be speaking, therefore, of fathers as mothers. Brian says, "both parents were very supportive, enthusiastic but not 'loving,'" and Sam says, "My parents set a tone for us, wanted us to 'be who we were,' and emphasized middle-class morals and life styles." With the exception of Hank and Christine, who are both slight anomalies, no other contributors made mention of their mothers.

Chapter 10

Frontispiece: Bartolome, F. and Evans, P.A.L., "Must Success Cost So Much?" in E. Collins (ed.), *Executive Success: Making It in Management,* New York: John Wiley & Sons, Inc., 1983, p. 77.

1. Roe, A. "A Psychological Study of Eminent Psychologists and Anthropologists, and a Comparison with Biological and Physical Scientists," *Psychological Monographs, 67,* 1953.

2. Mannheim, K. "The Problem of Generations." In P. Kecskemeti (ed.), *Essays on the Sociology of Knowledge,* New York: Oxford University Press, 1928/1952.

Chapter 11

Frontispiece: May, R., *Freedom and Destiny*, New York: W.W. Norton & Co., Inc., 1983, pg. 89.

1. Kagan, J., "Baby Research Comes of Age," *Psychology Today,* 1987, *21*(5), pg. 47.

2. In this regard Michael Reitter, a British psychiatrist, claims that despite difficult childhood environments there are factors that "protect" children, helping them to overcome even formidable obstacles, to become basically well-adjusted adults ("Resilient Children," in *Psychology Today*, March, 1984, 57–65).

3. Crozier, M., *The Bureaucratic Phenomenon*, Chicago: University of Chicago Press, 1964, p. 164.

Part IV

Frontispiece: Burns, J.M., *Leadership*, New York: Harper & Row, Publishers, 1978, pp. 19, 40.

Chapter 12

Frontispiece: Kotter, J., *Power and Influence*, New York: Free Press, 1985, p. x (page after Preface).

Chapter 13

Frontispiece: Wrapp, H.E., "Good Managers Don't Make Policy Decisions," in *Classic Advice on Aspects of Organizational Life, Vol. 1,* New York: Perennial Library, 1985, p. 13; Millay, E.S.V., "Ballad," in *Huntsman, What Quarry?*, New York: Harper & Row, Publishers, 1939, pg. 92.

Chapter 14

Frontispiece: Zaleznik, A., "Managers and Leaders: Are They Different?" in E. Collins (ed.), *Executive Success: Making It in Management,* New York: John Wiley & Sons, Inc., 1983, p. 127.

Chapter 15

Frontispiece: Personal communication, August, 1986.

Chapter 17

Frontispiece: Peters, T.J. and Waterman, R.H., *In Search of Excellence: Lessons from America's Best Run Companies,* New York: Harper & Row, Publishers, 1982, p. 75.

Epilogue

Frontispiece: Toffler, A. *The Adaptive Corporation*, New York: Bantam, 1985, p. 4.

Appendix B

1. On the importance of perceptions: "What man chooses to take in, either consciously or unconsciously, is what gives structure and meaning to his world. Furthermore, what he perceives is 'what he intends to do about it.'" (Hall, E.T., *Beyond Culture,* New York: Anchor, 1977, p. 88); this argument is traced back to Karl Lewin who argues that behavior is in response to the perception of reality rather than to some objective reality (*Principle of Topological Psychology,* New York: McGraw-Hill, 1936).

Index

235